THE HISTORY OF THE
KINGS &
QUEENS
OF ENGLAND & SCOTLAND

THE HISTORY OF THE
KINGS &
QUEENS
OF ENGLAND & SCOTLAND

ARMADILLO

First published in 2002 by Armadillo Books
An imprint of Bookmart Limited
Desford Road, Enderby
Leicester LE19 4AD, England

© 2002 Bookmart Limited
Reprinted 2003 (twice)

ISBN 1-84322-058-X

Production by Omnipress, Eastbourne

Printed in Singapore

CONTENTS

INTRODUCTION

IN THE GALAXY of monarchs who have reigned in Britain since the time of the Anglo-Saxons there has been a wide variety of people of different characters. Some, like the Norman, William the Conqueror, are remembered as strong leaders and innovators; others, like Edward II, are seen as victims of personal circumstances. Some, like Richard the Lionheart, are national warrior heroes; others, like Elizabeth I, are admired for their firm but diplomatic skill in government; and a few, like Lady Jane Grey, have left hardly a trace of their passing.

William the Conqueror

King Charles I

The character of the monarch has often mirrored the mood of the people, as with the resolution in the fact of foreign as well as personal problems shown by George VI. Sometimes the monarch's own stubbornness has created a tragic outcome for himself as well as the nation, as in the reign of Charles I and the Civil War.

British kings and queens are not pasteboard figures in a scrapbook but real people faced with the problems of their reign and their own personal reactions to the questions of their day.

Their private and public personalities have often had to compromise in order to preserve the peace and at the same time satisfy their subjects' yearnings. In the course of time these have covered an ever-widening variety of the British people united in their desire for the success of their nation and with personal ambitions as well.

Monarchs have always had the guidance of parliaments but they had the right to summon these at will: Henry VII only once called a parliament together. From the early eighteenth century, when the first Hanoverian kings spoke little or no English, parliament began to become a more powerful force in government, and the march towards democratic government began.

The monarchy lost much of its direct power but its moral influence remained, as in the reign of Victoria, and it became a symbol of Britain's belief in itself and its status in the world. Despite the doubters who daydream of a republican Britain, the people of Britain's interest in their monarchy and their support for royal occasions is evidence that monarchs have a greater appeal than presidents as representatives of the nation's whole life.

Henry VIII, born in 1491, was the second son of Henry VII and Elizabeth of York. The significance of Henry's reign is, at times, overshadowed by his six marriages. The court life initiated by his father evolved into a cornerstone of Tudor government in the reign of Henry VIII. After his father's staunch, stolid rule, the energetic, youthful and handsome king avoided governing in person, much preferring to journey the countryside hunting and reviewing his subjects.

micis defende

tib; suis ab eq̄s

coldic fomenti

dano q̇ n̄o long

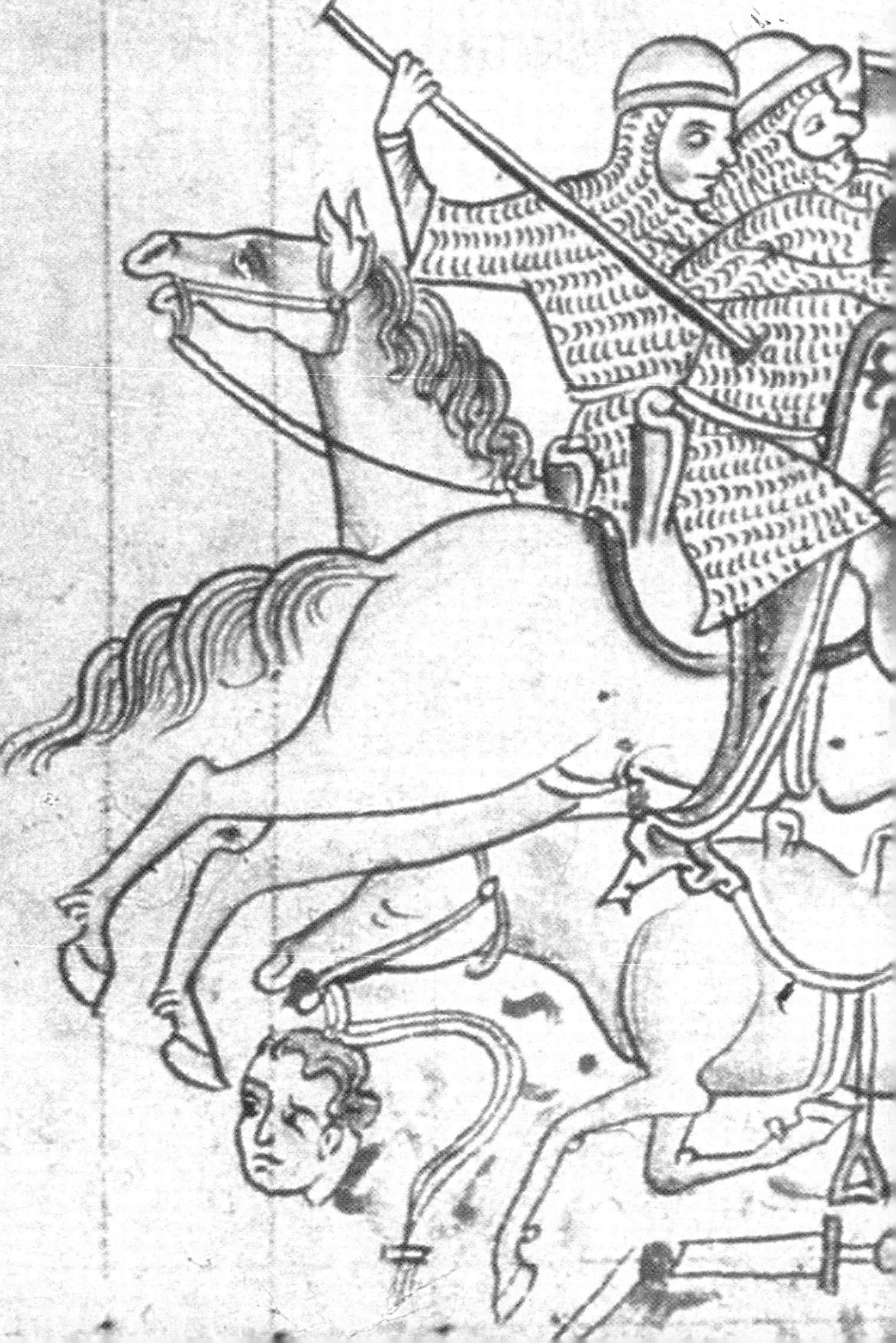

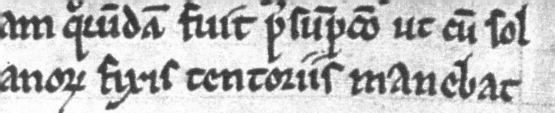

FIRST ENGLISH KINGS

After the Romans left, England was invaded by Jutes, Angles and Saxons from northern continental Europe, and the original British inhabitants were overrun and their leaders killed or driven out. There is little material evidence of these earlier cultures for they built in wood and their textiles perished. But once settled, their Christian influences emerged and they began to build stone churches. Their carvings reflected a people beginning to create an indigenous culture. Unfortunately, much of this was destroyed by the Normans.

EARLY SAXON KINGS

*c.*600–871

Anglo-Saxon men were tough and often brutal, but they tended to dress comfortably. Those who wore stockings decorated them with cross-garters.

BEFORE THE ARRIVAL of the Normans, and their efforts to unite England, there were poor communications and the populace was divided into regional groups ruled over by a local lord. There were seven regions, known as the Heptarchy, and comprising, Kent, Sussex, Essex, East Anglia, Wessex, Mercia and Northumbria. All of them were fertile for agriculture, and had abundant springs for settlements; they soon became self-contained kingdoms. Kent and Wessex were the most favoured for their southern position and access to the English Channel, and its warm Gulf Stream waters, which provided a temperate climate. These kingdoms and Northumbria were the first to be Christianized and profited from the administrative talent and knowledge of the educated clergy who arrived as missionaries.

Aethelfrith of Northumbria was one of the first to adopt the new religion. In his kingdom learning was encouraged and Bede, a scholar priest from the Jarrow and Monkswearmouth monasteries, near Durham, was one of the leading figures. The height of Northumbrian power came in the seventh century when King Oswy tried to unite his kingdom as one entity under his control. In East Anglia King Raedwald attempted to do the same and his power and influence are reflected in his funeral arrangements. He was buried in the traditional Viking manner in a longship surrounded by treasures which, when found in 1939 at Sutton Hoo, revealed the high skills that prevailed during the seventh century. The eighth century saw Mercia as the dominant kingdom of the Heptarchy under King Offa. His kingdom stretched to the edge of Wales, which remained

British, and he built a dyke along the foothills of the Welsh mountains to prevent their return into his territory. A man of vision and immense ambition, he made a pact with the Emperor Charlemagne to encourage trade between England and the Continent.

Further progress in Saxon England was now slowed down by the Danish Viking invasions and this brought Wessex to the fore as defenders of English territory. King Alfred's resolute opposition to the Danes made it the most important member of the Heptarchy and Alfred the monarch of all England.

TIME LINE OF THE PERIOD *c.600–871*

597
St Augustine settles in Canterbury and begins the conversion of the Kingdom of Kent to Christianity.

600
Augustine makes Paulinus Bishop of York.

613
The English defeat the Britons at the Battle of Chester, led by Aethelfrith of Northumbria.

632
Mercia and North Wales defeat Northumbria at Hatfield; Edwin, King of Northumbria and overlord of the English, is killed in the battle. Penda becomes King of Mercia.

641
Oswy becomes King of Northumbria.

685
Ecgfrith of Northumbria is defeated and killed by the Picts at the Battle of Nechtansmere.

716
Aethelbald becomes King of Mercia.

757
Offa becomes King of Mercia.

802
Ecgberht becomes King of Wessex.

829
Ecgberht becomes, in effect, King of all England.

839
Aethelwulf becomes King of Wessex and Athelstan King of Kent, Essex, Sussex and Surrey on Ecgberht's death.

866
Aethelred I becomes King of Wessex.

871
Aethelred I dies of his wounds a month after defeating the Danes at Merton.

ALFRED THE GREAT

871–899

ROYAL BIOGRAPHY

BORN: Wantage, Berkshire, c.849. PARENTS: Aethelwulf of Wessex and Osburga.
ASCENDED THE THRONE: 4 April 871. CROWNED: Possibly Kingston-upon-Thames, 871.
MARRIED: Ethelswitha, a Mercian princess. CHILDREN: Three daughters and three sons,
including Ethelfleda, or Aethelfleda, of Mercia and King Edward the Elder.
DIED: c.26 October 899. BURIED: Newminster Abbey, Winchester.

One of the best known stories of Alfred concerns him 'burning the cakes'. The story tells that when his fortunes were at their lowest ebb Alfred sought refuge in a woodcutter's hut. One day, the woodcutter's wife asked him to watch over the cakes which she had placed in the oven. Alfred, preoccupied with his own problems, neglected the cakes, and allowed them to burn. On returning the woodcutter's wife yelled at King Alfred and said, 'Now, none of us will have any supper because of you.' When the woodcutter came home, he recognized the stranger by the stove. He said to his wife, 'This is King Alfred'. The woodcutter's wife bowed to King Alfred's feet and said, 'I'm sorry that I shouted at you'.

BY 796 WESSEX, on the Celtic fringe of western England, was ruled by Ecgberht, sometimes thought of as the first King of England. Ecgberht's grandson was Alfred, known as the Great for his dominant personality and relentless defence of his kingdom against Viking invaders from Scandinavia. After routing the Danes, he allowed them to stay in the settlements that they had created in the north and east of England. Alfred agreed that a line between London and Chester would define their respective territories, though Alfred would remain overlord of the northern section, as well as King of Wessex. In 886 Alfred captured London and so confirmed his title as King of all England. He also made a treaty with King Offa to combine their forces against invaders and began the construction of a fleet to ward off incursions from the sea.

Alfred was an educated man who could read and write, and translated works from Latin into Anglo-Saxon. There were few like him, though scholars could be found in monasteries. One of these was Bede who wrote the *Ecclesiastical History of England.* Another history, compiled under Alfred's rule, was the *Anglo-Saxon Chronicles*, a history of England from before the arrival of the Romans. Alfred encouraged learning and craftsmanship, especially gold and silver work. During his reign there was considerable activity in the translation from Latin manuscripts, and the encouragement of the building of churches and monasteries. He was on good terms with the Church and an admirer of Pope Gregory, who was a shrewd politician, and had written a book of advice to bishops called *Pastoral Rule.* Alfred translated the book finding in it good advice for all those in power over others. His study and concern of kingship and its duties and responsibilities was one of his best qualities.

TIME LINE OF THE REIGN 871–899

871
Alfred succeeds his brother Aethelred as King of Wessex.
876
Southern Northumbria is colonized by the Danes.
877
Mercia is partitioned between the English and the Danes.
878
Danes invade Wessex. Alfred takes refuge on the Isle of Athelney and prepares his forces against the Great Army of Guthrum. The questionable story about Alfred burning the cakes took place during this period. Alfred defeats Guthrum's army at Ethandune in Wessex.
886
Alfred captures London and fortifies the city.
890
Alfred builds the first permanent fleet of warships in England, ready to engage Viking ships.
891
Alfred starts to compile the *Anglo-Saxon Chronicle*. Written in Anglo-Saxon, the language spoken by the people, rather than Latin, the language of the Church.
894–5
Alfred translates Orosius's *Historia Adversus Paganos* and Bede's *Ecclesiastical History of the English Nation* into Anglo-Saxon.
899
Death of Alfred, probably in Wessex.

VIKING INVASIONS

899–1016

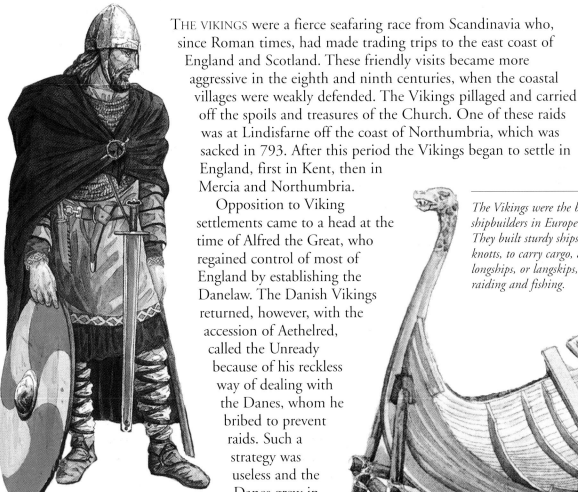

THE VIKINGS were a fierce seafaring race from Scandinavia who, since Roman times, had made trading trips to the east coast of England and Scotland. These friendly visits became more aggressive in the eighth and ninth centuries, when the coastal villages were weakly defended. The Vikings pillaged and carried off the spoils and treasures of the Church. One of these raids was at Lindisfarne off the coast of Northumbria, which was sacked in 793. After this period the Vikings began to settle in England, first in Kent, then in Mercia and Northumbria.

Opposition to Viking settlements came to a head at the time of Alfred the Great, who regained control of most of England by establishing the Danelaw. The Danish Vikings returned, however, with the accession of Aethelred, called the Unready because of his reckless way of dealing with the Danes, whom he bribed to prevent raids. Such a strategy was useless and the Danes grew in power, and under Sweyn Forkbeard,

The Vikings were the best shipbuilders in Europe. They built sturdy ships, or knotts, to carry cargo, and longships, or langskips, for raiding and fishing.

Viking men treasured their weapons. They fought furiously in battles, and the fiercest fighters were called 'berserkers'.

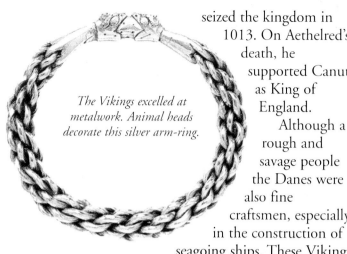

The Vikings excelled at metalwork. Animal heads decorate this silver arm-ring.

seized the kingdom in 1013. On Aethelred's death, he supported Canute as King of England.

Although a rough and savage people the Danes were also fine craftsmen, especially in the construction of seagoing ships. These Viking longboats, which were 80 feet long, enabled the Danes to cross the North Sea and even to sail to North America with Leif Eriksson, whose maps of a landfall called Vinland are said to be a proof of his voyage to a new continent in the year 1000. Vikings were also good administrators and once they had settled in England contributed to social progress.

The first permanent centre for the Vikings was York and

from here they spread into Mercia and East Anglia. Once the Danes were settled and had developed their administrative systems it was possible to negotiate with them and thus the Danelaw was established, creating a stable relationship between Danes and Anglo-Saxons.

AETHELRED THE UNREADY

978–1016

BORN: *c.*968. PARENTS: King Edgar and Elfrida. ASCENDED THE THRONE: 18 March 978. CROWNED: Kingston-upon-Thames, April 978. AUTHORITY: King of England. MARRIED: (1) Elfleda, or Elgiva, daughter of an ealdorman, (2) Emma, daughter of the Duke of Normandy. CHILDREN: With (1), eight sons, including Edmund II, and five daughters; with (2), two sons, including Edward the Confessor, and one daughter. DIED: 23 April 1016. BURIED: St Paul's Cathedral.

Right: The last Viking King of Northumbria was Eric Bloodaxe. This silver penny bears an unsheathed sword, a symbol of his heathen rule in Northumbria.

THE TITLE 'the Unready', or more accurately 'the Ill-Advised', given to Alfred's successor derives largely from the writer of the *Anglo-Saxon Chronicle* who was an admirer of Alfred and disappointed in his successor. Aethelred was slow and ineffectual in dealing with the Danes, and the Viking invasions intensified during his reign despite his efforts to contain them by enlarging his navy. Recent studies of Aethelred show that he was an able administrator and constructive in dealing with legal and financial matters of government. What he lacked was Alfred's warrior character and, despite a stand at the indecisive battle of Maldon, he found it difficult to protect his people from Danish attacks.

The idea of buying them off with money came from his adviser Archbishop Sigeric, and the method by which the

St Dunstan crowning King Edward the Martyr in 975 and his murder at Corfe Castle by the household of Aethelred the Unready at the instigation of his mother Alfreda.

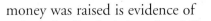

money was raised is evidence of Aethelred's administrative skill.

The money was collected from towns and villages by Aethelred's tax collectors as protection money, not unlike the money or services paid by tenants to their lords under the feudal system.

Aethelred's patience with the Viking hordes must have worn thin by 1002, for he decided to deal with the invaders by a surprise coup. He ordered a massacre of all Danes on St Brice's Day 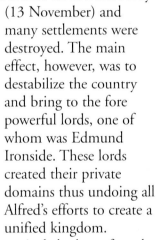 (13 November) and many settlements were destroyed. The main effect, however, was to destabilize the country and bring to the fore powerful lords, one of whom was Edmund Ironside. These lords created their private domains thus undoing all Alfred's efforts to create a unified kingdom.

Aethelred was forced into exile in Normandy with his wife Emma, but was recalled for an ineffective end to his reign. The end came with Sweyn Forkbeard's arrival in England and the takeover of the English throne by Canute, a Danish king, on the death of Aethelred.

TIME LINE OF THE
REIGN 978–1016

978
King Edward the Martyr is murdered at Corfe Castle; he is succeeded by Aethelred II (the Unready). Edward is revered as a martyr.
980
The Danes raid England and succeed because of Aethelred's inability to unite the English.
988
Dunstan dies and is succeeded by Athelgar as Archbishop of Canterbury.
990
Athelgar dies and is succeeded by Sigeric Serio as Archbishop of Canterbury.
991
Battle of Maldon. Byrhtnoth of Essex is defeated by the Danes under Olaf Tryggvesson.
994
The Danish King Sweyn leads an attack on England. Archbishop Sigeric dies.
1012
The Danes raid Kent, burning Canterbury Cathedral and murdering Archbishop Alphege.
1014
Battle of Clontarf. Brian Boru, the Irish king, defeats Danish raiders. Sweyn Forkbeard dies at Gainsborough and is succeeded by his son Canute.
1016
Aethelred dies and is succeeded by his son Edmund II, Ironside. Edmund and Canute fight for the kingdom.

CHRISTIANITY

St Francis of Assisi, founder of the Franciscan order.

CHRISTIANITY, WHICH HAD been accepted in the Roman Empire by the Emperor Constantine in 313, had arrived in England before Augustine arrived in Canterbury with Roman priests in 597 with the intention of converting the pagan Anglo-Saxons. The first sprinkling of the new religion probably arrived through traders long before and there is evidence that Christian priests from London, York and Colchester attended the council of Arles in 314. The budding new religion did not last long in its first flowering, however, for it was overwhelmed by the Viking incursions and their warlike gods Wotan and Thor. Except, that is, in the Celtic territory to the west.

Augustine's mission was a more organized and determined one, as was Columba's with its headquarters in Iona in 563. Each of them brought other missionaries to support their efforts. At first they were rivals with different forms of worship, but the two streams came together at the Synod of Whitby 664.

Unlike other countries, where priests were persecuted for introducing a concept foreign to the ethnic culture, missionaries in Britain seemed to find a ready acceptance. The secret of their success was that they brought not only spiritual comfort but material benefits such as education, technical skills, and administrative talent.

Their contribution to an agricultural society improved farming methods and brought bigger yields. Their schools trained young people to become useful clerks and managers, their knowledge of Latin helped in the study of law, and their philosophy gave to the common people a meaning of life.

Monasteries became centres of learning and culture and filled the gaps that kings had neither the time or the knowledge to deal with. In time the Church became an instrument of government and high clerics were appointed the Chancellors of kings. The secular power of the monarch was difficult to separate from the political power of the Church of Rome, and there soon developed a rivalry between them – especially as the wealth of the church was gathered through church levies and lands acquired by landowners, who were attempting to avoid the kings taxes by donating land to the Church.

Battle of the Christians and Saracens at Damietta.

KING CANUTE

—— 1016–1035 ——

ROYAL BIOGRAPHY

BORN: *c*.995. PARENTS: King Sweyn and Gunhilda of Poland.
ASCENDED THE THRONE: 30 November 1016. CROWNED: Possibly St. Paul's Cathedral,
London, *c*.1017. AUTHORITY: King of England, Denmark (from 1019) and Norway (from 1028).
MARRIED: (1) Elgiva, daughter of the Ealdorman of Deira, never consecrated, (2) Emma of
Normandy, widow of Ethelred II. CHILDREN: With (1), two sons, Harold Harefoot and Sweyn;
with (2), one son, Harthacanute, and two daughters; several illegitimate children.
DIED: Shaftesbury, 12 November 1035. BURIED: Winchester Cathedral.

ON THE DEATH of King Aethelred the Unready, who gained his name from playing a waiting game with the Danes, including bribing them with money to stop their raids, there were two rivals for the throne. Canute who was Danish and Edmund Ironside, the Saxon. After several fierce battles the two claimants agreed to a peaceful settlement by sharing the kingdom between them. Ironside died soon after, leaving Canute as sole king. Canute married Emma of Normandy and divided his kingdom into four earldoms: Northumbria, Mercia, East Anglia and Wessex. By this means he hoped to have four loyal lords guarding his own and the interests of England as a united country.

A religious man, who also understood the usefulness of the Church, Canute encouraged the spread of

Christianity and appointed both Saxon and Danish priests to positions of trust and authority. In 1027 he attended the coronation of the Pope in Rome, which indicates the degree of his acceptance by the centre of universal spiritual power and, therefore, by the Church in his own country.

He treated both Saxons and Danes equally and tried to make laws that would be acceptable to both sides. On his death much of his work was undone as his sons Harefoot and Harthacanute competed for the kingship. The two brothers died in 1040 and 1042, and were succeeded by Edward the Confessor, son of Aethelred II. When Edward married Edith, the daughter of Godwine, Earl of Wessex, he established a connection that was to prove troublesome. Having quarrelled with Godwine, and exiled the family, Edward promised his succession to the Duke of Normandy. He later changed his mind and supported the cause of Harold of Wessex to the English crown. This was however unacceptable to William of Normandy, who in 1066 prepared to claim his rights.

The meeting of Edmund Ironside and Canute on the Isle of Alney in the Severn, in 1016. When Canute invaded England in 1015, Emund led the fighting against him. However, the people apparently felt that he was a rebel against his father, Aethelred the Unready, for he found it hard to gain a following without his father's aid.

TIME LINE OF THE REIGN *1016–1035*

1016
Aethelred dies and his son, Edmund II and Canute fight for the kingdom. At the Battle of Ashingdon, in Essex, Canute defeats Edmund and they agree to divide the kingdom into two – Canute controlling the north and Edmund the south.
Edmund is murdered and Canute is chosen to rule as King of all England.

1017
Canute marries Emma of Normandy, the widow of Ethelred II. Canute divides England into four earldoms: Northumbria, Wessex, Mercia and East Anglia.

1020
Lyfing dies and is succeeded by Athelnoth as Archbishop of Canterbury.

1027
William the Conqueror is born in Normandy. Canute makes a pilgrimage to Rome to demonstrate his alliance with the Church, and attends the coronation of the Pope.

1028
In addition to his existing kingdoms, Canute becomes King of Norway.

1035
Canute dies at the age of 40, and his huge North European empire disintegrates.

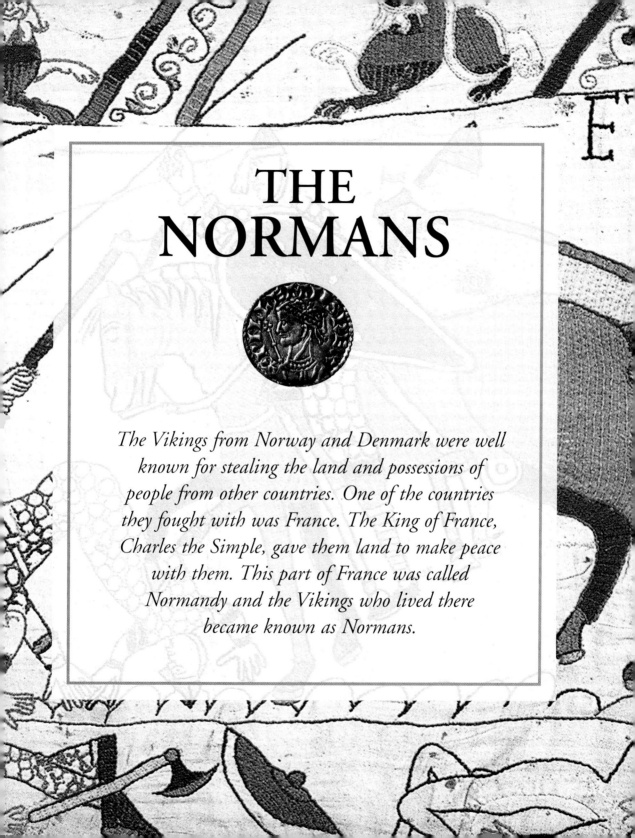

THE
NORMANS

The Vikings from Norway and Denmark were well known for stealing the land and possessions of people from other countries. One of the countries they fought with was France. The King of France, Charles the Simple, gave them land to make peace with them. This part of France was called Normandy and the Vikings who lived there became known as Normans.

BATTLE OF HASTINGS

WILLIAM I, Duke of Normandy, invaded England on 28 September 1066 because Edward the Confessor had drawn back from his promise to give William the English crown on his death. William, a determined and active man, gathered a fleet of over 100 ships, crowded with soldiers in suits of mail and their horses, and landed on a beach in Pevensey Bay. This caught Harold of Wessex, who expected to succeed Edward, by surprise for he was in the north of England fighting a Viking force under Harold Hadrada. Hurrying south from his victory at Stamford Bridge, Harold found that William and his army had already advanced some miles into Sussex and the force of 300 mounted knights and 2,000 foot soldiers and archers were waiting for battle.

Part of the Bayeux Tapestry, before 1082, which was wool embroidery on linen.

On 14 October, Harold, with a similar number of soldiers, took up a position on a ridge on the site of Battle Abbey to repel a cavalry charge. The advance was successfully repelled but, cheered by their success, his troops followed the retreating Normans downhill only to find themselves set upon by soldiers with battle axes. Archers fired at Harold's soldiers who were retreating or still formed at the hilltop. One of these arrows pierced Harold in the eye, upon which his dismayed and now leaderless troops began to retreat.

After the battle William ordered an abbey, called Battle Abbey, to be built to commemorate his victory. His success was not as conclusive as he might have wished, however, for the Saxon nobles now gathered together another army to support Edgar the Atheling's claim to the throne. This was in vain, for William, moving with his usual determination and speed, defeated his rivals and

had himself crowned King at Westminster Abbey on Christmas Day in the same year. No one could have imagined at the time, that the battle of Hastings was more than an episode in the rivalries between barons. It was in fact a significant moment in the destiny of England. The history-making battle was recorded for posterity in a woven tapestry which was probably ordered by Odo, Bishop of Bayeux. This tapestry shows in vivid detail scenes of the Channel crossing and the battle, and is one of the main attractions for visitors to Bayeux today.

EDITH OF THE SWAN NECK

Although they actually never married, the love of Harold's life was Edith of the Swan Neck, who gave him five children. She was devoted to him and helped Harold to prepare for the Battle of Hastings. In fact, Edith and Harold's mother, Gytha, travelled down to Hastings to watch the battle. They watched and waited under a massive oak tree, which later became known as the 'Watch Oak'. They must indeed have been sickened to the heart by what they saw. In fact the old lady Gytha lost three sons and a nephew on that very day. The corpses on the battlefield were so mangled and jumbled together that she simply couldn't recognize any of them. It was left to Edith of the Swan Neck to undo the chain mail on one of the victims. It was only then that she could identify the tattoos on the body, and inform the world that this was indeed the man who had loved her.

Despite the pleas by Gytha, William the Conqueror refused to give Harold a proper burial. His body was simply wrapped in royal purple and placed under a rough cairn of stones on the cliffs at Hastings.

Many years later, however, his body was reburied in Waltham Abbey in Essex, and he was given a tomb of plain grey marble.

WILLIAM I

—— 1066–1087 ——

ROYAL BIOGRAPHY

BORN: Falaise, 1027 or 1028. PARENTS: Robert, Duke of Normandy and Herleva, a tanner's daughter. ASCENDED THE THRONE: 25 December 1066. CROWNED: Westminster Abbey, 25 December 1066. AUTHORITY: King of England and Duke of Normandy. MARRIED: Matilda, daughter of the Count of Flanders, *c.*1050. CHILDREN: Four sons, including the future kings, William II and Henry I, and six daughters. DIED: 9 September 1087. BURIED: St Stephen's Abbey, Caen, Normandy.

WILLIAM OF NORMANDY was the illegitimate son of Robert, Duke of Normandy, and though his inheritance of his father's title was agreed by Norman lords, he had to contend with other rivals throughout his early years. This no doubt served to harden his character and made him the leader best able to take on the conquest of England.

He became known as the Conqueror after he landed with his army at Hastings and defeated Harold of East Wessex in 1066. His claim to the English throne was based on a promise made to him by Edward the Confessor, after William had protected Edward during a period of exile in Normandy.

Crowned King on Christmas Day 1066 William immediately set about getting control of his new kingdom. He had brought members of the Norman nobility and clergy with him to help him in his task and rewarded them with lands confiscated from the Anglo Saxons. He also tried to create a body of administrators which included Anglo-Saxons but this failed, and he reverted to ruling the land with members of the Norman nobility. A brilliant military leader, William put down revolts against his rule by Edwin of Mercia and Hereward the Wake in East Anglia. He also invaded Scotland and obliged Malcolm III to accept his overlordship.

During his reign William brought about the unity of England and introduced the French language, thus creating a mixture of Saxon and French which is the basis of modern English. He also introduced the feudal system and kept an eye on his important lords by means of the Domesday book, which recorded in two volumes the wealth and properties of important estate owners.

William also kept order by building castles in strategic places and encouraged the building of churches by his allies in the Roman clergy. He died after a fall from his horse in Nantes in his kingdom of Anjou.

A penny coin commemorating William I The Conqueror, King of England.

TIME LINE OF THE REIGN 1066–1087

1066
William and his Norman army defeats Harold II and the Saxons at the Battle of Hastings. Harold is killed and William is crowned King of England in Westminster Abbey on Christmas Day.

1067
William suppresses a Saxon revolt in Kent, led by Eustace of Boulogne.

1068–69
Rebellion against the Norman invasion breaks out in Mercia and Northumbria.

1070
William dismisses Stigand as Archbishop of Canterbury. Lanfranc of Bec is appointed in his place.

1071
William defeats a revolt led by Hereward the Wake in East Anglia, thus putting an end to Saxon resistance to his rule.

1072
William invades Scotland.

1079
William's eldest son, Robert, leads a rebellion in Normandy, but is defeated by his father at the Battle of Gerberoi.

1086
The Domesday Book is completed.

1087
William dies of his injuries after falling from his horse while besieging the French city of Nantes.

THE DOMESDAY BOOK

HAVING CONQUERED England and installed himself as King, William wasted no time in getting a firm hold on the administration and imposing his will on a resentful population and its barons. One of the essential tasks to be accomplished was to record the lie of the land and the centres of power. William needed to know who the important landowners were, how much land they owned, the numbers of their tenants and servants, and even the amount of their livestock. This enormous task was given to surveyors who travelled the length and breadth of England recording all the information required. The data was collected by juries which gathered evidence from shires and courts, in seven circuits of England allotted to the surveyors.

There were two Domesday books, the Great book which included all the land to the south of the rivers Ribble and Tees and another solely for Norfolk, Suffolk and Essex. The final records were presented to William in 1086 in preparation for the Salisbury Oath, a gathering to which he had invited all noble and important landowners to pay homage to their new King. It was a significant and historic occasion for, by appearing before them, William seized the opportunity to impress them with his presence. He underlined the fact that his government intended to keep a close eye on their wealth and to demand contributions for the good of a unified England. It was a good start, but it would be years before barons would be brought into line.

Though the results were not immediate, the Domesday Book continued to be immensely useful throughout subsequent history by giving a clue to various legal matters regarding tenure of land and to geographers mapping out the English countryside. It was the first record of the country's welfare which is now contained and administered by innumerable Whitehall departments.

Unfortunately King William did not live to see the completion of the survey which took approximately two years, although thought to be finished by the end of AD 1086. Today the original manuscript of the Domesday Book is stored securely in the Public Records Office in London.

THE COUNTIES IN THE DOMESDAY BOOK

This is a listing of the all the counties mentioned in the Domesday Book:

Bedfordshire
Berkshire
Buckinghamshire
Cambridgeshire
Cheshire
Cumberland
Cornwall
Derbyshire
Devonshire
Dorset
Essex
Gloucestershire
Hampshire
Herefordshire
Hertfordshire
Huntingdonshire
Isle of Wight
Kent
Lancashire
Leicestershire
Lincolnshire
Middlesex
Norfolk
Northamptonshire
Nottinghamshire
Oxfordshire
Rutland
Shropshire
Somerset
Staffordshire
Suffolk
Surrey
Sussex
Warwickshire
Westmorland
Wiltshire
Worcestershire
Yorkshire (E)
Yorkshire(N)
Yorkshire(W)

WILLIAM II

1087–1100

ROYAL BIOGRAPHY

BORN: Normandy, *c.*1056. PARENTS: William I and Matilda of Flanders.
ASCENDED THE THRONE: 9 September 1087. CROWNED: 26 September 1087,
Westminster Abbey. AUTHORITY: King of England.
MARRIED: Unmarried. DIED: New Forest, Hampshire, 2 August 1100.
BURIED: Winchester Cathedral.

WILLIAM II, known as Rufus because of his ruddy complexion and pale hair, was the third son of William the Conqueror. He was unswervingly loyal to his father, who chose him to inherit his kingdom, rather than his elder son Robert, whom he made Duke of Normandy. The existence of two strong men in charge of two parts of the Norman kingdom gave rise to difficulties for William, for the lords who owned estates in both territories were worried about the conditions of tenure from each ruler. William II had strong character and continued his father's transformation of England into a unified and well organized kingdom. In 1088 he put down a rebellion of barons who supported his brother Robert and repelled an invasion by the Scots led by Malcolm III. He also suppressed a rising of lords in North Wales. Thanks to Robert's enthusiasm for the First Crusade and his need of money for the enterprise, William gained a hold on Normandy by giving his brother a mortgage on the duchy. This gave him increasing authority abroad.

Like his father, William was a builder of castles and began, in London, by building Westminster Hall, a centre of government. During his reign several great churches were started, notably Durham Cathedral, but William was not a notable supporter of the Church from which he extracted taxes to pay for his own schemes for the government of England. He also confiscated Church property to distribute among his friends. This led to quarrels with the powerful Anselm, Archbishop of Canterbury, who went into voluntary exile, to protest against the confiscation of Church properties.

One of the few portraits we have of William II is on this coin which was minted during his reign.

William was an active man, fond of sport, and was killed by an arrow fired by his friend Walter Tyrrell while hunting in the New Forest. Walter incautiously aimed an arrow at a stag, which missed the stag, and pierced the King in the breast. It has been suggested that this was not an accident and that Tyrrell was acting under orders of Henry I, William's brother, present at the scene and who succeeded William to the throne.

William II 'Rufus', engraving by George Vertue.

TIME LINE OF THE REIGN 1087–1100

1087
William II accedes to the throne on the death of his father, William I.

1089
Archbishop Lanfranc dies – the archbishopric remains vacant for four years.

1090
William wages war on his brother Robert in Normandy.

1091
William defeats an invasion of England led by Malcolm III of Scotland.

1093
Malcolm III and the Scots invade England again. They are defeated and Malcolm is killed at the Battle of Alnwick. Anselm is appointed Archbishop of Canterbury.

1095
William suppresses a baronial revolt in Northumbria.

1097
Following a row with William, Anselm is exiled to Rome and William seizes his estates. King Donald Bane of Scotland is deposed and is succeeded by Edgar, son of Malcolm III.

1098
William invades North Wales to suppress a Welsh rebellion against the Norman border lords.

1100
William is killed by an arrow while out hunting with friends in the New Forest.

WESTMINSTER ABBEY

WESTMINSTER ABBEY was originally the abbey church of a Benedictine monastery in London, which closed in 1539. Not only is it one of England's most important Gothic structures, it is also a national shrine. The first church on the site, originally a gravel island in the marshy floodplain, is believed to date from early in the 7th century. It was erected by Æthelbert, King of Kent. Edward the Confessor began *c.*1050 the building of a Norman church, which was consecrated in 1065. Miracles claimed at the Confessor's shrine confirmed the site's sanctity as a focus for the monarchy.

In 1245, Henry III began to demolish the edifice and to build a new eastern portion. The fine octagonal chapter house was built in 1250, and in the 14th century the cloisters, abbot's house, and principal monastic buildings were added. The nave was completed in the 16th century. Henry VIII finished the Lady Chapel, which was a dedication to Henry VII, early in the 16th century. This chapel, in Perpendicular style, is noted for its superb fan vaulting. The two western towers were built (1722–40) by Sir Christopher Wren and Nicholas Hawksmoor. In the late 19th century Sir George Gilbert Scott supervised extensive restoration. From that time memorial statues by many academic Victorian sculptors have been added to the decor.

The present church is cruciform in plan; both nave and transept have side aisles. The choir is semicircular in plan, and its ring of chapels exhibits the only complete chevet in England. French influence is also seen in the height of the nave, the loftiest in England, and in the strongly emphasized flying buttresses.

Nearly every English king and queen since William I has been crowned in Westminster, and it is the burial place of 18 monarchs. England's most notable statesmen and distinguished subjects have been given burial in the Abbey since the 14th century. In the Poets' Corner in the south transept rest the tombs of Chaucer, Browning, Tennyson and other great English poets.

THE BELLS

Westminster Abbey has had bells since 1220 and the bells in use today include one 13th century and two 16th century bells. The Westminster Abbey Company of Ringers provides ringing at the Abbey for major church festivals, Royal and civic events. The half-muffled Abbey bells were included in the worldwide broadcast of the funeral service for Diana, Princess of Wales.

THE TOWER OF LONDON

THE TOWER OF London is an ancient fortress at the eastern edge of the City of London, on the north bank of the Thames, and covering about 13 acres. It was built in a simple timber-and-earth style by William the Conqueror a few months after his victory at Hastings in October 1066. The Tower is enclosed by a dry moat, within which are double castellated walls surrounding the central White Tower. Although Roman foundations have been discovered, the White Tower was built c.1078 by Gundulf, Bishop of Rochester, as a royal residence and fortress. Construction began in 1078 and was completed some twenty years later. The residential suite for the royal family, as well as a great dining hall and the Chapel of St John, were in the top part of the tower. The exterior was restored by Sir Christopher Wren.

Various towers subsequently built were used as prisons – one of them now houses a collection of medieval arms and armour. The Tower was not originally built to be a prison, and for centuries was only used to confine the privileged few. The first successful attempt at escape was made by Ranulf Flambard, Bishop of Durham, who escaped in 1101. Another, not so lucky escapee, was Prince Gruffydd of Wales, who, in 1244, fell and broke his neck whilst trying to escape from the Tower.

The crown jewels are displayed in the Waterloo Block, a former barracks. The Traitors' Gate (giving access by water from the Thames) and the Bloody Tower are associated with many historically noted persons, including Queen Elizabeth I (when still princess), Sir Thomas More, Anne Boleyn, Catherine Howard, Lady Jane Grey, the 2nd Earl of Essex, Sir Walter Raleigh, and the Duke of Monmouth. Many persons beheaded within the Tower precincts, or on the neighbouring Tower Hill, were buried in the Chapel of St. Peter ad Vincula.

The Yeomen of the Guard, dressed in Tudor style, still guard the Tower today.

HENRY I

— 1100–1135 —

ROYAL BIOGRAPHY

BORN: Selby, Yorkshire, *c.*September 1068. PARENTS: William I and Matilda of Flanders.
ASCENDED THE THRONE: 2 August 1100. CROWNED: 5 August 1100, Westminster Abbey.
AUTHORITY: King of England and Duke of Normandy (from 1106).
MARRIED: (1) Matilda (born Edith), daughter of Malcolm III, King of Scots, and (St) Margaret,
(2) Adelicia, or Adelaide, daughter of Geoffrey VII, Count of Louvain.
CHILDREN: With (1), two sons and two daughters; other illegitimate children.
DIED: St Denis le Fermont, near Rouen, 2 December 1135. BURIED: Reading Abbey.

THE SPEED WITH which Henry was crowned, a few days after his brother, William Rufus's death, and with which he took possession of the royal treasure gives credence to the suggestion that he planned William's death.

Once in power Henry proved to be an able and conscientious King concerned with administration and reform of existing laws. His right to be King was challenged by Robert, Duke of Normandy, whom he defeated at the battle of Tinchebrai and imprisoned at Cardiff castle. He then assumed the title of Duke of Normandy in addition to that of King of England.

Henry's ambition to restore the Angevin possessions, lost under Robert, were not a success, despite several attempts which were foiled by the growing power of Louis IX, King of France. Such commitments increased his debts, however, and as a major

Henry I receiving news of the drowning of his son.

part of these were with the Papacy, he feared ex-communication for non payment.

Henry now devoted himself to the good government of England and became known as Beauclerc for his talent for administration and his knowledge of both Latin and English. With Roger Salisbury as his Chancellor in the court of the Exchequer he set about reforms and the control of crown finances. The system known as Pipe Rolls continued in use until June 1834.

Henry married Edith, daughter of Malcolm III, who was also the niece of Edgar the Aethling, and thereby strengthened his ties with Scotland and the existing English establishment. Henry's only legitimate son and

heir to the throne was drowned while crossing the Channel from France. Returning from Normandy aboard the White Ship, William lost his life when the pilot, who was drunk, steered the vessel onto a rock, where it quickly filled with water.

Henry, though heartbroken, set about assuring the continuity of his dynasty by trying to persuade the barons to accept his daughter, Matilda, as their queen.

TIME LINE OF THE
REIGN 1100–1135

1100
Henry I succeeds his brother, William II. Ranulf Flambard, Bishop of Durham and chief adviser to William II, is imprisoned by Henry in the Tower of London. Henry marries Edith, daughter of Malcolm III.

1101
Robert of Normandy invades England in an attempt to wrest the throne from his brother, Henry. Robert signs the Treaty of Alton, which confirms Henry as King of England and Robert as Duke of Normandy. Henry appoints Roger Salisbury as Chancellor.

1106
War breaks out between Henry and Robert of Normandy. Henry defeats Robert at the Battle of Tinchebrai and imprisons him in Cardiff Castle for the rest of his life.

1109
Anselm, Archbishop of Canterbury dies.

1118
Death of Matilda.

1120
Henry's 17-year-old son and heir, William, is drowned.

1121
Henry marries Adela of Louvain.

1128
Henry's daughter, Matilda, marries Geoffrey Plantagenet, Count of Anjou.

1135
Henry I dies of food poisoning near Rouen, in France.

NORMAN CASTLES

THE FIRST CASTLE built by William as a stronghold from
which to govern in England was made of earth and timber.
In the course of the next hundred years buildings became a
symbol of Norman power and the White Tower rising above
the Thames was the first of many which rose throughout the country much as Roman camps
had done. They were strongholds occupied by ruling lords and bodies of troops and imposed
the royal will. Once the initial towers were built, often on mounds of earth or existing
hillocks, their perimeter was expanded. A defensive wall was added with towers from which
archers could snipe at enemies and the ditches were deepened and widened and filled with
water to make a moat.

The lords and their courts lived in the central building and around them were living
quarters for troops, stables and all the services required for a self-contained community that

Carlisle Castle, Cumbria showing the Norman Keep, c.1160.

Ludlow Castle, Shropshire.

might have to withstand a siege. In many cases such as Dover and Chepstow further walls and buildings were added until the castle took on the appearance of a village.

Norman architecture was solid, with thick walls and rounded arches in the Romanesque style. However, once Gothic architecture had made its appearance in north eastern France, the Normans adapted the new style and later Norman castles in England have a lighter appearance.

The Norman's built some 2,000 castles in England and they fulfilled a useful purpose until the fifteenth century, as a means of keeping order and collecting taxes from a sometimes troublesome population. The end of feudalism and of private armies, and the increased power of monarchs through administrative systems, made castles less essential and the use of gunpowder diminished their effectiveness as strongholds.

In the 13th century the castle became increasingly sophisticated. Living and administrative quarters were moved from the keep into new buildings raised within the bailey. The keep, made smaller and stronger, became the final defensive position within a series of battlements.

A castle was often built on the edge of an impregnable cliff, ideally at a bend in the river where it could command a view of the surrounding countryside. The Château Gaillard, built by Richard I, King of England, in Les Andelys, France, is an example of a strategically located castle. The use of gunpowder in projectiles brought to an end the impregnability of the medieval castle. After 1500 the construction of castles was no longer feasible, and 'castle' became a term for an imposing residence.

THE FEUDAL SYSTEM

THE FEUDAL SYSTEM, about which there has been much controversy, was characteristic of medieval society in England. It is associated with the rule of Norman Kings who founded the system whereby everyone was subject to, or had power over, the various levels of society. It was a practical means of controlling the population and also a useful system for extracting money or service, in the form of armed troops, from landowners. This system bound the society together for everyone was in *fief* to someone and ultimately to the King. In return for their allegiance, people were protected by those more powerful, and could receive advice on practical agricultural matters or legal disputes, and help from the educated priesthood that served the lords.

After years of disorder and local feuds following the withdrawal of the Romans and Roman law from England, the populace were, on the whole, grateful for a system that allowed them to carry on their lives peacefully. It was only the lords who resented the growing power of the King to whom they were obliged to show allegiance and give financial support. This included paying for warlike activities, the

celebration of marriages of the King's sons and daughters, and raising ransom money if the King or lord was captured in battle. This led to a series of rebellions against monarchy and the growth of private armies, made up of tenants of the great lords like Warwick, Northumberland, Somerset and other

regions. These violent quarrels culminated in the Wars of the Roses which weakened lordly power, strengthening in contrast that of Kings who began to prohibit private armies and exploited one or other baronial power in their own interest.

The abolition of the feudal system took place on 4–5 August, 1789, and was caused by the reading of a report on the misery and disorder which prevailed in the provinces. The report declared: 'Letters from all the provinces indicate that property of all kinds is a prey to the most criminal violence; on all sides chateaux are being burned, convents destroyed, and farms abandoned to pillage . . .'

Peasants at work on a feudal estate by Limbourg Brothers (fl. 1400–1416).

THE TENURES OF THE FEUDAL SYSTEM

Land ownership in ancient England, as with most objects, depended primarily on possession. You had it, you owned it. You wanted it, you fought for it. You found it, you kept it. There were no courts or police force ready to recognize or enforce 'legal rights' as we know them today.

Tenures were known as 'estates' and ran for certain periods of time:

The **fee simple estate** was the most extensive and allowed the tenant to sell or to convey by will or be transferred to the tenant's heir if he died intestate. In modern law, almost all land is held in fee simple and this is as close as one can get to absolute ownership in common law.

Fee tail estate meant that the tenure could only be transferred to a lineal descendant. If there were no lineal descendants upon the death of the tenant, the land reverted back to the lord.

The **life estate** was granted only for the life of the tenant, after which it reverted automatically to the lord.

STEPHEN AND MATILDA

1135–1154

ROYAL BIOGRAPHY — STEPHEN

BORN: Blois, *c*.1097. PARENTS: Stephen, Count of Blois, and Adela, daughter of William I.
ASCENDED THE THRONE: 1 December 1135. CROWNED: 26 December 1135,
Westminster Abbey. AUTHORITY: King of England. MARRIED: Matilda, daughter of Eustace
III, Count of Boulogne. CHILDREN: Three sons and two daughters.
DIED: Dover, 25 October 1154. BURIED: Faversham Abbey.

ROYAL BIOGRAPHY — MATILDA

BORN: London, February 1102. PARENTS: Henry I and Matilda of Scotland.
ASCENDED THE THRONE: (1 December 1135). CROWNED: Never crowned.
MARRIED: (1) Henry V, Holy Roman Emperor, (2) Geoffrey IV, Count of Anjou.
CHILDREN: With (2), three sons, including Henry II DIED: Normandy, 10 September 1167.
BURIED: Fontrevault Abbey.

THOUGH MATILDA was to have been Queen on the death of her father, Stephen usurped the throne with the support of the barons. He had been brought up at the court of Blois and his uncle Henry I had favoured him by giving him extensive estates which strengthened his conviction that he had a claim to the throne. He also had a claim through his parents the Count of Blois and his mother Adela, daughter of William the Conqueror. This was no more substantial a claim than Matilda's, however, but the English lords decided to back him. After a while, however, some lords, acknowledging that they had picked the wrong sovereign, switched their allegiance and thus created a civil war situation which lasted for

Matilda claimed the crown was hers; Stephen knew it was his.

Stephen taken prisoner by forces of Matilda in 1141.

nineteen years. The first clash between the supporters of each claimant occurred in 1138 when David I, King of Scotland, invaded England to support his niece Matilda. He was defeated by Stephen's forces at the battle of the Standard in Yorkshire. After several other encounters, the issue was undecided for neither side could muster the strength, or the money, for an outright victory. After several defeats and victories for each side Matilda gave up the struggle in 1148, and returned to France to join her husband Geoffrey, Count of Anjou, and her son Henry Plantagenet.

This was not the end of the conflict between the rivals, however, for there was the matter of the succession to be decided. Matilda had full support from the Normandy dukes, and from Robert of Gloucester in England. Meanwhile, Matilda's son Henry had received the support of the Pope and had become Duke of Normandy. He now felt that he had a strong claim to the English throne. He invaded England in 1153 to assert his claim and met Stephen at Wallingford, on the Thames, where an agreement was reached by which Henry would become King on Stephen's death.

This agreement brought the civil war, sometimes called the Nineteen Long Winters, to an end.

TIME LINE OF THE REIGN 1135–1154

1135
Henry I dies near Rouen. Coronation of King Stephen, followed by civil war between supporters of Stephen and supporters of Matilda.
1136
The first baronial revolts against Stephen begin in Norfolk and Devon.
1138
David I of Scotland invades England to support the cause of Matilda, but he is defeated at the Battle of the Standard in Yorkshire.
1139
Theobold of Bec becomes Archbishop of Canterbury. Matilda leaves France and lands in England.
1141
Matilda's forces defeat and capture Stephen at Lincoln. Matilda is made Queen.
1147
Earl Robert of Gloucester dies. The Second Crusade begins.
1148
Matilda abandons the fight and leaves England.
1151
King Stephen's wife Matilda dies.
1152
Henry of Anjou, later Henry II, marries Eleanor of Aquitaine.
1154
Stephen dies and is given an 'iron age' river burial at Faversham, Kent.

THE
PLANTAGENETS

For much of the long Plantagenet era the kings were involved in costly and, on the whole, unproductive wars with France and Scotland. They were also frequently immersed in struggles for power with over-mighty barons at home. As a dynasty, the Plantagenets made their greatest and most permanent contributions in the development of English law. Especially so in the unique Common Law, and by sponsoring a splendid architectural heritage that combined the best of contemporary European styles with distinctive English ideas.

HENRY II

—— 1154–1189 ——

ROYAL BIOGRAPHY

BORN: Le Mans, 5 March 1133. PARENTS:
Geoffrey of Anjou and the Empress Matilda.
ASCENDED THE THRONE: 24 October 1154.
CROWNED: Westminster Abbey, 19 December
1154. AUTHORITY: King of England, Duke of
Normandy, Duke of Aquitaine, other titles.
MARRIED: Eleanor, daughter of William X, Duke of
Aquitaine, and former wife of King Louis VII of
France. CHILDREN: Four sons, including the
future kings Richard I and John, and three
daughters; other illegitimate children.
DIED: Chinon, near Tours, 6 July 1189.
BURIED: Fontrevault Abbey.

Generous to the poor, a pillar of justice and an intellectual giant, Henry was the greatest of the Plantagenets.

HENRY PLANTAGENET was ruler of the largest kingdom in Europe of his day. He was the Duke of the Angevin Empire, King of England, and through his wife, Eleanor of Aquitaine, he had inherited all south-western France as far as the Pyrenees. This vast domain, in which independent-minded barons were reluctant vassals, provided a never-ending challenge to a King determined to unite his kingdom.

His able lieutenant in England was the priest Thomas Becket, whom he made first Chancellor, then Archbishop of Canterbury. Henry was not a King who would allow the Church to usurp his authority, however, and in 1164 he introduced the Constitution of Clarendon which limited Church power. Clarendon also introduced trial by jury and laid the foundations of English common law.

The royal seal of Henry II.

Though controlling the powerful Church, Henry did not contemplate a break with Rome, and to aid Pope Adrian IV, he undertook an invasion of Ireland in order to restore Irish church connections with Rome. This led to later invasions for more secular reasons which paved the way to Henry being accepted as Lord of Ireland.

A year earlier Henry's relationship with Becket, who had gone into exile as a protest at the Constitution of Clarendon, had come to a tragic end. The reason was that some of Henry's knights misinterpreting his irritable comment about being rid of his troublesome priest, had assassinated Becket in Canterbury Cathedral. This dealt a serious blow to Henry's reputation which he attempted to redeem by a public show of penance in front of Canterbury Cathedral.

There were more difficulties to contend with at the end of his reign, as his wife Eleanor encouraged her sons to rebel against their father. Although his family never succeeded in overthrowing him, Henry felt sufficiently threatened to keep Eleanor in a state of virtual imprisonment for the last 15 years of his reign. Henry died a sad man at the Château de Chinon on the river Vienne a tributary of the Loire.

TIME LINE OF THE REIGN 1154–1189

1154
Henry II accedes to the throne upon the death of his second cousin, Stephen.

1155
Henry appoints Thomas Becket Chancellor of England.

1162
Henry appoints Thomas Becket as Archbishop of Canterbury.

1164
Henry introduces the Constitutions of Clarendon which leads to a violent quarrel between Henry and Thomas Becket.

1166
The Assize of Clarendon establishes trial by jury for the first time. Henry orders an enquiry into all the crimes commited since the beginning of his reign.

1167
The Empress Matilda dies. Oxford University is founded.

1170
Henry and Becket are reconciled, but quarrel again. Becket is killed in the north transept of Canterbury Cathedral on 29 December.

1171
Henry invades Ireland. Henry is accepted as Lord of Ireland.

1173
Becket is canonized.

1173–4
Henry's sons lead a rebellion against him.

1189
Henry dies at Chinon Castle in Anjou.

ELEANOR OF AQUITAINE

*c.*1122–1204

ELEANOR WAS A beautiful and strong-minded woman and heir to Aquitaine, the region encompassing Gascony and south-west France. She was married to Louis VII of France but the marriage failed and she then married Henry of Anjou (Henry II of England). Between the two they now had an empire covering the whole of western France.

She bore Henry eight children, but this did not prevent her taking an active part in the affairs of her kingdom. This led to disagreements with her husband who was as strong and independent-minded as she was, and who spent much of his time travelling about his kingdom, and hers, and ordering matters as he thought best for a united Anjou. The problem was that the various regions of the Angevin Empire were very different, with their own traditions and culture, so there was plenty of room for disagreement. Also, Henry's short-tempered and untrusting nature, found it difficult to divide the responsibilities for his domain and future inheritance among his sons. This led Eleanor to plot with her children to oust Henry. He was, however, too clever and well informed and, learning of the plot, he confronted his wife and sons and took Eleanor prisoner.

Her prison was in the large and powerful Château de Chinon, which gave her freedom within its walls above the River Vienne, but did not allow her to mingle with those who might have

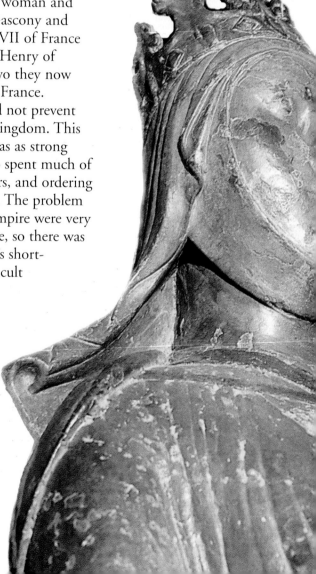

been her allies. While there she undoubtedly spread the Romance culture of southern France, in whose courts a more civilized form of life had been adopted. With gallant behaviour expected from the rough knights, troubadours entertained in castle halls and cultural pursuits became a social grace.

On Henry's death Eleanor resumed her political life and became a formidable ruler of her son Richard's kingdom while he was away on Crusades. She survived her son Richard, and saw her other son John crowned as his successor, and then went back to Aquitaine and arranged a splendid marriage. This was for her granddaughter Blanche of Castile to the grandson of her former husband, King Louis.

Eleanor was energetic to the end. Eleanor travelled constantly, even in her old age. Running from one end of Europe to another, she often risked her life in her efforts to maintain the loyalty of the English subjects, cement marriage alliances, and manage her army and estates. By this time she had many grandchildren, earning Eleanor the title of 'Grandmother of Europe'.

Eleanor died in 1204 at her favourite religious house, the abbey of Fontevrault, where she had retreated to find peace during various moments of the life. Her tomb in Fontevrault, next to her husband Henry II, has a magnificent effigy, a tribute to a great Queen.

The casts of three famous tombs have been placed in Falaise Castle chapel. They represent Henry II, his Queen, Eleanor of Aquitaine and their son Richard I. The originals lie at Fontevrault. The tomb of Eleanor is particularly lovely. Some people believe that Maud de Saint Valery, William de Braose III's wife, once served Eleanor as a hand maiden.

ELEANOR OF AQUITAINE 1122–1204

Eleanor's long life was quite spectacular and filled with every kind of excitement. She was brought up in France, where the arts were truly appreciated. She brought a new dimension to the English court, due to her very different tastes, morals and lifestyle. Two things really stood out about Eleanor, she was outstandingly beautiful and very rich.

Eleanor was Queen of France before she ever came to England. She accompanied her first husband, King Louis, to the Holy Land on the Second Crusade and ended up leading a special 'ladies' crusade.

Eleanor found life with Louis extremely dull and he soon realised he was completely out of his depth in the marriage. Eleanor indulged in a passionate love affair with her uncle, and enjoyed the attentions of a young Saracen emir. Eleanor's life changed dramatically when she met Henry Plantagenet. The passion was mutual and she quickly divorced Louis. Six weeks later Henry and Eleanor were married, Eleanor being already five months pregnant.

Two years later, Henry and Eleanor were crowned, gloriously, in Westminster Abbey. Everyone was astonished by the very elaborate ornaments and fabrics she wore, all from exotic lands.

RICHARD I

—— 1189–1199 ——

ROYAL BIOGRAPHY

BORN: Beaumont Palace, Oxford, 8 September 1157. PARENTS: Henry II and Eleanor of Aquitaine. ASCENDED THE THRONE: 6 July 1189. CROWNED: Westminster Abbey, 3 September 1189. AUTHORITY: King of England, Duke of Normandy, Duke of Aquitaine, other titles. MARRIED: Berengaria, daughter of Sancho V of Navarro and granddaughter of Alfonso VII of Castile. CHILDREN: Two illegitimate sons DIED: Limousin, 6 April 1199. BURIED: Fontrevault Abbey.

RICHARD, SON OF Henry II and Eleanor of Aquitaine, is a King whose reputation is legendary. He was a hero King and great warrior who comes only second to St George as a national icon, but whose contribution to the development of his English kingdom seems rather sparse. Known as the Lionheart for his courage in battle, Richard, who, like his father, spoke, and

wrote in French, spent little time in his English kingdom. One of his uses for his cross Channel domain was for the extraction of revenue for his crusading zeal. In 1189 he set off with Philip of France on the Third Crusade and took Acre, then defeated the Saracen King Saladin at Jaffa.

During his journeys in the Holy Land and in France to protect his Angevin kingdom from ambitious barons, Richard left his English affairs in the hands of William Longchamp and his youngest brother John Lackland. Some authorities regarded John as a treacherous ally, inclined to plot against his brother with the King of France. One of the events which led to this conclusion was the shipwreck and capture of Richard on his return from a Crusade. He was captured by Duke Leopold of Austria, who sold

Richard the Lionheart, John of Gaunt, Edward III, Joan Plantagenet and Philippa of Hainault.

him to the Emperor Henry VI of Germany, for potential ransom money. According to one version, his brother's absence was taken advantage of by John to further his own ambitions. In another version John raised the 100,000 marks for his brother's release which, according to some, Richard managed alone by the charm of his presence. The ransom money was raised by selling Church lands and town charters and aggravated the strained relationship between John, the Church and barons.

Thus the story of Richard is a confusion of fact and legend distorted by his admirers. A splendid statue of the warrior King was erected before the Houses of Parliament in Westminster.

The fact is that Richard was more French than English, and spent only six months of his reign in his English kingdom. Moreover, when he died he bequeathed his body to Fontevrault Abbey on the River Loire where his sarcophagus lies alongside that of his mother, Eleanor of Aquitaine, and his father Henry II.

TIME LINE OF THE REIGN 1189–1199

1189
Richard I becomes King of England upon the death of his father, Henry II. William Longchamp is appointed Chancellor of England and governs the country while Richard is abroad. Richard sets out with Philip of France on the Third Crusade to the Holy Land.

1191
Richard captures the city of Acre, in Palestine, and defeats Saladin at Arsouf, near Jaffa.

1192
The Third Crusade ends without regaining Jerusalem. On his way back to England from Palestine, Richard is captured by the Duke of Austria, who hands him over to Henry VI. Henry demands a ransom of 100,000 marks from England for Richard's release from prison.

1193
Hubert Walter becomes Archbishop of Canterbury.

1194
The ransom is raised in England and paid to Henry. Richard is released from captivity. He returns home for a brief period before leaving to fight in France.

1198
Hubert Walter reintroduces the idea of a land tax.

1199
Richard dies from a crossbow wound received while besieging Chaluz Castle, in France.

PLANTAGENET FRANCE

THE PLANTAGENET ERA consisted of fourteen kings, including the houses of York and Lancaster, spanning 331 years. Interestingly enough all of these kings shared one common family trait, a volatile spirit coursing through their veins. Richard I is said to have stated, 'from the Devil we sprang and to the Devil we shall go'.

Although the name was not used until the mid-15th century the surname Plantagenet came from Henry II's father Geoffrey Count of Anjou. It was said that Geoffrey used to wear a sprig of flowers upon himself as a badge (*planta genista*), a habit thought to have originated when, retrieving his hat which fell off one day while out hunting, he scooped up a handful of yellow broom flowers.

The reign of the Plantagenet kings plunged the country into eternal warfare, not only with France, and Scotland, but with internal family conflicts as well. Angevin, French for Anjou, was the name of two medieval dynasties originating in France. The first ruled over parts of France and over Jerusalem and England; the second ruled over parts of France and over Naples, Hungary, and Poland, with a claim to Jerusalem. Geoffrey Plantagenet inherited Anjou. He married Matilda of England, daughter of the English

King Henry I, and conquered Normandy. Their son became the first Angevin (or Plantagenet) King of England as Henry II. His successors were Richard I, John, Henry III, Edward I, Edward II, Edward III, and Richard II, after whom the English branch split into the houses of Lancaster and of York.

The second house of Anjou was a branch of the Capetians and originated with Charles, a younger brother of King Louis IX of France. Charles was made Count of Anjou by Louis, acquired Provence by marriage, and in 1266 was invested by the Pope with the kingdom of Naples and Sicily as Charles I. Charles lost Sicily but retained Naples. His successors were Charles II, Robert, and Joanna I of Naples and Provence.

Three Plantagenet Tombs: Henry II, Eleanor of Aquitaine and Richard I in Fontevrault Abbey.

THE PLANTAGENETS
1154–1399

House of Plantagenet

Henry II   (1154–1189)

Richard I   (1189–1199)
(The Lionheart)

John (Lackland) (1199–1216)

Henry III   (1216–1272)

Edward I   (1272–1307)
(Hammer of the Scots)

Edward II   (1307–1327)

Edward III   (1327–1377)

Richard II   (1377–1399)

House of Lancaster

Henry IV   (1399–1413)

Henry V   (1413–1422)

Henry VI   (1422–1461)

House of York

Edward IV   (1461–1483)

Edward V   1483

Richard III   (1483–1485)
(Crookback)

JOHN

—— 1199–1216 ——

ROYAL BIOGRAPHY

BORN: Beaumont Palace, Oxford, 24 December 1167. PARENTS: Henry II and Eleanor of Aquitaine. ASCENDED THE THRONE: 6 April 1199 CROWNED: 27 May 1199, Westminster Abbey. AUTHORITY: King of England and Ireland, other titles.
MARRIED: (1) Isabella of Gloucester (annulled 1199), (2) Isabella, daughter of the Count of Angoulême. CHILDREN: With (2), two sons, including the future Henry III, and three daughters; other illegitimate children. DIED: Newark, 19 October 1216. BURIED: Worcester Cathedral.

John's favourite pastime was hunting, as shown in this 14th-century illustration.

JOHN'S REPUTATION as an inept King who lost many of his father's possessions in France and the royal war chest and treasure in The Wash, Norfolk, is not entirely merited. Though the belief that he murdered, or arranged the murder, of his nephew Arthur may be true. While his brother Richard was abroad during most of his reign, John administered the affairs of England, and opposed Church pressure on English society.

His quarrels with the Church had a chequered history, dating from 1206 when he refused to accept Stephen Langton as

Archbishop of Canterbury. In 1209 the Pope excommunicated the King, after banning all church services except baptism. He also declared that John had no right to the English crown. Under pressure from the power of Rome John gave way, and was later rewarded by being relieved by the Pontiff of the obligations of the Magna Carta.

The signing of the Magna Carta, a document limiting royal power, marked a crisis point between John and the barons. They had never been happy with Norman control, and had obliged John to sign at Runnymede, on the Thames near Windsor, on 15 June, 1215. The conflict with the barons continued, however, until in desperation, they called on the assistance of the Dauphin Louis of France. Louis invaded in May 1216 and obliged John to accept the barons demands.

Despite these mishaps, history has shown that John was a King who continued the work of his predecessors. He extended the network of castles which secured peace for a country that was growing in strength and prosperity. However, John's reputation has been up against that of two warrior heroes, his own brother, Richard I, and that of Robin Hood, a legendary outlaw of Sherwood Forest. Robin was supposedly loyal to Richard, and stole from the rich to give to the poor. Against such charismatic figures John fades into insignificance.

TIME LINE OF THE REIGN 1199–1216

1199
John accedes to the throne on the death of Richard.
1204
England loses almost all its possessions in France.
1206
John refuses to accept Stephen Langton as Archbishop of Canterbury.
1208
Pope Innocent III issues an Interdict against England, banning all church services except for baptisms and funerals.
1209
Pope Innocent III excommunicates John for his confiscation of ecclesiastical property.
1212
Innocent III declares that John is no longer the rightful King of England.
1214
Philip Augustus of France defeats the English army at the Battle of Bouvines.
1215
John is compelled by his barons and prelates to sign the Magna Carta at Runnymede.
1216
The barons seek French aid in their fight against John; Prince Louis of France captures the Tower of London.
1216
John dies unexpectedly at Newark of a fever.

THE MAGNA CARTA

— 1215 —

SINCE THE ARRIVAL of William the Conqueror, the lords and earls of England had resisted attempts to force them to conform to the efforts of kings to unify England. They also objected to the King's arbitrary power to extract money by taxation and his rights over private property. John had incurred general hostility. His expensive wars abroad were unsuccessful, and to finance them he had charged excessively for royal justice, sold church offices, levied heavy aids, and abused the feudal incidents of wardship and marriage. He had also appointed advisers from outside the baronial ranks.

After long and quarrelsome negotiations John bowed to the barons demands. These included a curtailment of royal power, an agreement not to arbitrarily change principles on which the feudal system was based, and to set standards for royal behaviour in writing. The charter referred only to the King and the ruling classes. It was by no means a document which established rights for the people.

John met the barons and signed the charter on the island of Runnymede, on the river Thames near Windsor, on 15 June 1215. He immediately, with the Pope's scheming, decided that he was not obliged to abide by its principles. This provoked uprisings by the barons which continued until the reign of Henry III, when the charter was once more brought up for discussion. Nevertheless, something had been achieved and the Magna Carta had set a standard for future relationships between rulers and their lords.

Furthermore, as the power of barons declined in later centuries and the power of burgesses increased, it became the document on which demands for the rights of the people were based. It was recognized by Parliaments and the law courts, and some of its chapters remain on the statute books as enduring benchmarks in the evolution of British law.

qu er eis summoniti nolint vel nequeant in
air et firmum quod maior pars eorum qui pre-
erit vel preceperit ac si omnes viginti quin-
sent et predicti viginti quinque iurent quod
iter obserbabunt et pro toto posse suo facient
chil impetrabimus ab aliquo per nos nec per
a istarum concessionum et libertatum retro
t si aliquid tale impetratum fuerit irritum sit
a eo utemur per nos nec per alium Et omnes
ignationes et rancores orige inter nos et homi
t laicos a tempore discordie plene omnibus re-
mus Preterea omnes transgressiones factas
cordie a pascha anno regni nostri sertodecimo
matam plene remisimus omnibus clericis et
nos pertinet plene condonabimus Et insuper
ras testimoniales patentes domini Stephani
omini Henrici Dublin' archiepiscopi et epis-
a et magistri Pandulfi super securitate ista
fatis Quare volumus et firmiter precipimus
sia libera sit et quod homines in regno nostro
nnes prefatas libertates iura et concessiones
et quiete plene et integre sibi et heredibus
edibus nostris in omnibus rebus et locis in
dictum est Iuratum est autem tam ex parte
e baronum quod hec omnia supradicta bona
enio obserbabuntur Testibus supradictis et
per manum nostram in prato quod vocatur
Clundelesorum et Stanes quinto decimo die
stri septimo decimo.

THE MISSING THUMB

John's one wish was to be buried in Worcester Cathedral, near his favourite saint, Wulfstan. This wish was granted, and his effigy there is beautifully preserved.

When his tomb was opened in 1797, his body was found to be wrapped in robes of crimson damask and a monk's cowl. John's body was replaced after having been thoroughly inspected, but not before one of his thumb bones had been evilly taken.

However, the person who took the bone must have had a guilty conscience, for it was returned shortly afterwards. It didn't seem worthwhile disinterring John again to replace his thumb, so for many years this grisly object was on display, mounted in gold, in a nearby case. However, even this has now disappeared.

So it is a sad fact that the hand that put the seal to the Magna Carta will be missing a thumb for ever.

HENRY III

—— 1216–1272 ——

BORN: 1 October 1207, Winchester. PARENTS: King John and Isabella of Angoulême. ASCENDED THE THRONE: 19 October 1216. CROWNED: 28 October 1216, Gloucester Cathedral. AUTHORITY: King of England, Ireland and parts of France. MARRIED: Eleanor, daughter of Raymond Berenger IV, Count of Provence. CHILDREN: Six sons, including the future Edward I, and three daughters. DIED: 16 November 1272, Westminster. BURIED: Westminster Abbey.

ROYAL BIOGRAPHY

JOHN'S SON BECAME King at the age of nine but did not take on the government of England until 1227. During his childhood his kingdom was governed by Regents: William the Marshal, and Hubert de Burgh. Both men dealt successfully with the attempts by the French Dauphin, later Louis VIII, to take England by force.

On reaching his twentieth year Henry dismissed de Burgh and appointed Peter de Riveaux as Chancellor and Peter des Roches as Bishop of Winchester. The appointment of Frenchmen to important posts did not please the barons who rebelled under William Marshal, Earl of Pembroke. Their revolt did not succeed, but there was another more valiant opponent waiting to oppose the King. This was Simon de Montfort, Earl of Leicester, who was married to Eleanor, Henry's sister and obliged him to sign yet another document to limit his power. This was the Provisions of Oxford which, having signed, Henry repudiated. A civil war now broke out and Henry was defeated at Lewes in 1264. After his victory De Montfort called together a parliament but differences of opinion between its delegates doomed it to failure. Henry's son Edward now entered the fray and killed de Montfort in battle at Evesham in 1265, and thus ended the first attempt at parliamentary government.

Earlier in his reign Henry had also been faced by a Welsh revolt under Owain Glendower who had survived and kept north Wales independent for eleven years with French help.

Though not a clever or forceful King, and prone to offending friends and enemies alike, Henry's reign was one of political progress and prosperity. Henry encouraged learning and three Oxford colleges were founded in his reign.

The arts of writing and illustration flourished, notably in the person of Matthew Paris, the historian, who drew up the first map of England.

Despite all the difficulties he faced during his reign, Henry died in 1272 leaving behind him a kingdom that was prosperous, united and prepared to accept the rule of his son, Edward I.

Henry III had few of the personal qualities required to command respect, he always seemed to alienate enemies and advisers alike. However, in some way he redeemed himself by patronizing the arts, and inspiring improvements to Westminster Abbey and the construction of Salisbury Cathedral.

TIME LINE OF THE REIGN 1216–1272

1216
Henry III is crowned King of England at the age of nine upon the death of his father, John. England is temporarily ruled by two regents – William the Marshal and Hubert de Burgh.

1217
Battle of Lincoln in May. Battle of Dover in August. The French under Louis, later Louis VIII, are driven out of England. The Treaty of Lambeth establishes peace between France, the English barons and supporters of Henry.

1219
William the Marshal dies.

1227
Henry takes full control of the government of England, but retains Hubert de Burgh as his principal adviser.

1232
Peter des Riveaux is appointed Treasurer of England and Hubert de Burgh is dismissed.

1236
Henry marries Eleanor of Provence and three of her uncles become ministers in England.

1264
The Baron's War breaks out and Henry is defeated by de Montfort at the Battle of Lewes.

1265
De Montfort summons the first English parliament, but is killed at Evesham.

1272
Henry III dies in the Palace of Westminster.

EARLY PARLIAMENTS

THE FIRST STEPS in the forming of parliament occurred in the 13th century. The long, slow process of evolution began with the *Curia Regis*, the king's feudal council to which he summoned his tenants in chief, the great barons, and the great prelates. This was the nucleus from which Parliament and, more specifically, the House of Lords developed.

The House of Commons originated in the 13th century, in the occasional assembly of representatives of other social classes of the state – knights and burgesses – usually to report the consent of the counties and towns to taxes imposed by the King. Its meetings were often held in conjunction with a meeting of the great council, for the early 13th century recognized no constitutional difference between the two bodies. The forming of Parliament as a distinct organ of government took at least another century to complete.

During the Barons' War, Simon de Montfort summoned representatives of the counties, towns, and lesser clergy in an attempt to gain support from the middle classes. His famous Parliament of 1265 included two representative burgesses from each borough and four knights from each shire. This was the first time that all classses, with the exception of serfs, were represented in Parliament. Before a century had passed, Parliament had the right to make laws and levy taxation, and the knights and borough representatives had begun to sit as a separate body, the Commons.

The division of Parliament into two houses did not come about until the 14th century. The lawful position of Parliament was at first not very different

The present Houses of Parliament are situated beside the River Thames. They were built between 1840 and 1860 and incorporate part of the medieval Palace of Westminster.

The seal of Simon de Montfort.

from that of the great council.

In the 14th century, Parliament began to gain greater control over grants of revenue to the King. Statute legislation arose as the petition form was gradually replaced by the drafting of bills sent to the King and ultimately carried out by Commons, Lords, and King together. Impeachment of the King's ministers, another means for securing control over administrative policy, also derived from Parliament's judicial authority and was first used late in the 14th century.

In the 15th century Parliament wielded wide administrative and legislative powers. In addition a strong self-consciousness on the part of its members led to claims of parliamentary privilege, notably freedom from arrest and freedom of debate. With the growth of a stronger monarchy under the Yorkists and especially under the Tudors, Parliament became essentially an instrument of the monarch's will.

THE BARONS' WAR 1263–1267

The Barons' War was between King Henry III and his barons. In 1261, Henry III renounced the Provisions of Oxford (1258) and the Provisions of Westminster (1259), which had vested considerable power in a council of barons, and reasserted his right to appoint councillors. The barons led by Simon de Montfort, Earl of Leicester, finally resorted to arms in 1263 and forced the King to reaffirm his adherence to the Provisions. In 1264 a decision in favour of the crown by Louis IX of France as arbitrator led to a renewal of war. Montfort defeated Henry's forces in the battle of Lewes, and the King once again submitted to government by council. Early in 1265, Montfort summoned his famous representative Parliament to strengthen his position.

This was threatened by the possibility of an invasion by Henry's supporters abroad. The invasion did not take place, but an uprising against Montfort of the Welsh Marchers led to his defeat by the King's son (later Edward I) at Evesham. Montfort was killed in the battle, but some baronial resistance continued until 1267. The barons had failed to establish their own control over the crown, but they had helped prepare the way for the constitutional developments of the reign of Edward I.

EDWARD I

—— 1272–1307 ——

BORN: 17 June 1239, Westminster. PARENTS: Henry III and Eleanor of Provence.
ASCENDED THE THRONE: 16 November 1272. CROWNED: 19 August 1274, Westminster Abbey.
AUTHORITY: King of England, Wales, Scotland and Ireland. MARRIED: (1) Eleanor, daughter of
Ferdinand III of Castile, (2) Margaret, daughter of Philip III of France (1299).
CHILDREN: With (1) four sons, including the future Edward II, and 12 daughters; with (2) two
sons and one daughter. DIED: 7 July 1307, Burgh-by-Sands, Cumbria.
BURIED: Westminster Abbey.

ROYAL BIOGRAPHY

EDWARD, KNOWN AS 'Longshanks' because of his height, and the 'Hammer of the Scots' because of his success against the Scots, was a man of enormous energy. He finally subdued Wales in 1284, making his son Prince of Wales. Edward had sixteen children by Eleanor of Castile, one born while he and his wife were on a Crusade. Edward's love for his wife is confirmed by the fact that, on her death in Nottingham, Edward had her body brought to London and erected stone crosses at every one of the twelve stops on the way. He married for the second time and had three children by his second wife Margaret of France.

One of the 12 memorials to Eleanor of Castile.

His activities covered every aspect of government and continued his predecessors' efforts to curb Church and baronial power. The reason was that this interfered with the unification of the nation under a monarch. In 1279 he set up the Statute of Mortmain to prevent landowners giving their lands to the church in order to avoid taxation, and to ensure their place in heaven. In 1285 he created the positions of Justices of the Peace, a measure designed to curb banditry and violent crime. He also summoned, in 1295, lords, clergy and burgesses from each shire thus furthering the concept of a parliament. This was known as the

A 19th century engraving of Edward I.

1272
In Sicily, returning home from a Crusade, Edwards hears that, on the death of his father Henry III, he has become King.

1274
Edward returns to England to be crowned in Westminster Abbey.

1277
Edward invades North Wales.

1282
Edward invades North Wales again and defeats Llywelyn.

1284
Welsh independence ended by Statute of Rhuddlan.

1285
Statute of Winchester institutes the first Justices of the Peace.

1290
Death of Eleanor of Castile at the age of 54.

1292
Edward chooses John Balliol to be King of Scotland.

1296
Edward invades Scotland and defeats and deposes Balliol.

1298
Edward invades Scotland again and defeats William Wallace at the Battle of Falkirk.

1299
Edward marrries Margaret of France.

1305
Wallace is betrayed, tried and executed in London.

1307
Edward invades Scotland again, but dies on his way north.

Model Parliament, first proposed by Simon de Montfort. Edward's energy was tinged with the ruthlessness needed to govern in a country still finding its feet. Having chosen John Balliol as King of Scotland in 1296, he then deposed him and removed the Stone of Scone to Westminster. Traditionally Scottish kings had always been crowned on the Stone. His one setback was a defeat by William Wallace, the Scottish patriot, at Stirling but he took his revenge at Falkirk in 1305 and Wallace was taken prisoner and later hanged, drawn and quartered.

THE CRUSADES

THE STRENGTHENING OF Church power in Europe created an ambience in which Church activity was rife in all levels of society. There was an increase in monastic life, the building of churches, and in pilgrimages to holy places. It became essential to go on a Crusade to the Holy Land to free biblical places from domination by disbelievers.

These holy expeditions were launched at the Council of Trent in 1095, and soon everyone from the poorest to the most powerful and wealthy, were wending their way to the Middle East. Even the very young joined the disastrous Children's Crusade. The object of the Crusades was to rid the Holy Land of the Saracens, but the journeys soon became a social necessity and a commercial venture. The grand Crusaders took with them not only an army, but retainers,

Battle of the Christians and Saracens at Damietta during the Crusades, by Matthew Paris.

clerics, scholars and merchants – all of whom had their own interest for going along. The usual port of embarkation was Venice which soon grew rich providing ships, provision and mercenaries for the enterprises.

The east had always been an exotic place since the time of Marco Polo, and was the source of fine works of art, textiles, architectural techniques and learning. Many of the old Roman texts, lost during the Dark Ages, had disappeared in the west but had been preserved in Arabic. Thus the Crusades became, not only a means for material gain, but a channel through which knowledge flowed into Europe. Sciences, including arithmetic, algebra, astronomy, chemistry and physics, changed European learning. Building with a pointed arch launched the European age of Gothic architecture.

Crusades became a business as well as a holy mission. Commerce triumphed over the spiritual life to such an extent that the Fourth Crusade, which followed Richard the Lionheart's Third Crusade, deviated from its original aim to free the Holy Land and sacked Byzantium instead.

THE KNIGHTS TEMPLAR

The Knights Templar were a military Religious Order, or to put it simply 'fighting monks'. They were founded in 1119 AD to protect Christian pilgrims visiting the Holy Land and in particular the Temple of Solomon in Jerusalem – hence the name.

The Knights Templars were formed after the crusaders had captured the Holy Land. Ostensibly their task was to protect pilgrims from the still frequent Islamic attacks, however some claim that this was a cover, right from the start. They were a highly secretive organization and have, therefore, positively invited much speculation. Amongst the more famous speculations are those regarding devil worship, retention of the treasures of Jerusalem and retention of the Holy Grail. All weird and wonderful stories but, many think, totally fabricated.

The Templars had a rule that they could acquire wealth as a body, through their Templar activities, but not individually. Over the years, for services rendered, and possibly with the Jerusalem treasure as a starting fund, the group became very rich. Eventually, they became extremely arrogant and considered themselves even superior to monarchy or at least, outside its control and answerable only to the Pope.

EDWARD II

1307–1327

ROYAL BIOGRAPHY

BORN: 25 April 1284, Caernarfon. PARENTS: Edward I and Eleanor of Castile.
ASCENDED THE THRONE: 8 July 1307. CROWNED: 25 February 1308, Westminster Abbey.
AUTHORITY: King of England, other claims. MARRIED: Isabella, daughter of Philip III of France.
CHILDREN: Two sons, including the future Edward III, and two daughters.
DIED: 21 September 1327, Berkeley Castle. BURIED: Gloucester Cathedral.

THE STORY OF Edward II has the elements of a grand horror story, with marital treachery and a gruesome death. The only surviving son of a powerful father, Edward I, he was brought up in a household of female siblings and this may well have conditioned his character.

His reign was not a happy one for he had a weakness for surrounding himself with unsuitable and incompetent advisers. One of these, Piers Gaveston, was executed by the barons who were deeply dissatisfied by Gaveston's influence on the king.

Edward's forays against the Scots, whom his father had dealt with energetically, were a failure. His army was defeated at Bannockburn by the forces of Robert Bruce.

Though Edward was able to quell a rebellion by barons at Boroughbridge in Yorkshire, his troubles were not over. His wife, Isabella of France, who had borne him four children, deserted him for Roger Mortimer and ran away to France. Here she and her lover raised an army which sailed to the Suffolk coast and defeated Edward. This act forced him to abdicate in favour of his son Edward, later to become Edward III, during whose childhood Isabella and Mortimer would be regents. Edward was deposed with the consent of Parliament and imprisoned in Berkeley Castle in Somerset. Attempts were made to rescue him until, on his wife's and Mortimer's orders, he was murdered by hired killers who were told that no mark should be visible on his body. The only way of doing this was by pushing a red-hot poker up his anus, which at the time was a conventional, but gruesome death for homosexuals. In 1330 when he was eighteen, Edward's son decided to take up the reins of power. Mortimer was tried and executed and Isabella was imprisoned at Castle Rising in Norfolk for the rest of her life.

ISABELLA OF FRANCE (1292–1358)

Isabella was Queen to Edward II of England. She was known as Isabella the Fair, and later as the She-Wolf of France. As soon as she arrived in England, aged only twelve, to marry Edward, Isabella noticed that Piers Gaveston, to whom Edward had entrusted the 'care' of England, was wearing rings and jewels which her own father had just given to Edward. Edward and his gay companion were publicly kissing and embracing. Isabella wrote home in her misery, describing herself as the most wretched woman in the world. Realizing that she could do nothing about the situation, she gritted her teeth and became a loyal and supportive consort. She bore Edward four children, and helped him on his admittedly unsuccessful military campaigns. Eventually, when Isabella had had enough of his strange relationships, she took herself a lover, Roger Mortimer. Aiming to revenge herself on Edward, Isabella recruited an army in France and after a struggle Edward was defeated.

TIME LINE OF THE REIGN 1307–1327

1307
Edward accedes to the throne on the death of his father Edward I.

1308
Edward's favourite, the Gascon noble Piers Gaveston, is exiled for misgovernment.

1309
Gaveston returns from exile in France. Robert Bruce holds his first parliament at St Andrews.

1310
Parliament sets up a committee of Lords Ordainers to control the King and improve administration. The King's cousin, Thomas, Earl of Lancaster, takes control.

1312
Gaveston is kidnapped by the King's opponents and is beheaded.

1314
Edward and the English army are routed at the Battle of Bannockburn by Robert Bruce.

1320
Edward takes two new favourites, Sir Hugh Despenser and his son Hugh.

1322
Barons' rebellion, led by Thomas, Earl of Lancaster, is crushed at the Battle of Boroughbridge. Edward has Lancaster beheaded.

1326
Edward's wife Isabella seizes power with her lover Roger and deposes Edward. The Despensers are both put to death.

1327
Edward is murdered in Berkeley Castle.

THE CONQUEST OF WALES

—————— 1277–1284 ——————

THE MOST SIGNIFICANT figure in Welsh history was Llewelyn ap Iorwerth (Llewelyn I the Great), Prince of Wales from 1194 to 1239, when he retired to a monastery. He died in 1240. On his son Dafydd's death in 1246 there were four claimants to the Welsh crown: Owen and Llewelyn (Llewelyn II ap Gruffydd), the sons of Griffith; Ralph Mortimer, who had married Gladys, daughter of Llewelyn the Great, and who at his death left his estates and claim to his son, Roger; and Edward, the son of Henry III, later to become Edward I. Llewelyn declared war on the English in 1256. A settlement was reached in 1267 when Henry and Llewelyn met at Montgomery, where they ratified a treaty that gave Wales peace under the recognized rule of Llewelyn.

On the death of Henry III in 1272 Llewelyn refused to take the oath of loyalty or to pay homage to Edward I, who at that time was absent on the crusades. After his return to England, Edward appeared with an army at Chester (1275). The following year Edward made great preparations for a war of annihilation against Llewelyn and in 1277 his army closed round Wales. Llewelyn realized the hopelessness of continuing the struggle and submitted to the humiliating terms of the Treaty of Rhuddlan on the 10 November 1277. He did homage to Edward at Westminster in 1278, but a few years later again led a revolt. Edward once again invaded Wales and overran the country. Finally, in 1282, Llewelyn was killed in a chance encounter.

From this date Wales ceased to have any separate political existence. The conquest of the country brought into the king's hands the government of the principality and of those chieftains in South Wales who had become Llewelyn's adherents. In all these lands government by princes was replaced by that of the king's officials. Llewelyn's principality became six shires: Anglesey (the former island of Mon), Caernarfon, Merioneth, Flint, Cardigan, and Carmarthen. New castles ringed the land. The young prince, the future Edward II, born at Caernarfon, was the new Prince of Wales, and to him was given the honour of offering Llewelyn's coronet at the shrine of Edward the Confessor at Westminster.

LEFT: Harlech Castle, completed in 1290, is sited on a crag commanding views over the Lleyn peninsula and Snowdonia. In 1404 it was captured by Owain Glyndwr and was used as a base for his lengthy rebellion against Henry IV.

RIGHT: A slate monument stands outside Builth in mid-Wales, in memory of Llwelyn Yr Ail, the last independent Prince of Wales. He was ambushed and killed on a bridge near the town on 11 December 1282.

TIME LINE OF WALES
1277–1284

1246–82
Llywelyn ap Gruffydd (the Last), Prince of Gwynedd rules much of Wales.
1267
Treaty of Montgomery signed by Henry III, ratifying Llywelyn ap Gruffydd's claim to the title 'Prince of Wales'.
1270–1320
Tintern Abbey built.
1276–77
First War of Welsh Independence.
1277
Llywelyn signs Treaty of Aberconwy, ending the First Welsh War and reversing the gains of the Treaty of Montgomery. Edward I begins Aberystwyth, Flint and Rhuddlan Castles.
1282–83
Second War of Welsh Independence. Llywelyn's brother Dafydd rises up against Edward I.
1283
Caernarfon, Conwy and Harlech Castles started.
1284
Treaty of Rhuddlan signed by Edward I.

THE CANTERBURY TALES

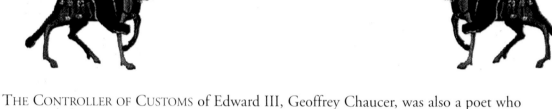

THE CONTROLLER OF CUSTOMS of Edward III, Geoffrey Chaucer, was also a poet who wrote a tale of pilgrims going to Canterbury to visit the tomb of St. Thomas Becket. This has become a world classic.

The tale records the members of the party which travelled along the North Downs in a group, for company as well as safety. They were a mixed crowd, from all walks of life and cultural backgrounds, and give a vivid picture of medieval England. Each evening as they stopped at an inn one of the company would tell a tale to entertain the others. There was a miller whose stories, Chaucer remarks, were 'filthy in the main', and a Prioress who wiped her upper lip so clean that 'not a trace of grease was to be seen'. There was a monk whose favourite sport was hunting, and a poor Oxford student 'with a hollow look and sober stare'. In fact a whole gallery of characters, who are as alive today as when Chaucer first wrote about them.

Through Chaucer's superb powers of characterization the pilgrims – such as the earthy wife of Bath, the gentle knight, the worldly prioress, the evil summoner – come intensely alive. Chaucer was a master storyteller and craftsman, but because of a change in the language after 1400, his technique was not fully appreciated until the 18th century.

Chaucer, whose patron was John of Gaunt, wrote *The Canterbury Tales* while Gaunt was away on foreign business. Chaucer himself began to be sent on missions abroad by the King and, while on his travels, he practised his French, Italian and Latin, and indulged his thirst for knowledge of astronomy, and medicine. He no doubt studied another story teller Bocaccio who must have been an inspiration for *The Canterbury Tales*.

On the death of Edward, Chaucer was temporarily out of favour, as the Regent for the young Richard II was not a lover of poetry, and gave his own friends such posts as the Controller of Customs. However, when Richard took over as King, Chaucer returned to favour with the King who used to give him a tun of wine every year. He died on 25 October 1400 and is buried in Westminster Abbey.

Portrait of Geoffrey Chaucer

THE TALE OF THE PRIORESS

An extract from 'the Canterbury Tales':
The Prioress

Ther was in Asye, in a greet citee,
Amonges Cristene folk, a Jewerye,
Sustened by a lord of that contree
For foule usure and lucre of
vileynye,
Hateful to Crist and to his
compaignye,
And thurgh this strete men myghte
ride or wende,
For it was free and open at eyther
ende.

A litel scole of cristen folk ther
stood
Doun at the ferther ende, in which
ther were
Children an heep, ycomen of
Cristen blood,
That lerned in that scole yeer by
yeer
Swich manere doctrine as men used
there,
This is to seyn, to syngen and to
rede,
As smale children doon in hir
childhede.

Among thise children was a
wydwes sone,
A litel clergeon, seven yeer of age,
That day by day to scole was
his wone,
And eek also, wher as he saugh
th' ymage
Of Cristes mooder, he hadde in
usage
As hym was taught, to knele
adoun, and seye
His Ave Marie, as he goth
by the weye.

EDWARD III

1327–1377

BORN: 13 November 1312, Windsor Castle. PARENTS: Edward II and Isabella of France. ASCENDED THE THRONE: 25 January 1327. CROWNED: 29 January 1327, Westminster Abbey. AUTHORITY: King of England, other claims. MARRIED: Philippa, daughter of the Count of Hainault. CHILDREN: Eight sons, including Edward the Black Prince and John of Gaunt, and five daughters. DIED: 21 June 1377. BURIED: Westminster Abbey.

ROYAL BIOGRAPHY

THE CONFLICT WITH France known as The Hundred Years War began ten years after Edward III became king, and asserted his claim to the throne of France. The war began well with the Battle of Crécy and then Poitiers. This is where the French King John II was taken prisoner by Edward's son, the Black Prince, who was regarded as one of the most formidable knights in Europe. After the victory Edward signed a Treaty of Bretigny by which he gave up a claim to the French throne in exchange for Calais, Guienne, Gascony and Poitou.

While his son waged war Edward devoted himself to the unification and strengthening of his English kingdom. Unlike his father, he picked good advisers, one of whom was his own wife Philippa of Hainault. Philippa bore him thirteen children. He also took advice from Parliament which he divided into Lords and Commons and in which English was the spoken language rather than French.

Among the members of his court was the remarkable Controller of Customs, Geoffrey Chaucer, who wrote *The Canterbury Tales*, a book which was a product of the mixture of Saxon and French which was to be the rich and varied English tongue of Shakespeare.

A setback to a successful reign was the Black Death from 1348 to 1350. This was a plague which killed off a third of the inhabitants of England and brought agriculture and other activities to a standstill. It did not, however, stop the momentum of Edward's reign during which much was done to iron out grievances between the King and the barons and increase Parliament's right to look into public abuses.

The last years of Edward's reign mirrored the first, in that a woman again dominated him. Philippa died in 1369 and Edward took the unscrupulous Alice Perrers as his mistress. With Edward in his dotage and the Black Prince ill, Perrers and William Latimer (the chamberlain of the household) dominated the court with the support of John of Gaunt. Edward, the Black Prince, died in 1376 and the old king spent the last year of his life grieving, dying at Sheen Palace in 1377.

The nature of English society transformed greatly during Edward III's reign. Edward learned from the mistakes of his father and affected more cordial relations with the nobility than any previous monarch.

THE HUNDRED YEARS' WAR

1337–1453

EDWARD III CLAIMED the French throne through his mother, Isabella of France when the line of Capetian kings was becoming extinct. His claims, however, were rejected, for England had long since lost its territories in France. The war was a half-hearted affair, however, involving the King's armies and those of lords with their personal axes to grind. There were frequent changes of local alliances throughout France and especially in Aquitaine, where castles and walled towns sprang up to affirm the dominance of local lords. These included Richard II and Simon de Montfort.

The first blow in the war was struck by the French King, Philip VI, who ordered the bombardment of Portsmouth. Edward quickly struck back by defeating the French fleet at Sluys to ensure a safe passage for an expeditionary army to France. In 1346 came a victory with the massacre of the French army at Crécy. This was followed in 1356 by the capture of the French King, John II, at Poitiers by the Black Prince, son of Edward III. Prince Edward was one of the most renowned warriors in Europe. The King was taken to England and treated with the usual courtesies extended to captured kings and nobility. A treaty followed and England gained once more the sovereignty of Calais, Guienne, Gascony and Poitou, in return for the renunciation by English kings of the French crown.

This success was followed by the victory of Henry V at Agincourt, and his marriage to Catherine de Valois, daughter of the King of France, Charles VI. This was no

On 26 August 1346 the English army scored a great victory over the French at the Battle of Crécy. The French lost over 10,000 men, while English deaths were less than 200.

doubt a clever move by Henry to re-establish a claim to the throne of France. It was, however, doomed to failure on the arrival of a peasant girl Joan of Arc on the scene of war.

Joan of Arc, also called the Maid of Orléans, was a national heroine and became patron saint of France. She united the nation at a critical hour and decisively turned the Hundred Years' War in France's favour. Although Joan had united the French behind Charles and had put an end to English dreams of hegemony over France, Charles opposed any further campaigns against the English. Therefore, it was without royal support that Joan conducted (1430) a military operation against the English at Compiègne, near Paris. She

was captured by Burgundian soldiers, who sold her to their English allies. The English then turned her over to an ecclesiastical court at Rouen to be tried for heresy and sorcery. After 14 months of interrogation, she was accused of wrongdoing in wearing masculine dress and of heresy for believing she was directly responsible to God rather than to the Roman Catholic church. On May 30, 1431 she was burned at the stake in the Rouen marketplace at only nineteen years of age. Henry's death accelerated the debacle of English fortunes and by 1453 all but Calais had been lost again.

TIME LINE OF THE WARS 1337–1453

1337
Edward III announces his claim to the French throne and declares war on France.
1338
Portsmouth attacked and burned by French fleet.
1346
Edward III and the Black Prince win the Battle of Crécy.
1347
Calais surrenders to Edward.
1350
John II accedes to the French throne upon death of Philip VI.
1356
Black Prince wins Battle of Poitiers and takes John II hostage.
1364
Charles V becomes King of France.
1369
Charles V declares war on England.
1347–1415
Long intervals of peace.
1413
Henry V is crowned King of England.
1415
Battle of Agincourt.
1420
Treaty of Troyes is signed.
1422
Death of Henry V and, shortly after, Charles VI.
1431
Joan of Arc declared a witch and is burned at the stake.
1453
The War comes to an end.

RICHARD II

—— 1377–1399 ——

ROYAL BIOGRAPHY

BORN: 6 January, 1367. PARENTS: Edward the Black Prince and Joan, the 'Fair Maid of Kent'. ASCENDED THE THRONE: 21 June 1377.
CROWNED: 16 July 1377, Westminster Abbey.
AUTHORITY: King of England. MARRIED: (1) Anne of Bohemia, daughter of the Emperor Charles IV, (2) Isabella, seven-year-old daughter of Charles VI of France. CHILDREN: None. DIED: 14 February 1400, Pontefract Castle.
BURIED: King's Langley, removed to Westminster Abbey in December 1413.

WHEN THE BLACK PRINCE died a year before his father, he left as their heir his nine-year-old son, Richard. During his childhood the kingdom was ruled by Regents: his uncle John of Gaunt, son of Edward III, and Thomas of Gloucester.

On reaching maturity Richard assumed his place as King and appointed William Wykeham, Bishop of Winchester as his Chancellor. For a few years Richard's reign was uneventful, thanks to the work of his predecessors. But there soon arose protests at his government initiatives and employment of foreign advisers. A poll tax instituted in 1381 led to a Peasants' Revolt, led by Wat Tyler. This was created by the difficult conditions after the Black Death and the government's very slow solution to the countryside problems. The revolt was brought to an end after Tyler was killed, and by Richard's brave appearance before the peasant marchers to persuade them to forego violence.

The still restless barons rose again in 1387 under Thomas of Gloucester, and his cousin Henry Bolingbroke, to oppose the King's will. Formed into a group calling themselves the Lords Appellant, they resented the continuing attempts to control the Lords. Richard rounded on them, murdering Gloucester and banishing Bolingbroke. On his father's death Bolingbroke became Duke of Lancaster, the house which later struggled with the Yorkists for the crown of England.

Richard travelled to Ireland in 1399 to quell warring chieftains, allowing Bolingbroke to return to England and be elected king by Parliament. Rushing back, Richard met Henry Bolingbroke at Pontefract but was defeated and imprisoned at Pontefract Castle. Henry Bolingbroke became the future Henry IV.

Deposed on 29 September, 1399, Richard was murdered while in prison at Pontefract the following February, the first casualty of the Wars of the Roses between the Houses of Lancaster and York.

The reign of Richard II shows the changing nature of the crown and society after the Black Death wiped out almost half the population from 1348.

TIME LINE OF THE REIGN 1377–1399

1377
Richard II succeeds his grandfather, Edward III.
1380
John Wycliffe begins to translate the New Testament from Greek into English.
1381
Poll Tax leads to the Peasants' Revolt.
1389
Richard takes control of the government. William of Wykeham is Lord Chancellor.
1394
Anne of Bohemia dies.
1396
Richard leads army to reconquer west of Ireland.
1396
Richard marries Isabella, daughter of the King of France.
1397
Richard takes revenge against Lords Appellant and exiles Henry Bollingbroke.
1398
Geoffrey Chaucer completes *The Canterbury Tales*.
1399
Bolingbroke becomes Duke of Lancaster on the death of John of Gaunt. Richard seizes his possessions. Bolingbroke returns from exile to claim his inheritance and seizes the throne. Richard returns from fighting in Ireland but is deposed and imprisoned in Pontefract Castle, where he dies in 1400.

WINDSOR CASTLE

The large circular tower at the heart of Windsor Castle was built during the reign of Henry II in the late 12th century. It is one of the oldest surviving parts of the building.

WINDSOR CASTLE, with its fairy tale turrets and towers, is the largest continuously inhabited castle in the world. Since it was begun by William the Conqueror in the 11th Century to its prestigious stature as the ancestral home of Queen Elizabeth II today, Windsor has stood for nearly a millennium.

Windsor originated as a motte and bailey fortification as part of a defensive programme instituted by William the Conqueror after his victory in 1066. It was built on the only naturally defensive site on a ridge above the Thames Valley. The castle was used primarily for defence purposes until Henry II rebuilt the castle in stone. Extensive expansions were added for Windsor's use as a State residence. The basic curtain wall and the Round Tower, were also begun by Henry II. Henry III is credited with the addition of five circular towers added to the curtain wall. He also remodelled his predecessor's State apartments and added a new Chapel to the castle.

The medieval reconstruction of Windsor Castle during the reign of Edward III reflects the era's ideal of Christian chivalric monarchy and this new gothic palace became the seat of the Order of the Garter. The extensive construction included the building of the College of St. George, an inner gatehouse with cylindrical towers, stone-vaulted undercrofts which supported new Royal apartments for the King and Queen, the Great Hall and the Royal Chapel. Significant alterations and improvements continued by successive monarchs throughout the medieval period.

The castle was seized by the Parliamentarians during the English Civil War in the mid-17th Century and was used as a prison, which lasted for about eleven years. King Charles I was buried under the Chapel of St. George following his execution at Whitehall in 1649 on the order of Oliver Cromwell, Lord Protector. The Restoration of Charles II in 1660 saw the reappointing of Windsor Castle as a Royal Palace. Architect Hugh May was appointed in 1673 to supervise the outfitting of the interior of the castle with richly Baroque trimmings while leaving the blocky, castellated exterior virtually unchanged.

The devastating fire in 1992 consumed the ceilings of George IV's St. George's Hall and Grand Reception Room and gutted the Private Chapel, the State Dining Room, the Crimson Drawing Room and other smaller rooms.

PEOPLE ASSOCIATED WITH WINDSOR CASTLE

Royal associations with Windsor Castle are so numerous that it would be impossible to list them all, but a few are given below:

Henry II began the very distinctive Round Tower.

Edward III was born here in 1312. When he became King he founded the Order of the Garter here in 1344.

Henry VI was born here in 1421.

George III, in his madness, died here. So did William IV and Prince Albert.

Much of the splendour of the interior was the inspiration of George IV. He personally supervised an extensive rebuilding programme in the 1820s. It was then that the Round Tower was increased in height.

King Charles I was buried under the Chapel of St. George following his execution at Whitehall in 1649.

There was a disastrous fire in 1992 which destroyed much of the Castle. It has since been skilfully and beautifully restored. It was reopened exactly five years afterwards, on 20 November 1997. Coincidentally, this marked the fiftieth wedding anniversary of Queen Elizabeth II and Philip, Duke of Edinburgh.

THE AGE OF CHIVALRY

THE WORD CHIVALRY originates in the French for mounted knights or *chevalerie* and denotes their high standing in the King's army. Most of them were high born and wealthy enough to sustain the accoutrements and entourage of a mounted knight, as well as being mighty warriors. Thus the term chivalry came to be associated with gallantry as well as courage. In England the idea of chivalry was associated with King Arthur and his Knights of the Round Table, but it was Edward III who gave it a focal point by creating The Most Noble Order of the Garter with its motto *Honi Soit qui Mal y Pense*, 'Shame on him with Evil thoughts'. This was allegedly a reference to a moment when the King replaced a garter that had slipped off a woman's leg at a court occasion.

Edward restricted the order to 24 knights whose loyalty he could trust and allowed them each their own coat of arms. Today the Queen, head of the Order, leads her knights through Windsor Castle to St George's Chapel, where all their banners hang above their personal stalls, for an annual ceremony. Though limited to a few participants the Ceremony of the Garter is one of the great pageants of the year.

Since Edward III founded the Order to reward the Lords and to bind them closer to the King, his example was followed by other countries. Scotland honours those whose lives have served the country best by The Most Ancient and Most Noble Order of the Thistle. The members of which gather on St Andrew's Day at St Giles Cathedral in Edinburgh. Other orders founded by later English sovereigns include The Order of the Bath, founded in the fifteenth century, The Order of St Michael and St George (1818) and the Royal Victorian Order 1896.

The education of a knight proceeded in a way similar to that of many medieval occupations. At an early age the prospective knight was apprenticed to serve as a page, or attendant, in a knight's household. In his teens the page graduated to the status

The Accolade, 1901, an oil painting by Edmund Blair Leighton.

COURTLY LOVE

Another major influence on chivalry was courtly love, the system that came to define relationships between knights and ladies in the feudal court.

The ideals of courtly love stressed that a knight should devote himself completely to a married or betrothed woman at court. In his lady's name, he waged war or jousted in tournaments, trying to win her favour. After a period of courtship, the two might consummate their love secretly.

Courtly love's influence among the feudal nobility was undeniable, despite the fact that its ideals ran counter to the Christian ideals of chivalry.

Courtly love helped refine relationships between men and women at court. To please their ladies, knights laboured to master the arts as intently as they did the skills of warfare. Writing poetry, singing love songs, and playing musical instruments became indispensable to the feudal knight hoping to entertain his lady.

The principal weapons used by knights were the lance and the sword.

of a squire and received more responsibilities. As a squire the boy tended his knight's horses and armour, but he also gained his first battle experience. To graduate to the status of a knight, a squire usually performed some heroic deed in battle. The squire was welcomed into the order of knights by being dubbed with a sword or slapped in the face by his lord.

THE PEASANTS' REVOLT
— 1381 —

THE LIFE OF A peasant in medieval England was one of endless toil from dawn till dusk. Each peasant had his Lord's lands to till, sow, reap and maintain, and his own small plot to grow the crops that were his livelihood. There were no labour-saving machines and there was no guarantee that the weather or marauding bands would not destroy the crops. Peasants had no means of complaint against the King or noble landowners and were subject to severe penalties if they broke the law, including the sentence of death for such misdemeanours as poaching on a Lord's land.

During the Black Death a third of the population died and the land was neglected owing to the shortage of labour. A misguided attempt to deal with this was the Statute of Labourers which limited wages to their level before the Plague, and forbade landlords from competing for agricultural workers by paying higher wages. A Poll Tax in 1381 aggravated the peasants' conditions and finally stirred them to protest by marching to London under the leadership of Wat Tyler. Tyler was a follower of John Ball, a supporter of Wycliffe's Lollards who believed in reform and practical Christianity. Unfortunately, the demonstration was not peaceful, houses were burned, Chancellor Sudbury, who was also the Archbishop of Canterbury, and Sir Robert Hales, the King's Treasurer, were murdered, and the lists of those subject to poll tax incinerated.

John Ball is shown here leading the rebels. Both groups carried the King's flag in the misguided belief that he would champion their cause.

On arrival in London the marchers were stopped and their leader, Wat Tyler, was killed by Mayor Walworth and a bloody chaos might have ensued except for the presence of the young King, Richard II. He calmed the rebels with promises that the tax would be repealed. This was only a ruse to restore order, and once the peasants had returned to the countryside, rebels were hunted down and John Ball was hanged. Though a failure in its immediate objectives the Peasants' Revolt was a warning to landowners and the King, and bore fruit later.

JOHN BALL

John Ball lived during the turbulent 14th century in England. A poor man and an itinerant, he was made a peasant priest by John Wycliffe, although Ball opposed some of the church's beliefs. As these disagreements existed between factions within the church and between the nobility and the peasantry, the governmental control was being tossed about in the royal courts, and claims to land was causing destructive wars. Wars between countries led to wars between social classes, and death became characteristic of these years.

An added mortal destructive force came from the presence of the Black Death which hit England first in 1348–49, and returned in 1362 and 1369. Although John Ball's birthdate is questionable, his death came as a result of his participation in the Peasant's Revolt in 1381–82.

John Ball was excommunicated in 1376 for his advocacy of 'ecclesiastical poverty and social equality' for priests, in direct opposition to the church's ideas. He was imprisoned at Maidstone by John of Gaunt.

HOUSE OF LANCASTER

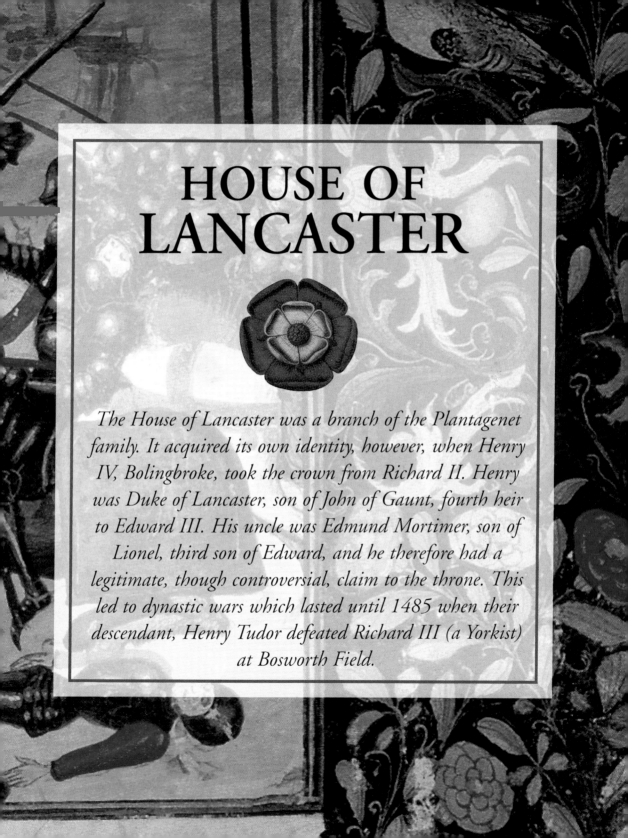

The House of Lancaster was a branch of the Plantagenet family. It acquired its own identity, however, when Henry IV, Bolingbroke, took the crown from Richard II. Henry was Duke of Lancaster, son of John of Gaunt, fourth heir to Edward III. His uncle was Edmund Mortimer, son of Lionel, third son of Edward, and he therefore had a legitimate, though controversial, claim to the throne. This led to dynastic wars which lasted until 1485 when their descendant, Henry Tudor defeated Richard III (a Yorkist) at Bosworth Field.

HENRY IV

— 1399–1413 —

ROYAL BIOGRAPHY

BORN: 4 April 1366, Bolingbroke Castle. PARENTS: John of Gaunt and Blanche of Lancaster. ASCENDED THE THRONE: 30 September 1399. CROWNED: 13 October 1399, Westminster Abbey. AUTHORITY: King of England. MARRIED: (1) Mary de Bohun, daughter of the Earl of Hereford, (2) Joan, daughter of Charles II of Navarre.
CHILDREN: With (1) five sons, including the future Henry V, and two daughters.
DIED: 20 March 1413, Westminster Abbey. BURIED: Canterbury Cathedral

THE UNPOPULARITY OF Richard II at the end of his reign made Henry an acceptable substitute as far as the barons were concerned. The barons were indifferent to the fate of their former King who was on a hunger strike in Pontefract Castle, where he had been imprisoned. In his youth Henry had travelled to Jerusalem and was a crusader renowned for his military prowess. He was also educated and sincerely pious, but his life as sovereign was not to be an easy one. First he had to deal with rebellions from dismayed supporters of Richard II, then Henry had to face a revolt from his former allies, the Percys of Northumbria. Their growing power drove them to challenge the King's authority over a matter of ransom for Scottish prisoners taken in battle. Harry Hotspur, son of the head of the Percy family, now attempted to join Glendower in Wales, but was intercepted and defeated in battle at Shrewsbury by his former close friend Henry, second son of Henry IV, who would become Henry V.

In 1404 the northern Welsh rebelled against the allegiance to England exacted by Edward I. Owain Glendower, the Welsh leader, succeeded in forcing Henry to accept a Welsh freedom from allegiance to England which lasted for eleven years.

Henry was a hard worker but poor at financial management and this often brought him to quarrel with his parliaments. They accused him of prodigal generosity to his friends and supporters.

Though his reign began well, the latter part faded as Henry dealt with challenges by his rivals. Even his son, Henry of Monmouth, set up a court in competition with his father.

By 1410, Henry was incapacitated by ill health. His power at court was diminished as his sons gathered supporters. They did not wish to challenge his authority, however, for they still admired his youthful energy and intelligence.

In stature, Henry IV was short and stocky with red hair. Henry was brave, energetic and in good health until his last years. He enjoyed sports and excelled in martial arts. He was also well read, an accomplished musician and encouraged the arts. In fact one of his first acts as King was to increase the pension of Geoffrey Chaucer. Henry was a very keen correspondent and kept in touch with many heads of state, including the emperors of Byzantium and Abyssinia. When he was young he travelled widely, fighting with the Teutonic Knights in Lithuania. He also made a pilgrimage to Jerusalem, visiting Prague, Cyprus, Rhodes and Venice.

The gilt effigy of Henry IV stands above his tomb in Canterbury Cathedral. When Henry's body was brought from London to Canterbury, it was taken by ship down the Thames Estuary to Faversham and from there to Canterbury to be finally laid to rest.

TIME LINE OF THE REIGN 1399–1413

1399
Henry returns from exile in France to reclaim his estates seized by Richard II. He claims the throne and is crowned. Richard is deposed and imprisoned in Pontefract Castle.

1400
Richard dies, possibly, from self-inflicted starvation, possibly murdered, in Pontefract. Geoffrey Chaucer, the poet, dies.

1401
Persecution of the Lollards. A new act permitting the burning of heretics is passed.

1401–15
Owain Glyndwr leads revolt in Wales.

1402
Manuel II, the Byzantine emperor, makes a state visit to England.

1403
First rebellion by the Percy family is defeated at the Battle of Shrewsbury.

1404
William of Wykeham dies. The French form an alliance with Wales.

1405
The second Percy rebellion.

1406
Henry contracts leprosy-like illness.

1407
Plague strikes England for the fifth time.

1408
Third Percy rebellion.

1413
Henry dies at Westminster.

HENRY V

—— 1413–1422 ——

ROYAL BIOGRAPHY

BORN: 9 August 1387, Monmouth. PARENTS: Henry IV and Mary de Bohun.
ASCENDED THE THRONE: 20 March 1413. CROWNED: 9 April 1413, Westminster Abbey.
AUTHORITY: King of England, Duke of Normandy (from 1417), Regent of France (1420).
MARRIED: Catherine de Valois, daughter of Charles VI of France (1420).
CHILDREN: One son, the future Henry VI. DIED: Vincennes, 31 August 1422.
BURIED: Westminster Abbey.

The morning of the Battle of Agincourt.

THE BATTLE OF Agincourt, dramatised by Shakespeare in his play *Henry V*, has made Henry into a heroic figure. However, his reign was too short for him to contribute meaningfully to the development of England. Even his success at Agincourt was to be short-lived for he died soon after, and his territorial gains were lost to the French army led by a girl, Joan of Arc.

As a military exploit Agincourt remains a glorious success and heartens English people even today. Henry had landed in France in August 1415 with the intention of laying siege to Harfleur, which would ensure his entry and exit from France. He had some 2,500 foot soldiers and 7,000 archers. As he marched towards his objective his men began to fall ill with dysentery. This meant that his army was considerably reduced in strength, which was desperately needed to face 20,000 Frenchmen, many heavily armed mounted knights.

Returning to Calais seemed a hazardous prospect so Henry decided to face the French at Agincourt. Here he drew up ranks of his well trained and disciplined bowmen and waited for the charge of the French knights. Fortunately for him the ground was wet, which slowed the galloping horses, and as the volleys of arrows struck them they slowed even further causing a jam of horses and knights. They consequently became victims of the English men at arms who advanced among them. The victory was complete and led Henry to believe that France was his.

Further victories convinced the French King to sign the Treaty of Troyes by which Henry became the heir to the French throne. To seal the treaty Henry married the King's daughter Catherine. Before he could enjoy the fruits of his victory, however, Henry had died, in 1422, and all dreams of recouping the French kingdom died with him.

Henry exhibited military genius, characterized by brilliant daring, patient strategy and diplomacy, and attentiveness to detail. His strong personality, his military successes, and his care for his less fortunate subjects made him a great popular hero.

The historian Rafael Holinshed, in the *Chronicles of England*, summed up Henry's reign as such:

'This Henry was a king, of life without spot, a prince whom all men loved, and of none disdained, a captain against whom fortune never frowned, nor mischance once spurned, whose people him so severe a justicer both loved and obeyed (and so humane withal) that he left no offence unpunished, nor friendship unrewarded; a terror to rebels, and suppressor of sedition, his virtues notable, his qualities most praiseworthy.'

Portrait of King Henry V by Benjamin Burnell

TIME LINE OF THE REIGN 1413–1422

1413
Henry accedes to the throne upon the death of his father, Henry IV.

1415
Henry thwarts the plot to replace him on the throne with his cousin. Henry renews the war against France, captures Harfleur and wins the Battle of Agincourt (25 October).

1416
Death of Owain Glyndwr. Henry makes a pilgrimage to St Winifrede's Well in Somerset.

1417
Henry V is victorious at the Battle of Caen. He takes Pontoise.

1418
The English army takes Louviers and Compiègne. The Siege of Rouen begins.

1419
The long siege of Rouen ends. Henry starves the inhabitants into submission. Henry meets Duke John of Burgundy at Meulan and falls in love with the Princess Catherine.

1420
Henry becomes Regent of France and heir to the French King Charles VI, under the Treaty of Troyes. Henry marries Catherine.

1421
Birth of Prince Henry, later Henry VI.

1422
Henry V dies at Vincennes in France of dysentery, before he can succeed to the French throne.

THE WARS OF THE ROSES

1455–1485

THIS COMPLEX CONFLICT between two dynastic houses of the Plantagenet line arose out of the incapacity of the mentally unbalanced Henry VI and the ambitions of John of Gaunt. John of Gaunt was the fourth son of Edward III, and Edmund, Duke of York was the fifth son. Richard, the son of Edmund, was Protector of England during one of Henry's bouts of insanity, but was dismissed when Henry recovered. Angered at this rebuff, Richard raised an army and, with a white rose as his emblem, attacked the King's Lancastrian forces at St Albans to the north of London. The Lancastrian forces had taken the red rose as their insignia. Having been defeated in their turn the Yorkists gained the support of the Earl of Warwick, who earned the name of 'the Kingmaker'. He

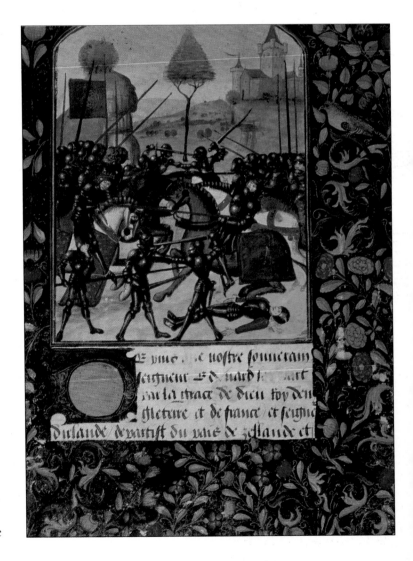

The Tudor rose

defeated Henry and, through his energetic and militant wife, Margaret of Anjou, managed to escape to Scotland.

Undeterred by the defeat, Margaret raised another army in Scotland and defeated the Yorkists and killed the Duke. His son, Edward, now took over defeating Margaret at Towton and becoming King after deposing Henry in 1461. This was not the end, however, for Warwick now quarrelled with Edward because of his choice of wife. He switched his allegiance to Margaret and attempted to restore Henry VI briefly to the throne. This was in vain, for Margaret and Henry's army was defeated at Barnet and a further defeat was inflicted on the Lancastrians at Tewkesbury. In 1471 Henry was imprisoned in the Tower of London and later murdered. This left Edward secure on his throne, which came to his brother Richard after the death of Edward's son in the Tower.

The last act in the dramatic years of the houses of Lancaster and York came with the reign of Richard III, and ended with his death and the replacement of the Yorkists by the Tudors.

LEFT: *In early 1471 Edward and Warwick met at the Battle of Barnet, where Warwick was slain.*

TIME LINE OF THE WARS 1455–1485

1454
Richard, Duke of York is appointed Protector of England during the mental incapacity of Henry VI.

1455
The Duke of York is dismissed. He raises an army and defeats the King's Lancastrian army at the first Battle of St Albans. The Duke of Somerset is killed. York takes over government of England.

1459
Battle of Blore Heath; Salisbury defeats a Lancastrian force. Battle of Ludford Bridge where the Yorkists are routed by Lancastrian forces headed by Henry VI.

1460
Battle of Northampton. The Yorkists win and Henry VI is taken prisoner by the Yorkist lords. King James II of Scotland dies and is succeeded by James III.

1461
Edward, son of Richard, defeats Lancastrian army at Mortimer's Cross. Henry VI is deposed. Coronation of Edward IV.

1464
Battle of Hexham; Henry VI is captured and brought to the Tower of London.

1469–70
Warwick falls out with Edward IV and defeats him at Edgecote. Henry VI is restored to the throne.

1471
Edward defeats and kills Warwick at the Battle of Barnet. Henry VI is captured and murdered in the Tower of London.

1485
Richard III is defeated at Bosworth Field (22 August) by Henry Tudor. The Wars of the Roses comes to an end.

THE LOSS OF FRANCE

SINCE THE DAYS of Henry II, England's hold on its French kingdom had been tenuous and challenged by French barons. The French king, however, lacked the power to deal either with his lords or the English. The mismanagement of the reign of John, son of Henry II, allowed the French to regain much of their territory, but lost it again to the energetic Henry V.

The instability of kingdoms in medieval Europe was due to the lack of national identities and lands which belonged to the King and barons. Anyone who aspired to creating a national kingdom had to overcome the hurdle of local power and interests. The change in attitudes in France was inspired by a woman, Joan of Arc, who claimed that she had been chosen by God to free France from the English. This idea, which coincided with a growing national desire for French unity and expansion of the royal kingdom, spread throughout France especially after Joan's meeting with the future King at Chinon. With his support and that of the Church, which had subjected her to an examination at Poitiers, Joan joined the French army on the Loire. She led it to Orléans which was under siege by the English. Having routed them she then led a force through the English lines to Reims where she had the Dauphin crowned King, as Charles

The Siege of Orléans took place in 1428–29 and dragged on for seven months.

VII of France. Joan now set out for Paris but was captured by Burgundian forces who were at war with the French. She was sold to the English for 10,000 crowns.

In view of her extraordinary success with the French troops it was not difficult for the English to brand her a witch. She was burned at the stake in Rouen on 24 May 1431. This did little good to the English cause, however, and by 1453 England had quit France forever.

Twenty-five years after Joan of Arc's death, the church retried her case, and she was pronounced innocent. In 1920 she was canonized by Pope Benedict XV; her traditional feast day is May 30.

Charles VII provided Joan of Arc with a suit of armour costing 100 écus, either 2,500 sols or 125 tournois pounds.

JOAN OF ARC AND HER 'VOICES'

Jacques d'Arc, Joan's father, was a small peasant farmer, poor but not needy. Joan seems to have been the youngest of a family of five. She never learned to read or write but was skilled in sewing and spinning. The popular idea that she spent the days of her childhood in the pastures, alone with the sheep and cattle, is quite unfounded. People spoke of her as a singularly pious child, grave beyond her years, who often knelt in the church absorbed in prayer, and loved the poor tenderly.

Great attempts were made at Joan's trial to connect her with some superstitious practices supposed to have been performed round a certain tree, popularly known as the 'Fairy Tree' (*l'Arbre des Dames*). However, the sincerity of her answers baffled her judges. She had sung and danced there with the other children, and had woven wreaths for Our Lady's statue, but since she was twelve years old she had held aloof from such diversions.

It was at the age of thirteen and a half, in the summer of 1425, that Joan first became conscious of her 'voices' or her 'counsel'. It was at first simply a voice, as if someone had spoken quite close to her, but it seems also clear that a blaze of light accompanied it. Joan was always reluctant to speak of her voices. She said nothing about them to her confessor, and constantly refused, at her trial, to be inveigled into descriptions of the appearance of the saints and to explain how she recognized them.

HENRY VI

—— 1422–1461, 1470–1471 ——

ROYAL BIOGRAPHY

BORN: 6 December 1421, Windsor Castle. PARENTS: Henry V and Catherine de Valois.
ASCENDED THE THRONE: 1 September 1422. CROWNED: 6 November 1429, Westminster Abbey;
repeated 13 October 1470 at St Paul's Cathedral. AUTHORITY: King of England.
MARRIED: Margaret, daughter of the Count of Anjou. CHILDREN: One son, Edward (died 1471).
DIED: 21 May 1471, Tower of London. BURIED: Chertsey Abbey, then removed to St George's
Chapel, Windsor, in 1484.

HENRY WAS ONE year old when his father died and he became King
of England. According to the Treaty of Troyes he also became King
of France on the death of Charles VI. During his childhood his
kingdom was ruled by the Duke of Bedford, who was Regent of
France and by Humphrey, Duke of Gloucester in England. This
glorious start to Henry's reign did not last long, for by the time he
was old enough to assume his role as King in 1437, England had lost
much of its land in France to the French troops inspired by Joan of
Arc. 1453 was a fateful year, not only because England had lost all its
French possessions, except Calais, but the King's mind also gave way. A
Protector, Richard Duke of York, was named to carry on the affairs of
state. On Henry's recovery in 1455 Richard was dismissed and in revenge
led an army against the King.

This was the beginning of what came to be known as the Wars of the
Roses. The two factions within the kingdom sided either with the King, the
Lancastrians, who took a red rose as their symbol, or with the Duke of
York who adopted a white rose as his emblem. In 1461 the son of the
Duke of York became King as Edward IV. He came to the throne
through the efforts of his father, as Henry VI became
increasingly less effective. However, the Earl of Warwick
proclaimed Henry King again in 1470, but less than a year

*This portrait of Henry VI is by an unknown artist. This painting hangs in
the library of Eton College, which was founded by Henry in 1441.*

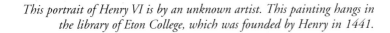

elapsed before Edward claimed the crown and had Henry executed in 1471.

Henry's temperament and delicate constitution was not suited to the rigours of kingship and he had paid little attention to court politics and administration. His interests were cultural and religious. He founded Eton College and encouraged the building of the beautiful King's College chapel at Cambridge.

After his death Henry's reputation as a good man and noble king grew and his burial place became a place of pilgrimage. In fact when Richard III became the Yorkist King, Henry's tomb was moved to Windsor so that Richard could keep an eye on the cult of Henry the 'saint'.

Little by little Margaret of Anjou must have realized just how weak-willed and foolish her husband was. He gave huge amounts of money to the poor, pardoned his enemies, and let people off their debts. And then of course he went completely mad for about eighteen months. Margaret gave birth to their only son, Edward, during the time when Henry was out of his mind. In fact when he recovered, she had to introduce him to his own baby and tell him what name she had chosen.

TIME LINE OF THE REIGN 1422–1471

1422
Henry becomes King of England on the death of his father Henry V. Two months later he becomes King of France on the death of his grandfather Charles VI.

1429
Joan of Arc begins to expel the English from France.

1431
Joan of Arc is burned at the stake by the English.

1437
Henry assumes personal rule of England. Catherine of Valois, Henry V's queen, dies.

1453
End of 100 Years' War. English driven out of France.

1454
Henry's cousin, Richard, Duke of York, is made Protector during Henry's mental illness.

1455
Duke of York is dismissed. He rebels against the King and takes over the government. Start of the Wars of the Roses.

1460
Henry is defeated at the Battle of Northampton and taken prisoner.

1461
Henry is deposed by Richard's son Edward, Duke of York, who is then crowned Edward IV.

1464
Henry VI becomes a fugitive.

1470–71
Henry is briefly reinstated on the throne.

1471
Henry is murdered in the Tower of London.

HOUSE OF YORK

The Yorkist claim to the throne came from the third and fifth sons of Edward III: Lionel, Duke of Clarence, and Edmund, Duke of York. Their claim had remained dormant while the King, Henry VI, had no heir. However, when one was eventually born, and Henry began to suffer from mental disorders, Yorkist supporters pressed for the popular Duke of York to take over the kingdom.

EDWARD IV

1461–1470, 1471–1483

BORN: 28 April 1442, Rouen. PARENTS: Richard, Duke of York, and Cecily, daughter of Ralph Neville, Earl of Westmorland. ASCENDED THE THRONE: 4 March 1461.
CROWNED: 28 June 1461, Westminster Abbey. AUTHORITY: King of England.
MARRIED: Elizabeth, daughter of Richard Woodville, Lord Rivers.
CHILDREN: Three sons, including the future Edward V, and seven daughters; four illegitimate children. DIED: 9 April 1483, Westminster. BURIED: St George's Chapel, Windsor.

ROYAL BIOGRAPHY

EDWARD TOOK THE crown from Henry VI at the Battle of Mortimer's Cross but lost it again when he was deposed by the powerful Earl of Warwick, 'the Kingmaker'. Warwick had disagreed with Edward's choice of wife, Elizabeth Woodville, a commoner. Warwick and Margaret, the wife of the mentally unstable Henry VI, now drove Edward out of England. He returned and defeated his enemies, killing Warwick at the Battle of Barnet. He defeated Margaret later, at the Battle of Tewkesbury 1471, the same year that her husband was murdered in the Tower of London.

Having established a firm grasp on his kingdom, Edward devoted himself to its administration. He personally addressed the House of Commons and instituted a court at which peasants could complain about the demands of greedy landlords. He encouraged his merchants and the progress

Edward became King at the age of 18. He was described by many as a beautiful young man.

Edward married Elizabeth Woodville in 1464. She was the daughter of a knight and the widow of an English commoner, which led to a major rift between Edward and Warwick.

of the wool trade, which was one of England's most lucrative sources of income.

He also came to an agreement with the Hanseatic League, which controlled trade at a number of north German ports, allowing them to trade in England. As a result of his government, England prospered and new industries evolved, including that of printing. This was a result of William Caxton setting up his printing press with moveable type, which made it possible to reproduce documents more quickly than by hand copying. This made learning more accessible to all literate people.

Though there was progress under Edward he tended to move cautiously, avoiding moves which would arouse his enemies and surrounding himself with trusted members of his household.

Though not renowned for his interest in the arts and architecture, he completed the building of St George's Chapel, Windsor, which became his mausoleum.

TIME LINE OF THE REIGN 1461–1483

1461
Edward defeats the Lancastrian army at Mortimer's Cross and is proclaimed King by his cousin Warwick.

1464
Edward marries Elizabeth Woodville, offending Warwick and other lords.

1469
Warwick breaks with Edward and joins Henry VI's wife Margaret to usurp Edward.

1470
Edward is briefly driven out of England to exile in Flanders when Henry VI is restored to the throne.

1471
Edward returns to England and defeats and kills Warwick at the Battle of Barnet (14 April). Battle of Tewkesbury (4 May). Henry VI is murdered in the Tower of London (21 May).

1475
Edward makes an alliance with the Duke of Burgundy against Louis XI.

1478
Edward falls out with his brother George, who is then murdered in the Tower.

1480
William Caxton prints *The Chronicles of England.*

1483
Edward dies suddenly and unexpectedly at the age of 40. Edward V and his brother are held in the Tower.

EDWARD V

1483

ROYAL BIOGRAPHY

BORN: 2 November 1470, Westminster. PARENTS: Edward IV and Elizabeth Woodville.
ASCENDED THE THRONE: 9 April 1483. CROWNED: Not crowned. AUTHORITY: King of England.
MARRIED: Unmarried. DIED: Probably in the Tower of London, c.September 1483. BURIED:
Tower of London; possible remains reburied in Westminster Abbey, 1678.

THE MYSTERY OF the fate of Edward V and his brother Richard has never been solved and casts a dark cloud over the reign of Richard III. Richard has always been considered responsible for their disappearance, but largely because of Tudor propaganda; Henry VII is also a suspect.

On the death of their father the two princes went to London in May, expecting Edward to be crowned in June. Arrangements for their residence were made by Richard of Gloucester, the man whose father had been the Protector during their childhood. They were lodged in apartments in the Tower of London and had the freedom of its grounds. Soon, however, Parliament declared the princes to be illegitimate because, when he had married Elizabeth Woodville, their father had already been betrothed to Lady Eleanor Butler. This was a condition regarded as virtually as binding as a marriage. Gloucester was then proclaimed King as Richard III. During this time the princes were seen in the gardens of the Tower and then suddenly disappeared. No explanation was forthcoming once Parliament had given its verdict, nor was there much interest in the young princes.

In 1674 the skeletons of two young boys were dug up in the grounds of the Tower, but there was no evidence to show how they had died or the

The Tower of London. It is assumed that the two princes were killed in the Bloody Tower and then buried in the Wakefield Tower, before reburial next to the White Tower.

This portrait of Edward V and his younger brother Richard, was painted by Sir John Everett Millais some 400 years after their death.

circumstances of their disappearance. Whoever was responsible had covered his or their tracks very well. In 1933 a further exhumation only confirmed that they were skeletons of young men. Nevertheless the remains were moved and reburied in Westminster Abbey.

Subsequent investigations have cast doubt on Richard III's involvement in the affair. He had already been named King by Parliament, and his bad reputation had been created, after his death, largely by the Tudors. The Tudors wanted to detract from the record of their predecessors, and by William Shakespeare, who like the other playwrights of his time depended on royal and noble patronage. The mystery of the Princes in the Tower remains, therefore, never to be solved.

TIME LINE OF THE
REIGN 1483

1483
Edward IV dies suddenly and unexpectedly at the age of 40. He is succeeded by his 12-year-old son Edward V. The Dukes of Gloucester and Buckingham join forces at Northampton. Gloucester takes possession of Edward V at Stony Stratford as his Protector.

Edward and his brother Richard arrive in London in early May and stay with the Bishop of London before moving to royal apartments in the Tower of London.

The two princes are held in the Tower. Bishop Stillington declares that the two boys are illegitimate, invalidating Edward's claim to the throne. Edward V is deposed. Accession of Richard III; his son Edward is created Duke of Cornwall.

The last sighting of the princes in the grounds of the Tower of London is in September. They are probably murdered around this time.

RICHARD III

1483–1485

ROYAL BIOGRAPHY

BORN: 2 October 1452, Fotheringhay Castle. PARENTS: Richard, Duke of York, and Cecily Neville. ASCENDED THE THRONE: 26 June 1483. CROWNED: 6 July 1483, Westminster Abbey. AUTHORITY: King of England. MARRIED: Anne Neville, daughter of the Earl of Warwick. CHILDREN: One son, Edward (died 1484); several illegitimate children. DIED: 22 August 1485, Bosworth, Leicestershire. BURIED: Greyfriars Abbey, Leicester; later disinterred and desecrated.

Richard III's seal.

ACCORDING TO POPULAR belief the most villainous King in English history was a hunchback who plotted all his life to become King. This relentless pursuit of the crown was done at any cost, even it seems down to the murder of the royal princes, the sons of Edward IV. Richard was the brother of King Edward IV and, like him, descended from Edward III through Edmund Duke of York. He was, therefore, in line for the crown with only the young princes standing in his way, although Parliament had already chosen him on his brother's death.

In the eyes of the nobles he was eminently suitable. He had proved to be courageous, distinguishing himself during the Battle of Barnet, in which Warwick the Kingmaker had been killed, protecting his brother's right to the throne. As a reward he had received the Neville estate and other royal rights in the north of England. He had also fought against the Scots and recovered the border town of Berwick. This was well thought of by his contemporaries.

As King he immediately set about improving the administration of the north by setting up a special council. He also created a bail system for defendants in court cases, and abolished the custom of obligatory gifts for the monarchy, which went under the name of Benevolence.

His reign was too short for much to be achieved, and in 1485 he had to face a challenge from the Tudors. The Tudors were led by Henry, son of Margaret Beaufort who was the granddaughter of John of Gaunt, who tried to claim the English throne. Richard rode into battle at Bosworth wearing the royal crown, but was defeated and killed. The crown, which had fallen off his head, was placed on that of Henry Tudor who became Henry VII. The much maligned Richard's body was left on the field of battle.

It is true to say that most of the Tudor writers elaborated Richard's ugliness and evil character. It was once said that he had spent two years in his mother's womb and, after a difficult birth, had emerged with hair down to his shoulders, and a full set of teeth!

He was a brave soldier, an able administrator and an extremely cultured man. If his kingship had not been contested he might have achieved much.

A portrait of Richard III by Italian School, 16th century.

TIME LINE OF THE REIGN 1483–1485

1483
Richard succeeds his brother Edward IV after confining his two nephews, Edward V and Richard, Duke of York, in the Tower of London.
The Duke of Buckingham, an ally of Richard, rebels against the King but is captured and executed (October).
Foundation of the College of Arms.

1484
Death of Richard's son Edward, Prince of Wales (9 April).
Richard creates the council of the North for better administration of the North of England. This survives until its abolition by Parliament in 1641.
Abolition of benevolences – the compulsory gifts from individuals to the monarch.
A bail system was introduced for defendants in court cases.
Parliamentary statutes written down in English for the first time.
Richard orders the body of Henry VI to be removed from Chertsey Abbey to St George's Chapel, Windsor (August).

1485
Death of Queen Anne (16 March). Henry Tudor lands at Milford Haven with 1800 French troops (7 August). Richard is killed and his army defeated at the Battle of Bosworth Field.

THE TUDORS

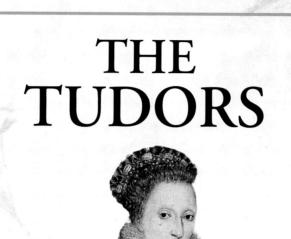

The Tudors claim to the crown was slight for it came through John of Gaunt, an illegitimate son of Edward III. Nevertheless the Tudor dynasty included the notable and strong-minded sovereigns Henry VII, Henry VIII and Elizabeth I. They were ruthless in dealing with challenges to the monarchy and moved England from a medieval society to one with international standing. Royal power was strengthened by the Reformation, the break with Rome, and military power by the growth of England's navy.

HENRY VII

1485–1509

ROYAL BIOGRAPHY

BORN: 28 January 1457, Pembroke. PARENTS: Edmund Tudor, Earl of Richmond, and Lady Margaret Beaufort. ASCENDED THE THRONE: 22 August 1485. CROWNED: 30 October 1485, Westminster Abbey. AUTHORITY: King of England. MARRIED: Elizabeth of York, daughter of Edward IV. CHILDREN: Four sons, including the future Henry VIII, and four daughters. DIED: 21 April 1509, Richmond, Surrey. BURIED: Westminster Abbey.

HENRY'S VICTORY OVER Richard III was a *fait accompli* as far as his claim to the throne was concerned, the victory was proof enough as far as he was concerned, and there was no one to deny him. This was typical of a man who is often underrated as a King, but who put an end to the wrangling between noble families that had prevented English unity for almost 100 years. He showed a certain talent for making the right decisions. For example, when he declared himself King before the death of Richard, in order to be able to accuse his enemies of treason, if it became necessary.

Dealing with the Lords who had become a nuisance to the later Plantagenets, Henry set up a Star Chamber which would deal with the misdemeanours of Lords who broke the law. Those who attempted to defy him were crushed. For example, the Earl of Lincoln who supported a rebellion by Lambert Simnel in 1457, and Perkin Warbeck in 1492.

The idea of reclaiming English possessions in France persisted for a while in Henry's mind but, having made threatening gestures towards the French King, Henry persuaded him to pay cash for the former English possessions by the Treaty of Etaples. With the money gained from this he turned his mind to more promising territories. Columbus had discovered America in 1492 and Henry now encouraged the Cabot brothers to explore further north, and he also began to expand the English fleet.

Though not a charismatic leader Henry knew how to make friends in the right quarters and to maintain peace at home. He also encouraged the spread of education by importing French scholars who helped to create the English Renaissance of the Tudor period.

Francis Bacon, in his *History of Henry VII,* described the King as such: 'He was of a high mind, and loved his own will and his own way; as one that revered himself, and would reign indeed. Had he been a private man he would have been termed proud: But in a wise Prince, it was but keeping of distance; which indeed he did towards all; not admitting any near or full approach either to his power or to his secrets. For he was governed by none.'

Henry was tall, dark, blue-eyed, well-built and athletic in appearance.

TIME LINE OF THE
REIGN 1485–1509

1485
Henry accedes to the throne after defeating Richard III at the Battle of Bosworth. Henry forms the Yeomen of the Guard.
1486
Henry marries Elizabeth of York, which unites the houses of York and Lancaster. John Morton becomes Archbishop of Canterbury.
1487
Henry founds the court subsequently known as the Court of the Star Chamber. Henry crushes a revolt by the Earl of Lincoln on behalf of Lambert Simnel, a claimant to the throne.
1491
Henry invades France but at the Treaty of Etaples agrees to withdraw English forces in return for a large sum of money.
1492
Perkin Warbeck claims the throne and attempts to overthrow Henry. He is defeated and put to death in 1499. Christopher Columbus discovers America.
1500
John Morton dies.
1503
Prince Arthur, Henry's oldest son, dies. Princess Margaret, Henry's eldest daughter marries James IV of Scotland. Henry's wife, Elizabeth of York, dies.
1509
Henry VII dies at Richmond Palace.

THE REFORMATION

THE ROME-BASED Catholic Church which had been a welcome ally of kings when they were struggling to impose their authority on their subjects, became too powerful and prone to interfere in monarchical rule. This, and the corruption in the ranks of Church leaders, brought about a revolt against Roman power and envy at its wealth.

This came to a head with Martin Luther (1538–1546) who published a protest against the arrogance and corruption of the Roman Church. This document spread through Europe and caused a split, with Catholicism entrenched in southern Europe and Protestantism taking root in the north. In England the Reformation was not as much a vital issue as on the Continent for, although Henry had broken with the Church, he had done so more for political than ideological reasons. Catholic rituals in churches went on much as before. However, many champions of the established church refused to take the Oath of Supremacy which acknowledged Henry VIII as Head of the English church. One of these was Thomas More, who, despite many entreaties to him to accept the new situation, was imprisoned and executed for treason in 1535. He was succeeded by Thomas Cromwell, a Protestant, who helped Henry VIII to dissolve the monasteries, and made their properties available to the King who consequently distributed them among his friends.

The Reformation in England was essentially a revolution in the way the state was governed, in the power structure of the Church, and its

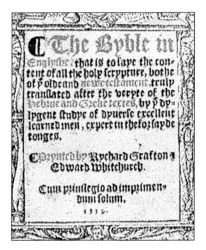

The first complete translation of the Bible into English was completed in 1535 by Miles Coverdale.

influence on the life of the nation. In the long term this meant that priests of a Catholic persuasion had to be removed from positions of authority, and the documents on which their spiritual authority rested had to undergo a change. Among these was the Bible, which was printed in English in 1549. Later, in the reign of James I, the Book of Common Prayer and an authorized version of the Bible were also produced. The Reformation also meant the dissolution of the monasteries and their physical destruction.

Thomas Cromwell was the administrative genius behind the English Reformation. His rise to power was extraordinary and occurred just when Henry VIII needed a minister of great administrative imagination and genius. Cromwell entered royal service in early 1530 and, from then on, rose rapidly.

THOMAS CROMWELL 1485–1540

Thomas Cromwell, Earl of Essex, was an English statesman. While a young man he lived abroad as a soldier, accountant and merchant. On his return to England in about 1512, he engaged in the wool trade and eventually became a lawyer. He entered Parliament in 1523 and soon became legal secretary to Cardinal Wolsey, for whom he managed the suppression of minor monasteries. He avoided being disgraced with Wolsey in 1529, and by 1531 was serving Henry VIII as a member of the privy council. By 1532 he had become the King's chief minister and was responsible for drafting most of the acts of Parliament by which the Reformation was effected. He was made a Baron and Lord Privy Seal in 1536, Lord Great Chamberlain in 1539, and Earl of Essex in 1540. He negotiated the King's marriage to Anne of Cleves as a means of securing the North German princes as allies against the Catholic Holy Roman Emperor Charles V. When Anne proved unattractive and the alliance failed, Henry allowed charges of treason and heresy to be brought against Cromwell by his bitter enemy, the Duke of Norfolk. The King's marriage was annulled (9 July, 1540) and Cromwell was condemned by act of attainder and beheaded (28 July, 1540).

THE MONASTERIES

THE FIRST CHRISTIAN community in Anglo-Saxon England was set up by Augustine in 597. A hundred years later these communities of holy and learned men had multiplied considerably. Rulers found themselves useful not only in establishing the spiritual life of the nation, but in such practical matters as agriculture, finance, education and craftsmanship. At the time of the Danish and Viking invasions, northern monasteries suffered from destruction and pillage and also by confiscation and theft by local lords.

The monasteries in the south of England fared better and Canterbury, Winchester, St Albans and Bury St Edmunds continued to increase in power and wealth. Under the Normans their growth continued and the political power of priests appointed by Rome, led to confrontations between kings and their advisers. These advisers were often highly trained academics, with high ranking in the Roman Church.

By the sixteenth century monasteries, as such, began to decline. The power of the Church, however, continued to grow, and this was exercised through chancellors and finance ministers of the courts of Europe and later, Cardinals

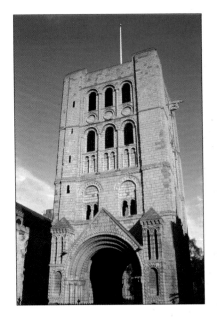

In 903 the remains of King Edmund were interred in a monastery in Bury St Edmunds, re-founded c.630, which later became a famous shrine and Benedictine abbey founded by Canute.

In 597, St. Augustine founded an abbey at Canterbury and became the first Archbishop of Canterbury and primate of all England.

Richelieu, Mazarin in France and Wolsey in England. As chancellor, Wolsey handled all the financial affairs of state, providing Henry with his financial needs of state – foreign affairs, palace building, etc.

When the crisis of his divorce from Catherine of Aragon arose, Henry VIII found little support from the Pope. The Pope was the nephew of Catherine, but at this time was a prisoner of the Emperor Charles V who had invaded Rome. Due to pressure from the Catholics who opposed his divorce and others, led by Thomas Cromwell, Henry broke with Rome and began to dissolve the monasterial system. Thomas Cromwell claimed that as God's representative, Henry could overrule the Pontiff. Henry felt that the monasterial system was a breeding ground for Roman clergy and the immensely rich.

By 1559 the monasteries had ceased to exist. Monks who accepted this change were given a pension. Others, who had opposed Henry, had been executed. Nuns were freed from their vows but forbidden to marry until the reign of Edward VI.

The monastic lands were distributed to the nobility, or important gentry, by the Court of Augmentations. Buildings were destroyed and their treasures distributed to Henry's supporters. Thus, the monastic system which had served a useful purpose for one thousand years disappeared.

HENRY VIII

— 1509–1547 —

ROYAL BIOGRAPHY

BORN: 28 June 1491, Greenwich. PARENTS: Henry VII and Elizabeth of York. ASCENDED THE THRONE: 21 April 1509. CROWNED: 24 June 1509, Westminster Abbey. AUTHORITY: King of England and Ireland. MARRIED: (1) Catherine of Aragon, (2) Anne Boleyn, (3) Jane Seymour, (4) Anne of Cleves, (5) Catherine Howard, (6) Catherine Parr. CHILDREN: Two daughters, one son and four other illegitimate children. DIED: 28 January 1547, Whitehall. BURIED: St George's Chapel, Windsor.

THE ACHIEVEMENTS of Henry VIII's reign have often been obscured in the popular imagination by the story of his many marriages. It is overlooked that by 1547, when he died, England had broken with the power of the Roman Papacy, had become established as a rival of the European powers headed by the Emperor Charles V and Francis I of France and laid the foundations for the golden age of Elizabeth I.

As a young man Henry was a predictable prince of his age: lusty, ambitious and a religious conformist, whose pamphlet *Assertio Septem Sacromentorum* earned him the title of Defender of the Faith, bestowed by Pope Leo X.

Henry's divorce from Catherine of Aragon, daughter of the Catholic monarchs of Spain, signalled Henry's lack of concern for political marriage alliances. Though, persuaded by Cardinal Wolsey his Chancellor, he attempted to make a pact with Francis I of France at the opulent meeting which came to be known as the Field of the Cloth of Gold in 1520. The failure of this rapprochement, Wolsey's ostentatious style of life (he built Hampton Court Palace), and his failure to procure for Henry a divorce from Catherine of Aragon, led to the Chancellor's fall from grace. Wolsey died in November 1530 before he could be executed.

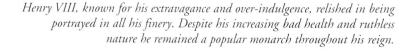

Henry VIII, known for his extravagance and over-indulgence, relished in being portrayed in all his finery. Despite his increasing bad health and ruthless nature he remained a popular monarch throughout his reign.

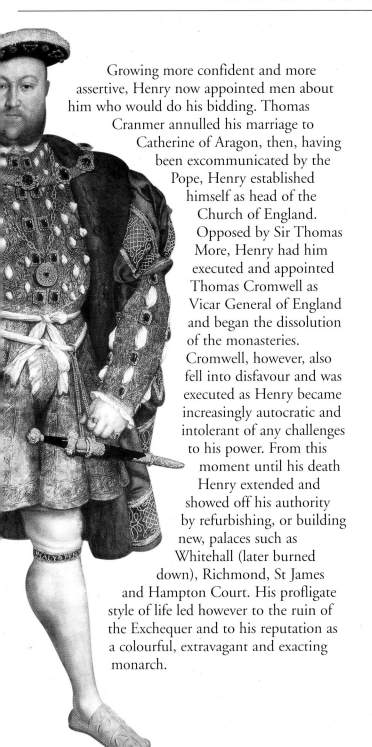

Growing more confident and more assertive, Henry now appointed men about him who would do his bidding. Thomas Cranmer annulled his marriage to Catherine of Aragon, then, having been excommunicated by the Pope, Henry established himself as head of the Church of England. Opposed by Sir Thomas More, Henry had him executed and appointed Thomas Cromwell as Vicar General of England and began the dissolution of the monasteries. Cromwell, however, also fell into disfavour and was executed as Henry became increasingly autocratic and intolerant of any challenges to his power. From this moment until his death Henry extended and showed off his authority by refurbishing, or building new, palaces such as Whitehall (later burned down), Richmond, St James and Hampton Court. His profligate style of life led however to the ruin of the Exchequer and to his reputation as a colourful, extravagant and exacting monarch.

TIME LINE OF THE REIGN 1509–1547

1509
Henry accedes to the throne on the death of his father Henry VII.
1509
Henry marries Catherine of Aragon.
1516
Catherine gives birth to Princess Mary.
1533
Henry's marriage to Catherine is annulled.
1533
Henry marries Anne Boleyn; Princess Elizabeth is born.
1533
Henry is excommunicated.
1534
Henry established as head of the Church of England.
1535
Thomas Cromwell made Vicar of England.
1536
Anne Boleyn is executed and Henry marries Jane Seymour.
1536
Cromwell begins dissolution of the monasteries.
1537
Jane Seymour gives birth to Edward (later Edward VI), but dies.
1540
Henry marries and divorces Anne of Cleves.
1540
Henry marries Catherine Howard.
1543
Henry marries Catherine Parr.
1547
Henry VIII dies.

EARLY TUDOR PALACES

THE IMPROVEMENTS IN the manufacture of gunpowder (limited to production within the walls of the Tower of London) and of cannons in warfare, diminished the protective role of castles in Tudor times. Moreover, the close control of Tudor kings on the nobility ensured political calm and a decrease in petty squabbles which disrupted the life of the country. Castles, therefore, became less belligerent and adopted features which made them more like palaces. Palaces were also a means of impressing the King's subjects by their size and splendour, and this was no doubt in the minds of Henry VII and Henry VIII as they embarked on an age of palace building which was only matched by the manor houses of the nobility.

One of the first and most splendid palaces was at Richmond on the River Thames. Only the gatehouse now remains but this was a much loved palace of King Henry VIII. It was built in 1500 by Henry VII on the site of an earlier royal palace. It was designed in the Gothic style around a central courtyard, and it was certainly one of the most imposing of the Tudor palaces.

A view of the great river was an asset and the position of Greenwich Palace, of which the splendid hall remains, gives a view of the river which, in Tudor times, was filled with shipping from all parts of the then known world. Henry VIII's Nonsuch Palace no longer exists, but St. James, by the once royal hunting ground now known as Green Park, is in its original state. It still has the initials of Henry VIII and Anne Boleyn visible on the entrance tower. The building of Nonsuch Palace was started by King Henry VIII in 1538. The site was occupied by the manor house, church and village of Cuddington, which was completely cleared, with suitable

Richmond Palace fell into disrepair during the mid-17th century, only the gatehouse survives today.

Hampton Court Palace was begun by Cardinal Wolsey in 1514 as his private residence. After his downfall it was taken (1530) by Henry VIII and remained a royal residence until the time of George II.

compensation for the owners. The structure of the palace was completed in 1541, but the famous external decorations took another five years. It is recorded that the total cost of the work up to the end of 1545 was £24,536, which was substantially more than Hampton Court which was built at the same period. Henry died in 1547 with the work still not quite finished

Many of Henry VIII's palaces were confiscated from ambitious clerics whose extravagance annoyed the King. Some had outlived their usefulness which had made the King turn a blind eye to their pretensions. The most famous of these was Cardinal Wolsey who had failed to convince the Pope to agree to Henry's divorce from Catherine of Aragon and who had built himself two grand palaces. One was these was the Whitehall palace where Henry installed Anne Boleyn. This later burned down, leaving only the Banqueting Hall and Hampton Court Palace by the Thames, the most splendid of all the palaces and later added to by William III.

THE WIVES OF HENRY VIII

CATHERINE OF ARAGON

ANNE BOLEYN

JANE SEYMOUR

WHEN HENRY VIII married Catherine of Aragon he was creating an alliance with one of the powerful ruling houses of Europe. By 1509 the Spanish Empire included large parts of Europe and the new continents of North and South America. Catherine was the daughter of the King and Queen of Spain and Henry's marriage was conditioned, not only by ambition for England's extended power, but by the need for an heir. When his wife failed to produce an heir but his mistress, Anne Boleyn, became pregnant, one of Henry's desires seemed within reach. But divorcing Catherine was a more difficult matter which led finally to a break with the Church of Rome. Anne Boleyn only produced a daughter (Elizabeth) and, though the evidence is not clear, Henry accused her and her brother and several attendants of treason and they were executed. Henry now pinned his hopes on one of Boleyn's ladies-in-waiting, Jane Seymour. Jane obliged him by giving birth to a son (Edward VI) but she died soon after, leaving Henry bereft and distraught.

After the failure of his marriage to Catherine of Aragon Henry seemed to be indifferent to

ANNE OF CLEVES

CATHERINE HOWARD

CATHERINE PARR

the idea of political marriages. He allowed himself to be persuaded to marry Anne of Cleves, a princess of a Protestant family. He had not met her and was disappointed on doing so, calling her a 'Flanders mare' and refusing to consummate the marriage.

Henry now turned his eyes to the English nobility and married Catherine Howard, niece of the Duke of Norfolk. The wedding took place on the day of the execution of his old ally Cromwell. This may have been a bad omen, for Catherine was soon to follow to the scaffold for disloyalty and indiscretion. Now in middle age and sick with various ailments brought on by his excesses Henry looked for a loyal and devoted woman to comfort his old age, and married Catherine Parr. The King saw her as an ideal stepmother for his three children and a woman who would show due consideration to him during his remaining years. Both expected few, if any, physical demands of each other. Catherine survived Henry, and within months of his death in 1547, she married Thomas Seymour, uncle to the new King Edward VI. Unfortunately she died in childbirth the following year.

An excerpt from a letter by Catherine Howard to Thomas Culpeper, in Spring 1541:

Master Culpeper,
I heartily recommend me unto you, praying you to send me word how that you do. It was showed me that you was sick, the which thing troubled me very much till such time that I hear from you praying you to send me word how that you do, for I never longed so much for a thing as I do to see you and to speak with you, the which I trust shall be shortly now . . .

EDWARD VI

— 1547–1553 —

BORN: 12 October 1537, Hampton Court. PARENTS: Henry VIII and Jane Seymour. ASCENDED THE THRONE: 28 January 1547.
CROWNED: 19 February 1547, Westminster Abbey.
AUTHORITY: King of England and Ireland. MARRIED: Unmarried.
DIED: 6 July 1553, Greenwich. BURIED: Westminster Abbey.

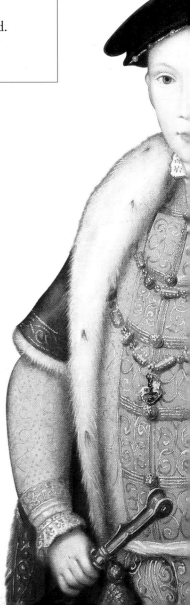

THE SON OF Henry VIII and Jane Seymour seems to have been a precocious and strong-willed child who might have been a powerful monarch had he not died of tuberculosis at the age of fifteen. Family life cannot have been easy for Edward. His mother, Jane Seymour, died a fortnight after his birth; his first stepmother, Anne of Cleves, was divorced from his father before he was three; his second stepmother, Catherine Howard, was beheaded for adultery when he was four; and finally his syphilitic father died when he was only nine.

After his accession at the age of nine, the kingdom was administered by Edward Seymour, Duke of Somerset, the Protector of England and Warwick, Duke of Northumberland. Somerset tried to arrange a marriage with Mary Queen of Scots but this was forcibly rejected at the Battle of Pinkie. Mary was a Catholic and in England Protestantism was being established firmly by the abolition of the Catholic mass, and the amendment of the book of Common Prayer, which was printed in English.

Northumberland, who disagreed with the idea of marriage to a Catholic, now ousted Somerset and put forward the suggestion that Edward should declare the Protestant Lady Jane Grey as his heir. Edward, who was an opinionated young man, agreed to this and when he died in 1553, Lady Jane Grey was proclaimed queen. Her reign was short-lived, however, for

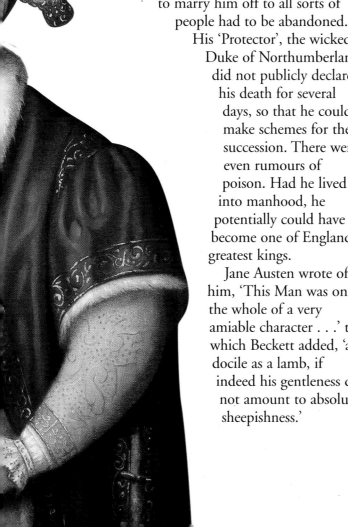

when Mary, daughter of Henry and Catherine of Aragon, heard about it, she and her supporters gathered an army and marched on London. Lady Jane Grey was arrested and executed soon after. She had been queen of England for only nine days.

Edward was a highly intellectual and pious boy who fell prey to the conspiracies of his powerful Council of Regency. His frailty led to an early death. He caught consumption and spent many months dying. Plans to marry him off to all sorts of people had to be abandoned. His 'Protector', the wicked Duke of Northumberland, did not publicly declare his death for several days, so that he could make schemes for the succession. There were even rumours of poison. Had he lived into manhood, he potentially could have become one of England's greatest kings.

Jane Austen wrote of him, 'This Man was on the whole of a very amiable character . . .' to which Beckett added, 'as docile as a lamb, if indeed his gentleness did not amount to absolute sheepishness.'

TIME LINE OF THE REIGN 1547–1553

1547
Edward VI accedes to the throne after the death of his father Henry VIII. Edward Seymour, Earl of Hertford, is invested as Duke of Somerset and Protector of England. The English army defeats the Scots at the Battle of Pinkie as part of an attempt to force a marriage between Mary, Queen of Scots, and Edward VI.

1548
The heresy laws in England are abolished. All craft guilds are abolished except for the London Guilds.

1549
The First Book of Common Prayer is issued, which changes the Church service from Latin to English.

1550
The Duke of Somerset is deposed as Protector of England and replaced by John Dudley, Earl of Warwick, who creates himself Duke of Northumberland.

1552
Somerset is executed. Christ's Hospital in London is founded by Edward VI.

1553
Thomas Cromwell becomes Lord Chancellor. The Duke of Northumberland persuades Edward to nominate Lady Jane Grey as his heir in an attempt to secure the Protestant succession. Edward VI dies at Greenwich Palace.

MARY I

—— 1553–1558 ——

ROYAL BIOGRAPHY

BORN: 18 February 1516, Greenwich Palace.
PARENTS: Henry VIII and Catherine of Aragon.
ASCENDED THE THRONE: 19 July 1553.
CROWNED: 1 October 1553, Westminster Abbey.
AUTHORITY: Queen of England and Ireland.
MARRIED: Philip II of Spain. CHILDREN: None.
DIED: 17 November 1558, St. James's Palace.
BURIED: Westminster Abbey.

THOUGH SHE HAS gone down in history as a merciless and despotic queen, Mary was more a victim of her times and circumstances than a cruel woman. As the daughter of Catherine of Aragon she had suffered from her father's rejection of her mother and had felt the subsequent humiliation deeply. When her half-brother nominated Lady Jane Grey as his heir, her bitterness grew, and when Edward died and Lady Jane acceded to the throne she marched to London and got rid of her rival.

Mary now set about restoring Catholicism in England and her first step was to marry the most Catholic monarch in Europe, Philip of Spain. This proved to be unpopular with her subjects and soon there were protests from leading clerics. Mary put these down energetically and Ridley, Latimer and Cranmer were burned at the stake in Oxford. In order to affirm her position, Mary now claimed that she expected an heir. But Philip, her husband, was occupied with a challenge to his domains in the Low Countries and it became evident that his marriage to

Mary had been to ensure that he had an ally on his northern flank. To add to Mary's anxieties, the French now took back Calais, the last English possession in France.

In a state of great mental anguish Mary declared that she was pregnant again and, when this was shown to be untrue, had to recant. She died soon after on a November day in 1558, a sad and despairing woman whose impossible dream had crumbled into ashes.

Mary died most piously, as she had always lived, a few hours before her staunch friend, Cardinal Pole. Her good qualities were many. To the very end she was a woman capable of inspiring affection in those who came in contact with her. Modern historians are almost unanimous in regarding the sad story of this noble but disappointed woman as one of the most tragic in history.

While Mary's strong Catholic faith gave her a great sense of purpose, it also made her obstinate and narrow minded. During her reign she had numerous Protestants burned at the stake for heresy.

TIME LINE OF THE REIGN 1553–1558

1553
Lady Jane Grey is proclaimed Queen by the Protector, Northumberland. After only nine days, Mary arrives in London, Lady Jane Grey is arrested and Mary is crowned. Edward VI dies of tuberculosis at Greenwich.

1554
After Mary declares her intention to marry Philip of Spain, Sir Thomas Wyatt leads a revolt to depose her. Wyatt's rebellion is crushed. Wyatt, Lady Jane Grey and her husband are executed. Mary marries Philip of Spain in Winchester Cathedral. The persecution of Protestants begins, the heresy laws are revived and England is reconciled to Papal authority.

1555
The Protestant bishops Ridley and Latimer are burned at the stake at Oxford for heresy.

1556
Cardinal Reginald Pole is made Archbishop of Canterbury. Thomas Cranmer, former Archbishop of Canterbury, is burned at the stake at Oxford for heresy.

1557
England declares war on France.

1558
The port of Calais – the last English possession in France – is captured by the French.

1558
Mary dies at St James's Palace in London.

SEA ADVENTURERS

AFTER THE SUCCESS of the Spanish and Portuguese sailors in voyages to South America and the East, freelance English sailors were encouraged to set off on their own voyages of exploration. The object was not only political but commercial, and the two aims often went hand-in-hand with piracy, as in the seizing of Spanish galleons loaded with the treasures of the American Indian empires.

One of the first English sea adventurers was John Hawkins who sailed to the West Indies in 1532 and was accompanied by Francis Drake on a later voyage in 1567. Late in 1577, Francis Drake left England with five ships, ostensibly on a trading expedition to the Nile. On reaching Africa, the true destination was revealed to be the Pacific Ocean via the Strait of Magellan. This was much to the dismay of some of the accompanying gentlemen and sailors. Still in the eastern Atlantic, a Portuguese merchant ship and its pilot – who was to stay with Drake for fifteen months – was captured, and the fleet crossed the Atlantic, via the Cape Verde Islands, to a Brazilian landfall.

Running down the Atlantic South American coast, storms, separations, dissension, and a fatal skirmish with natives marred the journey. Before leaving the Atlantic, Drake lightened the

Christopher Columbus persuaded the King and Queen of Spain to finance a voyage across the Atlantic.

expedition by disposing of two unfit ships and one English gentleman, who was tried and executed for mutiny. After rallying his men and unifying his command with a remarkable speech, Drake renamed his flagship, previously the *Pelican*, the *Golden Hind*.

Other routes round the world were being explored by other seafarers, notably Martin Frobisher who imagined that it would be possible to reach the east by a north west passage through Canada. Both Frobisher and Gilbert were given a patent of colonization enabling them to claim new lands for England in the name of Elizabeth. In 1595 Walter Raleigh travelled to Guiana on the north east coast of South America in order to find the route to the imaginary city of El Dorado, which was supposed to be a source of Spanish gold. Of course, Raleigh's big claim to fame these days is the story that he once gallantly threw his cloak over a muddy puddle so that Queen Elizabeth I wouldn't get her feet dirty. Like most of these stories, it is almost certainly untrue. He had another legend as well, much less well-known these days. He supposedly used a diamond to scrawl verses on a window pane in order to get the Queen's attention.

The search for a north west passage continued with Henry Hudson. Hudson was an English navigator, famous for four great voyages of discovery; a river and a bay in North America are named after him. Nothing is known of Hudson's life before 1607, the year in which he undertook his first expedition for the English Muscovy Company. Commanding a single ship, the *Hopewell*, Hudson touched the shores of Greenland and then sailed further north in an attempt to find a northeast passage by way of the Arctic Ocean to East Asia.

These voyages and many others were recorded by Richard Hakluyt (1552–1616) a geographer, in *The Principal Navigations, Voyages and Discoveries of the English Nation*. Hakluyt also wrote *Divers Voyages touching the Discovery of America* and introduced the globe in schools.

THE ELIZABETHAN THEATRE

THE RENAISSANCE IN Italy gave Europe its first taste of theatre, with *Commedia del Arte*, an art form often played indoors with scenery. These plays were undoubtedly familiar to English visitors to Italy who had become plentiful as people on business or as tourists. Shakespeare was familiar with the Italian scene as so many of his plays and their characters confirm.

In England, London's theatres were built outside the city walls and were, on the whole, opposed by the Mayor of London and the burgesses, though supported by the monarchs and the nobility. One of the first purpose-built theatres was erected by James Burbage, a carpenter who was also an actor, in 1576. This was probably north of the city, in Shoreditch, but was soon followed by others on the south bank of the River Thames which became a quarter where theatre, bear pits, taverns and brothels soon flourished. The *Globe*, the *Rose*, and the *Swan* with their circular open construction, soon attracted large crowds from all walks of life, who heckled the actors and slapped the boys who played female parts on the bottom with their swords.

It was in this environment that Shakespeare's plays were produced. His plays were received universal acclaim from the public, but his contemporaries such as Thomas Kydd, Christopher Marlow and Ben Jonson, who were educated university men, rather looked down on the popular playwright.

Theatre was supported financially by monarchs and the nobility, which patronage may explain Shakespeare's historical plays which look, with a jaundiced eye, on the squabbles of the kings before the Tudors. He has a low opinion for example of Henry IV and Richard III who is branded as a villain for all time, nor reflecting popular prejudice, is he sympathetic to the Jewish people whose skill in finance was a source of envy and dislike.

The establishment of Elizabethan theatre was one of the cultural achievements of the age, and it is surprising to know that manuscripts were not printed until a much later date. The English theatre was directly under the control of the government. Acting companies had to have a license, requiring the patronage of a noble. Provincial troupes were deprived of legal status, so theatre was concentrated in London.

The Globe Theatre, a London playhouse, was built in 1598. It was where most of Shakespeare's plays were first presented. It burned in 1613, was rebuilt in 1614, and was destroyed by the Puritans in 1644. A working replica opened in 1997.

THE ELIZABETHAN THEATRE

Usually the Elizabethan theatre interiors were a blaze of colour. As early as 1577, Thomas White describes the playhouses as 'sumptuous'.

To the Elizabethans, the theatre was an image of the universe. The stage was the earthly region where humans played out their comedies and tragedies. Beneath the stage lay Hell, out of which devils or ghosts would emerge through a central trap door.

The audience ate and drank throughout performances, interrupted at will, broke into fights and hissed and clapped the action. Reports probably highlight the more rumbustious incidents. Audiences must have felt safe since all sorts of people 'old and young, rich and poor, master and servant, papists and puritans' came to the Globe.
(John Chamberlain, 1624)

Those who stood below the stage payed a penny while the seated audience, who entered through a separate entrance, paid another penny. And those who wanted the best, cushioned seats, paid yet another penny.
(Thomas Platter, 1599)

ELIZABETH I

—— 1558–1603 ——

ROYAL BIOGRAPHY

BORN: 7 September 1533, Greenwich. PARENTS: Henry VIII and Anne Boleyn.
ASCENDED THE THRONE: 17 November 1558. CROWNED: 15 January 1559, Westminster Abbey.
AUTHORITY: Queen of England and Ireland. MARRIED: Unmarried.
DIED: 24 March 1603, Richmond Palace. BURIED: Westminster Abbey.

THE DANGERS OF political life must have imprinted themselves in Elizabeth's mind early in her childhood. Her mother, Anne Boleyn, was beheaded when she was three years old. After Wyatt's rebellion against her half sister, Mary, she was imprisoned in the Tower of London, then kept at Woodstock under house arrest.

Soon after her coronation in 1559 Elizabeth, who had been well educated in the classics and spoke French, Spanish and Italian, took a firm hold of the reins of government. Strong willed, she was also diplomatic and made friends with the Lords at court. Though she tried to avoid a confrontation on the religious issue, she confirmed England's position by the Act of Supremacy, which made her head of the English church. By 1559 all Catholic bishops had been replaced by Protestant ones. Where foreign policy was concerned she tried to avoid entanglements, but followed her father in building up the strength of the fleet. She also encouraged the half piratical, exploits of her sailors, Drake and Hawkins. She made Howard of Effingham the commander of the ships that routed the *Armada*, in 1588.

Elizabeth's most disturbing problem was the existence of Mary Queen of Scots. She was the daughter of James IV of Scotland, whose mother was a granddaughter of Henry VII and was herself, widow of the Dauphin of France. These connections gave Mary loyal supporters in both England and France and threatened Elizabeth's difficult position with the Catholic Scots and Continental Catholic rulers. Things came to a head when a page in Mary Stewart's household hatched a plot to kill Elizabeth. Reluctantly Elizabeth signed Mary's death warrant in 1587.

Elizabeth's last years were darkened by the revolt of her once favourite Earl of Essex, who was consequently executed. Her reputation remained intact, however, and was immortalized by the poet Edmund Spenser in his poem *The Faery Queen.*

Her reign was noted for the English Renaissance, an outpouring of poetry and drama led by William Shakespeare, Edmund Spenser, and Christopher Marlowe that remains unsurpassed in English literary history. She was the last of the Tudor monarchs, never marrying or producing an heir, and was succeeded by her cousin, James VI of Scotland.

TIME LINE OF THE REIGN 1558–1603

1558
Elizabeth accedes to the throne on the death of her half-sister Mary.

1559
Act of Supremacy makes Elizabeth head of the Church of England.

1560
Treaty of Berwick, between Elizabeth I and the Scottish reformers.

1562
John Hawkins and Francis Drake make first slave-trading voyage to America. Elizabeth gives aid to the Protestant Huguenots in the French Wars of Religion.

1563–4
17,000 die of the Plague in London.

1577–80
Francis Drake sails round the world.

1586
Mary Queen of Scots is brought to trial.

1587
Mary Queen of Scots is executed (8 February). Drake attacks the Spanish fleet in Cadiz Harbour.

1588
The English navy and bad weather defeat the Spanish Armada (21–29 July).

1595–6
Sir Walter Raleigh makes his first expedition to South America.

1601
Earl of Essex is executed for leading a revolt against Elizabeth's government (25 February).

1603
Elizabeth I dies at Richmond Palace, Surrey.

THE ARMADA

THE SPANISH ARMADA, under the command of the Duke of Medina Sedonia, sailed from Portugal in late May of 1588 heading for the British Isles. It reached the South West coast of England on July 19 and was very quickly challenged by the English fleet, commanded by Lord Howard and Francis Drake. The English vessels, avoiding close-in combat as the Spanish desired, hung on to the flanks of the Spanish ships as they sailed up the English Channel. The English harassed the Spanish in every way possible, doing much damage, until the Armada anchored at Calais. Here the Duke of Parma failed to show up and as a result the English saw an opportunity to attack the Spanish fleet. On July 28, 1588 the English used fire-ships to scatter the Spanish ships. On July 29 at the pivotal Battle of Gravelines an eight hour struggle ended with many Spanish ships lost or damaged.

The Spanish Commander, the Duke of Medina Sedonia, found himself in danger of total defeat and made a fateful decision to forgo the invasion and return to Spain via the North of Scotland and Ireland. For three days the English fleet pursued the Spanish into the North Sea then returned to England when they ran out of ammunition. The Spanish fleet fared disastrously rounding the coast of Scotland. Many Armada ships were wrecked by storms off the coast of Scotland and Ireland and the surviving Spanish ships limped back to Spain totally defeated and demoralized.

The defeat of the Spanish Armada marked the turning point between the era of Spanish world domination and the rise of Britain to the position of international supremacy. Thus this battle began the decline of Spain and the ascent of Britain – a sea change event.

Francis Drake was a vice admiral in the fleet that defeated the Armada in 1588.

REPORT ON THE SPANISH ARMADA

As there were no newspapers at this time, the news was carried by newsbooks published weeks or months after the events. One of the first accounts was in a 24-page newsbook printed in 1588 in Cologne by Michael Entzinger. The front page featured a woodcut representing the Spanish Armada sailing off the coast of England. The newsbook is in German and the front page translates as follows:

'A true account of the Spanish Armada or Armaments translated from the original Spanish edition into the high German including the story of how on the 29th and 30th of May the Armada under the command of the Duke of Medina Sedonia, departed from Portugal and how it then, at great risk, arrived in England and struggled in a strait on the 8th, 9th, and 10th of August and also how the Armada again encountered the Englishmen on the open sea after that, on the 22nd of the same month of August.'

This was quite a 'headline' and was only the introduction to a complete early account of the Spanish defeat. This newsbook represents one of the earliest 'first reports' of a significant historical event in a printed news vehicle.

NOBLE TUDOR HOUSES

THE PEACE AND prosperity of Tudor England created a large group of landed gentry, many of them profiting from Henry's distribution of monastic estates. Of these a number survive in their original architecture and reveal the more expansive times of the Tudor era. They have large windows, unprotected entrances and splendid chimneys for the huge fireplaces that kept them warm. They breathe an air of comfort and noble living that show how life under the Tudors had changed England.

Montacute in Somerset is one such place. Owned by Sir Edward Phelips who was Speaker of the House of Commons and Master of the Rolls. Another is Oxburgh Hall in Norfolk,

Mary Arden, Shakespeare's mother, lived in this tudor house in Wilmcote, Warwickshire.

which still has the character of a castle with its turreted tower, kept for decorative rather than defensive reasons. The Hall was started by Sir Edmund Bedingfield who was entrusted with the care of the young Elizabeth by Mary Tudor.

A smaller but very charming house is The Vyne in Hampshire, built by William Sandys, Lord Chamberlain to Henry VIII.

Compton Wynyates, also has the character of a home rather than a castle and the Compton family who built it have resided there since the thirteenth century. Another manor house on a pre-Tudor site, but with much Tudor architecture is Sulgrave Manor, the home of the family from which George Washington emerged. Yet another grand manor house is Knole in Kent, originally a gift from Elizabeth to Thomas Sackville in 1566, it had been greatly extended by Thomas Bourchier, Archbishop of Canterbury, 1454–86.

The wealth of palaces and manor houses in the English countryside continue to tell the

Garrick Inn and Harvard House, Stratford-on-Avon.

TUDOR ENGLAND

In Tudor England, a person's social status and prestige were determined by two main things: the lavishness of their standard of living and the number of their servants and attendants. The successful maintenance of a large household also indicated a person's ability to govern (albeit on a much smaller scale than the King).

A nobleman of sufficient rank and skill was often called to serve the monarch in London. To that end, they would purchase and maintain – often at great expense – town homes in or just outside London. In London, the most affluent street was known as The Strand. These homes were built on the riverside and so were equipped with docks. The nobles could travel by personal barge from their homes to various royal palaces.

Nobles also owned homes in the counties near their largest estates. Naturally enough, the maintenance of these various residences was expensive, and became increasingly so as the century progressed. But the greatest expense – and worry – was their principal estate, always situated in the countryside. At these estates, their spiritual, public, private, and economic worlds merged.

story of life in England through every period of its history but its beginning lies in the affluent times of the Tudors.

When someone mentions Tudor architecture, the image that most often comes to mind is the black and white timber/plaster constructions. While this style of building did occur during the reign of the Tudors, it was popular enough to continue as a building pattern to this very day. Most 'Tudor' black and white buildings do not date from the 16th century, but were built during 'revival' periods. However, some towns have managed to preserve their original buildings. Shrewsbury and Chester have fine examples of original 16th century building. Stratford-upon-Avon also has a number of preserved Tudor and Elizabethan buildings, such as Palmer's Farm which was formerly called Mary Arden's House.

In the 15th and 16th centuries, stone became more popular for building medium sized homes, and not just castles and cathedrals, especially in areas where wood was scarce or where local stone was plentiful. The limestone cottages of the Cotswolds are a familiar example of this.

THE SCOTTISH MONARCHY

In the eighth century the Viking invasions of the coasts of Scotland reached Oban and the Scots capital at Dunstaffnage. It forced a move eastwards for the Scot's leader Kenneth MacAlpin, creating the kingdom of Alba. Here at Scone, MacAlpin was crowned King of both Picts and Scots. By the tenth century the tribes were becoming a nation, though clan warfare was a thread that ran throughout Scottish history.

THE HOUSE OF ALPIN AND DUNKELD

843–1058

Silver coins depicting Viking longships.

OVER 1000 YEARS ago the House of Alpin, with their harsh rule, forged the path that became Scotland. Kenneth MacAlpin was the first in the line of Scottish Monarchs. Kenneth, although never truly crowned a King of Scotland was more responsible for the creation of Scotland by uniting the Scots and the Picts. Kenneth I died of cancer in 858, leaving his new Scottish Kingdom to his Brother Donald I.

Donald's short rule was not in vain, and before his suspicious death in 862, he managed to further Kenneth's attempts at law and helped secure further rule across the land. Despite his attempts, no less than ten of the fourteen kings who ruled during the period 943–1097 were murdered, and only then was the birth right of rule accepted.

The title of 'last of the Alpin rulers' fell to Malcolm II, and thankfully for Scotland Malcolm II had more on his mind than blood and war, and by 1034 a true and well-defined Scottish Kingdom had emerged.

On the death of Malcolm II, the House of Alpin failed in the male line. Malcolm had two daughters, and the only surviving descendant of his cousin and immediate predecessor Kenneth III, was a granddaughter. King Malcolm's grandsons and King Kenneth's grand-daughter were the leading characters in the drama with which the history of the new dynasty opened.

Duncan was the first of the royal House of Dunkeld. He added Strathclyde to his grandfather's, Malcolm II, kingdom, thereby being the first monarch of a united Scotland. The hereditary right to the throne of his two sons, Malcolm Canmore and Donald Ban was threatened by his cousin Macbeth who claimed the kingdom on the grounds of tanistry. The matter was settled in 1040 near Elgin when Macbeth killed Duncan in battle.

This piece of Celtic jewellery was found inside a bronze cup at Lochar Moss, Dumfriesshire.

TIME LINE OF THE HOUSE OF ALPIN & DUNKELD

843–858
Kenneth McAlpin.
858–862
Donald I.
862–877
Constantine I.
877–878
Aedh.
878–889
Gric and Eochain.
889–900
Donald II.
900–943
Constantine II.
943–954
Malcolm I.
965–962
Indulf.
962–966
Dubh.
966–971
Culen.
971–995
Kenneth II.
995–997
Constantine III.
997–1005
Kenneth III.
1005–1034
Malcolm II.
1034–40
Duncan I.
1040–57
Macbeth.
1057–58
Lulach (the Fool).

Macbeth was another grandson of Malcolm II and had as good a claim to the throne as Duncan. Shakespeare, using poetic license, has distorted the historical facts, by showing that Macbeth ruled Scotland for 17 years quite successfully. He was married to Kenneth III's granddaughter Gruoch, who had a son, Lulach, by a previous marriage, which strengthened his claim to the throne. In 1045 Macbeth defeated and killed Duncan's father Crinan at Dunkeld. His reign was peaceful for the most part and he was generous to the Church. He was defeated in 1054 by Malcolm Canmore at Scone and killed by Malcolm Canmore in 1057.

Lulach 'the Fool' was the final ruler in the Dunkeld reign. He was Macbeth's step-son, and after a few months of rule he was also killed by Malcolm Canmore

THE HOUSE OF CANMORE

1058–1290

Alexander I was described as a lettered and godly man but was nicknamed 'the Fierce' after dealing ruthlessly with an uprising.

MALCOLM III, though a powerful king, was faced with two threats, one from the English and the other from the Vikings who had settled on the coasts and islands of north and west Scotland. Hoping to achieve an understanding with the Vikings Malcolm married Ingibjorg, widow of Earl Thorfinn of the Orkneys. On her death he married Margaret whom he had met at the court of Edward the Confessor. St. Margaret was a devout Catholic and encouraged the growth of monasteries in Scotland. Her children, who subsequently became Kings of Scotland, carried on the systems of government introduced by William I in England with the help of the Church.

By 1124 Scotland had become a fully established kingdom under David I and flourished in peace, until the arrival of Edward I as King of England in 1274. He was ambitious to become overlord of Scotland, and when Alexander III, the descendant of David I, was killed falling from his horse, he left no heir. Edward saw this as an opportunity to gain control of Scotland and nominated John Balliol as his candidate for the kingship against that of Robert Bruce. The Bruce family refused to accept Edward's choice and rejected Edward's demand that Scotland should confirm allegiance to the English throne. Aware of Edward's real intention, Balliol now made an alliance with France, known as the Auld Alliance, in 1295, which infuriated Edward. He set about

Alexander II made Scotland stronger than it had ever been. He attended to parts of the country that were causing trouble.

TIME LINE OF THE HOUSE OF CANMORE

1058–1093
Malcolm III.
The reign of Malcolm III, or Canmore as he was known, began the rule of the house of Canmore. This house continued to preside for over two centuries.
1093–1094 & 1094–1097
Donald Ban.
May–November 1094
Duncan II.
1094–1097
Donald Ban and Edmund.
1097–1107
Edgar (the Peaceable).
1107–1124
Alexander I (the Fierce).
1124–53
David I (the Saint).
1153–65
Malcolm IV (the Maiden).
Malcolm was known as the Maiden because he never married and maintained a vow of chastity.
1165–1214
William the Lion.
1214–1249
Alexander II.
1249–86
Alexander III.
Alexander was only eight when he inherited the kingdom of Scotland from his father.
1286–90
Margaret Maid of Norway.
Margaret was only three years old when she became Queen of Scotland. Her death at the age of seven in Orkney ended the House of Canmore.

conquering Scotland by force and sent an army which rapidly took possession of all the castles between Roxburgh and Elgin. The Stone of Scone, the ancient symbol of Scottish sovereignty, was seized and taken to Westminster (July 1296).

Scottish resentment at Edward's arrogant behaviour led to revolts and uprisings notably by William Wallace, a semi outlaw who became a national hero when he recovered Stirling Castle. His success was short-lived, however, for Edward captured Wallace and took him to London where he was executed (23 August, 1305).

 # THE AULD ALLIANCE

SCOTLAND'S MOST famous connection with
Europe was the Auld Alliance with France.
First agreed in 1295/6 the Auld Alliance
was built on Scotland and France's shared
need to curtail English expansion. Primarily
it was a military and diplomatic alliance
but for most of the population it brought
tangible benefits through pay as
mercenaries in France's armies.

When John Balliol became King of
Scotland with the support of Edward I, to
whom he had sworn allegiance, he soon
realised that the support of the English King
meant that he was now more in his power
than before. The English intended that he
would be a puppet king. In order to protect
himself, Balliol made a pact with England's
enemies, the French, which came to be
known as the Auld Alliance.

The pact of mutual help was a deterrent
to English ambitions and not, at first, a
burden on the Scots. However, following the
English victory at Poitiers by Edward II's son
the Black Prince, the Scottish King David II
was made a prisoner. He was asked for a
£160,000 ransom, which, on the
impossibility of raising such a sum, was
traded by the Scottish King's right of
succession. This agreement was rejected by
the Scottish Parliament and led to another

invasion by the English. The Alliance continued until 1560 and served its purpose in preventing the English kings' attention to their Scottish ambition while they were fighting the French in the Hundred Years War.

In the end, however, treaties made directly between England and France, and an alliance between Scotland's James III and England in 1474, made the Auld Alliance unnecessary. Its existence, however, had laid a foundation of cultural interchange which has continued to the present day. This has taken the form of an interchange of scholars, scientist and artists which has given Scotland the lead in many fields of endeavour, though this was not always recognized in Scotland itself.

Under the Auld Alliance both Scottish and French coats of arms come together in battle against the common enemy – the English.

THE BATTLE OF FLODDEN 1513

Flodden was a disastrous and unnecessary confrontation for Scotland. James IV of Scotland was married to the sister of England's King Henry VIII and a treaty of friendship existed between their countries. The Auld Alliance between Scotland and France had been recently renewed. There had been English attacks made upon Scottish ships at the time when Henry VIII, on behalf of the papacy, invaded France.

James IV declared war immediately, with nothing to gain and ties to both England and France that their war neutralized. With the whole nation behind him, James amassed 20,000 men with ease, both Highlanders and Lowlanders. His fleet set sail and his army crossed the border into Northumberland with the intention of drawing upon England's numbers in France.

Norham Castle was among the places captured before confronting the English defenders. The Scots took the advantageous high ground. With slightly fewer numbers but superior equipment and artillery, the English moved around the Scots on their west and opened with cannon fire. They struck their target with great success, which the Scots could not match.

James IV was defeated and killed along with thousands of other Scots.

JOHN BALLIOL

— 1292–1296 —

ROYAL BIOGRAPHY

BORN: *c.*1249. PARENTS: Hugh de Balliol of Barnard Castle and Devorguilla of Galloway, a great-granddaughter of David I. ASCENDED THE THRONE: 17 November 1292.
CROWNED: 30 November 1292. REIGN: Four years.
MARRIED: Isabella de Warenne, a granddaughter of King John of England.
CHILDREN: Two sons, Edward and Henry, and one or two daughters.
DIED: Normandy, April 1313.

FOLLOWING THE death of King Alexander III, the succession was now open to many claimants, the strongest of whom were John Balliol and Robert Bruce.

King Edward supported John Balliol, who he believed was the weaker and more compliant of the two Scottish claimants. At a meeting of 104 auditors, with Edward as judge, the decision went in favour of Balliol, who was declared the rightful King in November 1292. The English King's plans for a peaceful relationship with his northern neighbour now took a different turn. In exchange for his support, Edward demanded that he should have feudal superiority over Scotland, including homage from Balliol. He also demanded judicial authority over the Scottish King in any disputes brought against him by his own subjects, and defrayment of costs for the defence of England as well as active support in the war against France.

Even the pathetic Balliol could not stomach these outrageous demands. Showing a hitherto unknown courage, he declared in front of the English King that he was the King of Scotland and should answer only to his own people. He refused to supply military service to Edward. Over-estimating his strength, he then concluded a treaty with France prior to planning an invasion of England.

Edward was ready. He went north to receive homage from a great number of Scottish nobles, as their feudal lord, among them none other than Robert Bruce, who owned many estates in England. Balliol immediately punished this treachery by seizing Bruce's lands in Scotland and giving them to his own brother-in-law, John Comyn. However, within a few months, the Scottish King was to disappear from the scene. His army was defeated by Edward at Dunbar in April 1296. Soon after at Brechin, on 10 July, he surrendered his Scottish throne to the English King, who took the Stone of Scone, which was the coronation stone of the Scottish kings. At a parliament, which he summoned at Berwick, the English King received homage and the oath of fealty from over 2,000 Scots. He seemed secure in Scotland.

John Balliol with his wife Isabella de Warenne.

TIME LINE OF THE REIGN 1292–1296

1292

The first interregnum in Scotland comes to an end. John Balliol succeeds to the Scottish throne, selected out of 13 competitors by Edward I.

1293

An Anglo-Gascon fleet defeats a larger Norman-French fleet off the coast of Brittany, and then sacks La Rochelle.

1294

Roger Bacon, the founder of experimental science, dies. War with France begins. Rebellion breaks out again in Wales. Robert Winchelsey becomes Archbishop of Canterbury.

1295

Treaty between Scotland and France begins the 'Auld Alliance'. The Earl of Warwick's troops defeat those of the principal Welsh leader, Madog ap Llewellyn, breaking the back of the Welsh rebellion.

1296

Edward I invades Scotland and deposes Balliol. As overlord of Scotland, he appoints officials to rule on his behalf. Edward seizes the Stone of Scone – on which the Scottish Kings sit at their coronation – and takes it to London, where it remains under the Coronation chair in Westminster Abbey until it is returned to Scotland in 1996.

Balliol was imprisoned in the Tower of London, but later released provided he went to France, where he eventually died.

THE STONE OF SCONE

THE STONE ON which the kings of Scotland have been crowned since the time of Kenneth MacAlpin has mystical significance for the Scottish people. Though there is controversy about its origins, it has acquired, over the centuries, the significance which attaches to objects of historical importance.

Its symbolism was appreciated by Edward I when he carried it off to Westminster and for centuries after it remained under the Coronation Chair, made by Edward I in 1301, on which all English (and Scottish, after 1603) kings and queens have been crowned. Cromwell transferred it to Westminster Hall for his installation as Protector of England.

Its significance has also made it vulnerable to militant groups intent on drawing attention to their dissatisfaction with government. Just before World War I, the Suffragettes drew attention to their just cause by the unconventional act of exploding a bomb in Westminster Abbey and causing the Stone to split, an act which raised cries of 'sacrilege' in the press. The damage done on this occasion was mended by another group whose only motive seems to have been that the Stone belonged in Scotland and not in England. They were a group of students who took the Stone from London to Arbroath where it was found in the cathedral. When returned to London, it was found that the split in the Stone had been repaired with pieces of metal and a note from the Assessor of the University of Glasgow reminded the world that the Stone had been stolen in 1296 and should be returned.

The Stone of Scone was eventually returned to Scotland by Prime Minister John Major, with the approval of Elizabeth II, in November 1996.

> The Celtic name of the Stone, now safely ensconced in Edinburgh Castle, is Lia Fail, 'the speaking stone', which named the King who would be chosen. Cambray in his 'Monuments Celtiques' claims to have seen the Stone when it bore the inscription: *Ni fallat fatum, Scoti quocumque locatum Invenient lapidiem, regnasse tenetur ibidem*: If the Destiny prove true, then the Scots are known to have been Kings where'er men find this stone.

*Edward I ordered the Coronation Chair to be made in
1301, five years after he had captured the Stone of Scone
from the Scots.*

THE FABLE OF THE STONE

*Except ald seers do fei~n
And wizard wits be blind
The Scots in place must reign
Where they this stone shall find.*

This fabled Stone has an obscure
history. Traditionally it is said to
have been 'Jacob's Pillow' or it
may have been the Royal Stone of
the Irish Kings brought from
Antrim to Argyll. It is possible
that it may have been the Royal
Stone of the Picts, or an altar
stone to some awesome but long
forgotten god.

We know the Stone was taken by
King Edward I from Scone Abbey
to Westminster Abbey in 1296,
and subsequently returned to
Scotland in 1996. Some say that
the Stone there is the Stone of
Destiny, others that it is not
Scone's famed Stone, but one
quickly hacked out by the monks
and palmed off on the King, the
real and greatly treasured Stone
being hastily hidden in an
underground chamber, where it
yet lies undiscovered.

A tantalizing mystery it may
always remain.

WILLIAM WALLACE

1270–1305

WALLACE, BORN at Elderslie in 1270, was the second son of Sir Malcolm Wallace who had refused to pay homage to Edward I. William Wallace grew up to become a powerful and sturdy young man, with a height of 6 foot 7 inches and a physique to match, he was in fact a giant of a man. Like his father he bore a grudge against the English from his early youth. He murdered the English sheriff of Lanark and thus became an outlaw and guerrilla fighter for the rest of his life.

Wallace's example aroused a national spirit of rebellion among his countrymen and he was able to gather round him other guerrilla fighters. This force of quick acting and determined men was successful in assaulting and taking a number of English strongholds, among them Aberdeen, Inverness and Montrose. Wallace's force was not well equipped, nor did it have the support of Scottish clan noblemen who preferred to remain neutral. With the exception, that is, of Andrew de Moray who became a staunch ally.

By 1297 Wallace and his men were besieging Stirling Castle, the chief English stronghold. This roused the English to send a powerful army under the Governor of Scotland, the Earl of Surrey.

The Earl with his formidable army of cavalry, archers and foot soldiers intended to crush Wallace at Stirling, but a change in

Wallace was reputed to be a very handsome man, although nobody knows actually what he looked like, since no portraits of him taken from life exist. But by all accounts he was very tall, strong and had a pleasing face. William Wallace was portrayed by the actor, Mel Gibson, in the epic film Braveheart.

There is a memorial to William Wallace in Stirling, Scotland which is accessed from the road below via a steep stepped slope. This spectacular monument has 4 floors reached by climbing, again, up a spiral staircase.

the weather made the ground soggy and slowed the cavalry charge that was intended to mow down the Scottish foot soldiers. Seizing their opportunity Wallace and his men advanced among the mounted enemy and drove them back in hand-to-hand combat, opening a path to the castle which fell to Wallace and his men.

Wallace now became Guardian of Scotland but without the support of the clan nobility his title was not confirmed. After a year Edward, taking advantage of a temporary truce with France, personally took charge of the campaign against the Scots and defeated and captured Wallace. He was taken to London where he was tried and convicted in Westminster Hall, and finally hanged, drawn and quartered as an example to other rebels. Nobody has any really knows where the remains of Wallace's body now lie.

TIME LINE OF WILLIAM WALLACE

1297
Treaty of Submission was signed by the Scottish nobles who took part in Wallace's rebellion. Wallace defeated English forces attempting to cross the Forth at the Battle of Stirling Bridge. Wallace elected to the office of guardian of the kingdom.

1298
Scotland was invaded by a large English force led by Edward I. Edward defeated Wallace's army in the Battle of Falkirk and Wallace was forced into hiding.

1299
King Edward I marries Margaret of France. John Comyn is placed at the head of a Regency for his absent uncle, John Balliol.

1303
John Comyn and his army defeat the English at Roslin. In retaliation, Edward I reduces Scotland for the third time, and then makes a treaty with Comyn.

1304
Scotland formally submits to Edward I.

1305
Wallace is betrayed. Sir John Menteith and 60 men surprise Wallace in his sleep at Robroystoun, capture him and take him to Carlisle. Wallace is given a show by trial by the English. Wallace is executed in London by hanging, drawing and quartering.

ROBERT BRUCE

—— 1306–1329 ——

BALLIOL'S TREATY with France, and Wallace's rebellion, aggravated the distrust and suspicion between Scotland and England and led to a war of attrition between the two nations. The death of Edward I brought Edward II to the English throne and he continued the attack, now against Robert Bruce who had stepped into the breach left by Balliol. Bruce, unlike Wallace, now had the support of Scottish nobles and bishops. In June 1314 Robert Bruce besieged Stirling Castle. The English King sent a huge army to relieve the castle and it encamped at Bannockburn, about two miles to the south. On 24 June the two armies met. Bruce's Scottish army was one-third the size of the English army, but by forming 'shiltrons' or rings of men with spears levelled at every point of assault, his soldiers managed to repel an attack and break the English lines. Although outnumbered the Scots dug themselves pits in which the spearmen waited for the charge of the English mounted knights. Not expecting resistance, the knights fell into the trap and were decimated and routed. As his army fell back Edward fled and narrowly escaped capture.

The Scottish victory was complete and Bruce followed it up with the Declaration of Arbroath (1320) which was sent to Pope John XXII in Rome, asking for his intercession and declaring Scotland's determination to fight to the death to keep its independence.

'For as long as one hundred of us shall remain alive we shall never in any wise consent to submit to the rule of the English, for it is not for glory we fight . . . but for freedom alone.'

A truce was agreed, but no treaty was signed until Bruce marched an army into England in the reign of the following King, Edward III. Bruce died a year after the treaty, a contented man who had achieved the recognition of Scotland as an independent nation.

The threat to Scottish independence, however, remained even after Bannockburn. Fighting continued until an invasion of England in 1327 persuaded the new King, Edward III, to recognize Scottish independence.

Edward III's agreement was only temporary, however, and soon another English army was on its way to defeat the Scots at Halidon Hill. The Scots now lacked firm leadership, for Robert Bruce's son had been deposed by the son of John Balliol.

TIME LINE 1306–1329

1306
Robert Bruce is crowned as Robert I at Scone but is immediately driven into hiding by the English occupation army of Edward I.

1307
Edward I launches his final invasion of Scotland but dies on his way north. Bruce begins his campaign to drive the English out of Scotland.

1314
Bruce besieges Stirling Castle. An English army sent to break the siege is routed at the Battle of Bannockburn.

1315
Edward Bruce, Robert Bruce's brother, is offered and accepts the crown of Ireland by Irish lords.

1320
Declaration of Arbroath is signed by nearly all the lords and bishops in Scotland and is sent to the Pope.

1323
Truce between Robert Bruce and Edward II fails to prevent continuing warfare between the two countries.

1327
Edward II is deposed and is succeeded by Edward III. Bruce launches an invasion of England to force English recognition of Scotland's independence.

1328
Treaty of Edinburgh.

1329
Death of Robert Bruce at Cardross Castle.

BRUCE AND THE SPIDER

Robert Bruce was hiding in a hut in the forest. His enemies were seeking him far and wide. Six times he had met them in battle, and six times he had failed. Hope and courage were gone, and Bruce had given up all as lost. Full of sorrow, he lay stretched out on a pile of straw in the poor woodchopper's hut. While he lay thinking, he noticed a spider spinning her web. The spider was trying to spin a thread from one beam of the cottage to another. It was a long way between the beams, and Bruce saw how hard a thing it was for her to do. 'She can never do it,' thought the King. The little spider tried it once and failed. She tried it twice and failed. The King counted each time. At length she had tried it six times and had failed each time. 'She is like me,' thought the King. 'I have tried six battles and failed. She has tried six times to reach the beam and failed.' Then starting up from the straw, he cried, 'I will hang my fate upon that little spider. If she swings the seventh time and fails then I will give up all for lost. If she swings the seventh time and wins, I will call my men together once more for a battle with the enemy.' The spider tried the seventh time, letting herself down upon her slender thread. She swung out bravely. 'Look! look!' shouted the King. 'She has reached it. The thread hangs between the two beams. If the spider can do it, I can do it.' The next time Bruce won his battle.

THE HOUSE OF STEWART

1390–1625

James I was only twelve when he became King in 1406.

THOUGH EDWARD III was engaged in the early stages of what came to be known as The Hundred Years War with France, he had the time and energy to deal with David II, son of Bruce, when he attempted to reclaim the throne of Scotland. David was defeated at Neville's Cross and made a prisoner at the Tower of London for eleven years until he was able to pay a ransom for his release. The raising of the ransom money had been made difficult by the Black Death, which had impoverished daily life, so Edward offered David his release in exchange for an agreement on the succession to the Scottish throne. The Scottish parliament were not prepared to accept the terms and the truce which had reigned during David's imprisonment came to an end.

On David's death his place was taken by Robert Stewart, grandson of Robert Bruce who became Robert II. He was followed by Robert III. There now followed a period of family rivalries and lawlessness as diverse groups competed for power. Then in 1406 the English once again put a Scottish King in the Tower of London. This time it was James, son of Robert III, and he was imprisoned for eighteen years.

The bitter rivalry between Scotland and England continued, with the Scots united in their desire to remain independent, and the English Kings determined to deprive them of it. In 1563 hope of a reconciliation rose again as a marriage was agreed between Margaret, daughter of Henry VII, and James IV of Scotland. Expectations were dashed, however, when James, responding to a call from his Auld Alliance ally the French King, challenged Henry VIII's army at Flodden and saw his army slaughtered.

This seemed to spell the end for Scottish independence but destiny had another card to play, when the next Scottish king, James V, married a French woman, Mary of Guise, in 1538.

In 1542, shortly after a Scottish army had suffered a crushing and shameful defeat at the hands of English Borderers at Solway Moss, Mary gave birth to a daughter who, days after her birth, became Queen of Scots on the death of her broken and demoralized father, James V.

When James V took control in 1528, he displayed courage and ruthlessness.

TIME LINE OF THE HOUSE OF STEWART

1390–1406
Robert III, married Annabella.
1406–1437
James I, married Joan, daughter of John Beaufort, Earl of Somerset.
1437–1460
James II, married Marie, daughter of Arnold, Duke of Gueldres.
1460–1488
James III, married Margaret, daughter of King of Denmark.
1488–1513
James IV, married Margaret, daughter of Henry VII.
1513–1542
James V, married Madelein, daughter of King of France and then Mary, daughter of Duke of Guise.
1542–1567
Mary, Queen of Scots, married King of France Henry Stuart (Lord Darnley), James Hepburn (Earl of Bothwell)
1567–1625
James VI, became James I of England, married Anne, daughter of King of Denmark.

THE SCOTTISH CLANS

IN MOUNTAINOUS territories there is a tendency for communities to develop with a strong sense of local patriotism for their valleys. This is true of Scotland where the clan system probably developed in about the sixth century, as the Scots spread over the land of the Picts and claimed territories for themselves. The head of each community became a chief and received a voluntary and willing allegiance from his clansmen. This led to rivalries between clans as their chiefs sought to extend their territories, and clan warfare became a feature of Scottish life. Clan chiefs began to take on the titles of kings as their kingdoms grew, and, by the fifteenth century, large areas had become the domains of the MacDonalds in the west, the Gordons in the north-east, the Mackenzies in the north Highlands and the Campbell's in the south-west.

By this time maintaining the independence of Scotland against the English had become more important. A sense of nationhood had emerged which led to various treaties and finally the marriage of a Scottish King to an English princess, Margaret Tudor. The Statutes of Iona in 1609 tried to stop clan rivalry, and more or less succeeded, though the last clan battle was at Keppoch in 1688.

The Highland clans had developed a distinctive dress which came to be known as a plaid. At first the plaid was a one-piece mantle, woven into a pattern of stripes and blocks of muted vegetable dyes, which was wrapped and pleated around the body. Later this was cut in several pieces and held together with a broad belt. Distinctive patterns, or setts, of colours came to be adopted by individual clans, giving rise to the tartans which have become such a feature of Scottish dress. Other distinctive features were the sporran and the *skean dhu*, a dagger inserted in the sock.

With the defeat of the last Jacobite rebellion at Culloden the clan traditions began to fade, though they were revived by the later Hanoverians, especially George IV and Queen Victoria. They believed it would provide a sense of national identity in Scotland, and were well aware of the fighting prowess of the tartan-clad Scottish regiments that became such a valuable part of British armies from the latter part of the eighteenth century.

CASTLE SWEEN, ARGYLL, SCOTLAND

Castle Sween (*above*) in Argyll is one of the oldest castles in Scotland. It was built in the 11th or 12th century, and has a curtain wall, enclosing a rectangular courtyard and a keep. It was held by the McSweens until it was captured by Robert the Bruce in 1315. It was then held by the McMillans, the Stewarts of Menteigh, the MacNeils of Gigha for the MacDonald Lord of the Isles, and in 1481 the Campbells became keepers for the Crown. During the time of the McMillans the western wall was dismantled and a round tower and a new rectangular building were added at the northwest corner. The tower is standing today, and is known as McMillan's Tower.

DEFINITION OF THE WORD 'CLAN'

Clan is the Gaelic word for children, but is more accurately translated as 'family' in the sense in which the word clan became accepted in the Scottish Highlands during the 13th century. A clan is a social group whose core comprises a number of families derived from, or accepted as being derived from, a common ancestor. Almost without exception, that core is accompanied by a further number of dependent and associated families who have either sought the protection of the clan at some point in history or have been tenants or vassals of its chief. That chief is owed allegiance by all members of the clan, but ancient tradition nevertheless states that 'the Clan is above the Chief'. Although Gaelic has been supplanted by English in the Lowlands of Scotland for nearly a thousand years, it is an acceptable convention to refer to the great Lowland families, like the Douglases, as clans, although the heads of certain families, such as Bruce, prefer not to use the term. Allegiance was generally given to a father's clan, but Celtic tradition includes a strong element of descent through, and loyalty to, a mother's line. In reality, the chief of a clan would 'ingather' any stranger, of whatever family, who possessed suitable skills, maintained his allegiance and, if required, adopted the clan surname.

MARY QUEEN OF SCOTS

1542–1587

ROYAL BIOGRAPHY

BORN: 8 December 1542, Linlithgow Palace. PARENTS: James V and Mary of Guise.
ASCENDED THE THRONE: 14 December 1542. CROWNED: 9 September 1543, Stirling Castle.
REIGN: 25 years. MARRIED: (1) Francis II of France (1558), (2) Henry Stewart, Lord Darnley
(1565), (3) James Hepburn, Earl of Bothwell (1567).
CHILDREN: With (2), one son, James VI and I. DIED: Fotheringhay Castle, Northamptonshire,
8 February 1587. BURIED: St George's Chapel, Windsor.

MARY WAS A victim of her own impulsive and self-willed character, and of her upbringing in the French court, but she has always attracted much sympathy from English and Scots alike. Betrothed to the Dauphin of France when she was six years old, Mary spent the next twelve years of her life in France, which at that time was torn by religious dissension. At the age of sixteen, in 1558, she married Francis, the French Dauphin, and became Queen of France when the Dauphin became Francis II.

On his death in 1560, she returned to Scotland which was being turned away from Catholicism by the Calvinist priest John Knox.

Mary then married Henry, Lord Darnley who was descended from Margaret Tudor and therefore was in line for the English throne. Elizabeth I of England, who had not been consulted about the Darnley marriage, was not pleased and was suspicious of Mary's motives. Particularly as Mary dismissed her trusted adviser, the Earl of Moray, and began to fill her court with foreigners. Among these was David Rizzio, who, when Darnley began to suspect that he was Mary's lover, was murdered in her presence. Mary now became pregnant with the son of Darnley. The child was destined to become James VI of Scotland and subsequently James I of England.

Mary hesitated to divorce Darnley as she was afraid that her child might be said to be illegitimate. She did not need to worry, however, for Darnley died in a mysterious explosion in a house where he lay ill in Edinburgh. One of the suspects of Darnley's murder was the Earl of Bothwell who, according to Mary, now kidnapped and raped her, in an effort to force her to marry him. Whatever the truth of the matter, it did not go down well with the Scottish lords or John Knox, who now named her the Scottish whore.

In 1567, her subjects turned against her and she was compelled to abdicate her position as Queen and was imprisoned at Loch Leven castle. She still had loyal supporters, among them Lord Douglas, who managed to rescue her and opened for her the escape route to England. This was where Mary hoped to find protection from her enemies with her cousin Elizabeth, whose legitimate heir she was. This was another of Mary's fatal miscalculations for, to Elizabeth, the Catholic Mary and her supporters were a threat to the throne of Protestant England.

Mary was to remain a prisoner in England for nineteen years before one Catholic plot too many persuaded Elizabeth that her cousin should be executed.

TIME LINE OF THE REIGN 1542–1587

1542
James invades England but is defeated at the Battle of Solway Moss and dies a few weeks later. His daughter, the one-week old Mary, succeeds.

1554
Mary of Guise takes over as Regent.

1558
Mary marries the French Dauphin in Paris.

1559
Mary becomes Queen of France.

1560
François II dies and Mary returns to Scotland in 1561.

1565
Mary marries her cousin, Henry, Lord Darnley.

1567
Darnley is murdered in an explosion in a house in an Edinburgh suburb. Mary is implicated, but nothing is proved. The Scottish lords rebel and defeat Mary, who abdicates and flees to England, where she is imprisoned. Mary's son becomes king as James VI and the Earl of Moray, her half-brother, becomes Regent.

1570
Moray is assassinated at Linlithgow.

1587
After being implicated in the Babington Conspiracy, Mary is tried and executed at Fotheringhay Castle.

THE STUARTS

By the time that the Earl of Bothwell, Mary Queen of Scots' husband, died in 1578 the Scottish Stewarts had begun to spell their name in the French way – Stuart. Thus, when James VI of Scotland became James I of England on the death of Elizabeth I, he adopted the name Stuart as the name of the dynasty. The union of the two crowns was in theory an admirable way to settle the political and religious disputes of the two nations. However, prejudices and deep-held beliefs die hard and it was not until the end of the Stuart period that differences were forgotten.

JAMES I

—— 1603–1625 ——

ROYAL BIOGRAPHY

BORN: 19 June 1566, Edinburgh. PARENTS: Mary Queen of Scots and Lord Darnley.
ASCENDED THE THRONE: 24 March 1603. CROWNED: 25 July 1603, Westminster Abbey.
AUTHORITY: King of Great Britain and Ireland.
MARRIED: Anne, daughter of Frederick II of Denmark and Norway (1589).
CHILDREN: Three sons, including the future Charles I, and five daughters.
DIED: 27 March 1625, Theobolds Park, Hertfordshire. BURIED: Westminster Abbey.

JAMES VI OF Scotland inherited the throne of England as the great-grandson of James IV's English wife, Margaret Tudor, and the legitimate heir of Elizabeth I, who had died childless. James inherited some of the worst characteristics of his parents, Mary Queen of Scots and Lord Darnley, being self-centred and prone towards setting up favourites as advisers. Although he was brought up in the belief of the Divine Right of Kings, he did try to rule his two kingdoms tolerantly. Working in England through Parliament, he attempted to relax penal laws. In 1605 a group of Catholic conspirators, including one Guy Fawkes, tried to blow up the Houses of

Parliament when he was present but they were caught and executed.

James's relationship with Parliament worsened after the Gunpowder Plot, which drove him to listen more closely to his advisers. The two principal favourites of James I were, in succession, Robert Ker and George Villiers. Both were good-looking and high-spirited young men. Ker had been the King's page and was created Earl of Somerset in 1613. He was also made a member of the Privy Council and entrusted with the King's most intimate business. However, he angered the nation by encouraging the King to make an alliance with Spain, and by helping him to raise unquestionable taxes. By 1616 the King had taken to George Villiers, who quickly became Earl of Buckingham. He was a Catholic, and had antagonised both the Anglican and Puritan factions in Parliament.

Politically, James hoped to bring about the union of England and Scotland but was defeated by the strong opposition of the English Parliament. The reign of James I was not entirely unsuccessful in foreign affairs. At home, Ulster ended its rebellion against the crown and accepted Protestant settlers and the magnificent Authorised Version of the Bible was published. The theatre flourished and Shakespeare wrote his greatest plays, including *King Lear*, and published his sonnets during the reign. James invited Dutch painters to England who had become skilled in the art of oil painting. Among them was Anthony Van Dyck who painted a full length portrait of James, which now hangs in Windsor Castle.

James also invited Dutch experts skilled in the reclamation of swampy land, a common problem in low-lying Holland. Their dykes and ditches began to turn East Anglia into arable land, though this task was not fully complete until the reign of William III. Some extreme Protestants were not happy with the religious attitudes of James' reign and a group of them, after an initial move to Protestant Holland, set off for the young colonies in America on a ship called the *Mayflower* in 1620.

TIME LINE OF THE REIGN 1603–1625

1603
James VI of Scotland becomes King James I of England after the death of Elizabeth I.

1604
Somerset House Peace Conference results in peace between England and Spain. The Hampton Court conference fails to settle doctrinal differences between the Anglican church and its Puritan critics.

1605
Gunpowder Plot attempts to blow up the King and Parliament. Shakespeare writes *King Lear*.

1607
The Earls of Tyrone and Tyrconnel end their rebellion against English rule of Ireland and flee to Europe. Ulster is colonized by Protestant settlers from Scotland and England.

1609
Shakespeare completes the *Sonnets*.

1611
Authorized Version of the Bible is published.

1612
Henry, Prince of Wales, dies of typhoid.

1616
Shakespeare dies.

1618
Walter Raleigh is executed for alleged treason at Westminster.

1620
Pilgrim Fathers set sail for America in the *Mayflower*.

1625
Death of James I.

THE GUNPOWDER PLOT

——— 1605 ———

THOUGH JAMES I had sympathy for the Catholics, and had tried to relax the penal laws by which Catholics could be imprisoned or fined, the opposition of Parliament forced him to change his mind. This caused Catholics to feel betrayed by their King, which, following the loss of support of the Spanish King after the establishment of peace between England and Spain, drove them towards the idea that violent measures were necessary to further their cause.

This took the form of a plan to attack the King and Parliament at the same time. The conspirators led by Robert Catesby, and Guy (Guido) Fawkes, who had served in the Spanish army, planned to blow up the Houses of Parliament during a State opening in November 1605, when the King would be present.

The plan required the introduction of barrels of gunpowder into the cellars of the Houses of Parliament without being observed. In order to do this the conspirators rented a house in which they could store the gunpowder, opposite the Parliament building. From here they dug a tunnel into the cellars of the Parliament building.

The plan might well have succeeded but for the fears of one of the conspirators who, fearing for the life of the members of Parliament, warned his brother, who was an MP, and who consequently passed the information to the Parliamentary guards. A search was made and Fawkes was arrested. Catesby and the other conspirators were tracked down at Holbeach House and attacked; Catesby was killed in the siege. Fawkes was tortured, tried, found guilty and subsequently executed.

The attempt on the King and government had a powerful effect on the nation. It had, by now, accepted the new religious order in England and disliked extremists on either side who tried to provoke religious dissension. The Fawkes/Catesby plot therefore passed into history so that even today the Fifth of November is remembered by fireworks throughout Britain and effigies of Guy Fawkes are burned on bonfires.

Bonfires are lit every year in Britain on the night of 5 November. This is in commemoration of the Gunpowder Plot, and sometimes an effigy of Guy Fawkes is burned on the top.

TRANSCRIPT FROM THE TRIAL OF GUY FAWKES

Then did Sir Edward Philips, Kt. his Majesty's Serjeant at Law; open the Indictment to this effect, as followeth:

The matter that is now to be offer'd to you my Lords the Commissioners, and to the Trial of you the Knights and Gentlemen of the Jury, is Matter of Treason; but of such Horror, and monstrous Nature, that before now, The Tongue of Man never deliver'd,
The Ear of Man never heard,
The Heart of Man never conceited,
Nor the Malice of hellish or earthly Devil ever practised . . .

Hearts judge the Horror of this Treason; to murder and subvert

Such a King,
Such a Queen,
Such a Prince,
Such a Progeny,
Such a State,
Such a Government,
So complete and absolute,
That God approves,
The World admires,
All true English Hearts honour and reverence,
The Pope and his Disciples only envies and maligns?

CHARLES I

1625–1649

ROYAL BIOGRAPHY

BORN: 19 November 1600, Dunfermline Palace. PARENTS: James VI and I and Anne of Denmark. ASCENDED THE THRONE: 27 March 1625. CROWNED: 2 February 1626, Westminster Abbey. AUTHORITY: King of Great Britain and Ireland. MARRIED: Henrietta Maria, daughter of Henri IV of France. CHILDREN: Four sons, including the future Charles II and James II, and five daughters. DIED: 30 January 1649, Whitehall. BURIED: St George's Chapel, Windsor.

CHARLES WAS James I's second son, and became his father's heir on the death of his much admired elder brother, Henry, Prince of Wales in 1612. His marriage to a French Catholic princess, Henrietta Maria, in 1623, caused some disquiet in the country. Like his father, Charles believed in the Divine Right of Kings. His reign began badly when he dissolved Parliament for trying to impeach the Duke of Buckingham, his father's adviser. Buckingham's murder in 1628 saved Charles from further confrontation with Parliament.

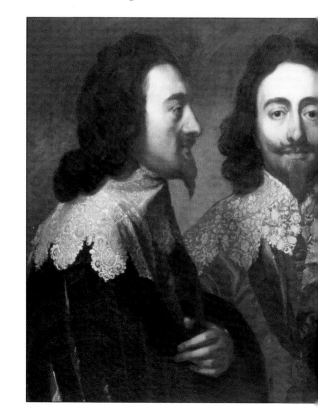

Charles' quarrels with his Parliaments were a constant source of friction during his reign. He was quite unable to accept the opinions of parliamentarians, and his insistence on tax money to support ill-advised wars against the French and Spanish did not help matters. The failure of his expeditions, the obvious influence over him of his Catholic wife, a fast-rising and anti-Puritan churchman William Laud, and a favourite, Thomas Wentworth, Earl of Strafford, and the militant mood of Parliament, eventually led to Charles having to agree to a Bill of Rights which stated that Parliament could not be dissolved without its own consent.

A crisis arrived when Charles made Laud Archbishop of Canterbury in 1633, in order to promote the high church party and to anglicize the Scottish church. This created more opposition to him and reduced his parliamentary support. Eventually, both Laud and Strafford were impeached and executed. Charles did regain some measure of support when his opponents in Parliament tried to deprive him of control of the army – a constitutional issue. The improved relations did not last long. Still influenced by his wife and others, Charles attempted to impeach his enemies in Parliament by entering the House of Commons with armed guards to arrest them, only to find that they had fled.

Alone against Parliament, Charles now withdrew from London and mustered an army with his nephew Prince Rupert. Raising his standard at Nottingham, he set up a

headquarters near Oxford, in defiance of Parliament and thus launched the Civil War. During this long and bitter conflict in which the whole nation became involved, Charles showed courage and military ability, but was outmatched by Cromwell's superior numbers and disciplined Model army. After losing the war, Charles foolishly made a secret treaty with the Scots, who promised to reinstate him. This led to his trial for treason and inevitably to his execution, which he faced with courage and dignity.

TIME LINE OF THE REIGN 1625–1649

1625
Charles I succeeds his father James I.

1626
Parliament attempts to impeach Buckingham and is dissolved by Charles.

1627
England goes to war with France, but the Duke of Buckingham fails to relieve the besieged Huguenots at La Rochelle.

1628
The Duke of Buckingham is assassinated. The Petition of Right is presented to the King, who agrees to it under protest.

1629
Charles dissolves Parliament and rules by himself until 1640.

1632
Van Dyck settles in England as the Court painter.

1637
Charles tries to force new prayer book on the Scots, who resist by signing National Covenant.

1640
Charles summons Short Parliament, which lasts 3 weeks.

1641
The Star Chamber and Court of High Commission are both abolished.

1642–9
Civil War.

1649
Charles is tried and executed by Parliament.

THE CIVIL WAR

1642–1649

The Battle at Marston Moor in Yorkshire on 2 July 1644, was between the Royalists, under Prince Rupert and the Duke of Newcastle, and the Parliamentarians, under Lord Fairfax of Cameron, Oliver Cromwell and the Earl of Leven. It resulted in the first major victory for the Parliamentarians in the English Civil War.

THE ENGLISH CIVIL War was the result of a protracted conflict between Charles I, who believed in the Divine Right of Kings, and Parliament. The King depended on Parliament for his finances, including the upkeep of a standing army. In 1629 Charles, despairing of obtaining Parliamentary support, dismissed it, planning to rule alone. However on trying to impose English religious practice on the Scots he met with rebellion. This led to the Bishops' Wars, to combat which he was obliged to open Parliament again in search of funds. But this time he was refused. As a result of his minister Strafford's dealings with an Irish rebellion, and a rumour that Charles was encouraging a Catholic revival in Ireland, the opposition to him grew. So much so that when he tried to arrest five members of Parliament, among them Oliver Cromwell, they flared up into open defiance.

Charles' response to this was to withdraw from London and gather an army in Nottingham to impose his will, either by force or threat. He was joined by his nephew Prince Rupert of the Rhine, a handsome young man who created the image of Charles's Cavaliers against that of Cromwell's Roundheads. At first things went well, with a resounding victory at Edgehill in

This hat was worn by the Parliamentarian John Bradshaw during the Civil War. It was lined with metal to protect his head.

Warwickshire. This was followed by a defeat at Marston Moor, Yorkshire, the decisive Royalist defeat. Cromwell, who was firmly in charge of the Parliamentary forces, now reorganized the army expelling all lords and parliamentary politicians. He created the Model Army which, with its morale boosted by Cromwell's religious indoctrination and regular pay, defeated Charles at the Battle of Naseby in 1645. Charles was later captured and handed over to Parliament by a Scots army. Charles as a defeated leader now began protracted negotiations for peace, but royalist uprisings in Kent, Essex and Wales did little to help his case, and drove Parliament to carry out his trial and execution.

The Death Warrant of Charles I.

OLIVER CROMWELL

1599–1658

THOUGH HE WAS instrumental in bringing about the death of a King and changing the framework of government, Oliver Cromwell was a somewhat difficult figure to categorize. He was also responsible for bringing all the countries of Britain into one Commonwealth. He was a leader who ruled by military force, a dictator, and a man of masterful energy and considerable personal charm. Cromwell was, for his time, amazingly tolerant of religious and political dissent, but his image faded after his death.

Convinced that it was impossible to deal with a stubborn King, Cromwell urged Parliament to take control of the army and enforce its views on the right way to govern England. In order to achieve his object Cromwell set about creating a new 'model' army, from which all peers and members of Parliament would be barred. He appointed himself second-in-command in this new force, which was to be headed by Thomas Fairfax, a parliamentary general who had distinguished himself in an early battle against the Royalist forces. Though Parliament, and especially the royalist members disagreed, Cromwell broke up the groups opposing him and obtained complete control. With his new army he was able to quell revolts in Kent, Sussex and Wales, and put down a revolt in Ireland with such ferocity that his name is abhorred there to this day.

Like the King, Cromwell believed he was divinely inspired and was ruthless about achieving his dream of a new republican England. In order to ensure full support in Parliament, he reduced the number of members to those he could count on. This Parliament, which came to be known as 'The Rump', was more manageable and voted eventually for the death of King Charles.

The death of the King, however, did not solve Cromwell's problems. In 1653, after the expulsion of the Rump Parliament, Cromwell became Lord Protector of the Commonwealth. The Commonwealth proper, however, ended with the establishment of Cromwell's Protectorate (1653–58), which was characterized by religious toleration, profitable commercial treaties with several foreign powers, and several successful wars. The Protectorate endured, however, only while Cromwell lived, and collapsed after his incompetent son Richard alienated both the Army and Parliament in his attempt to succeed him.

Without Cromwell's lead, the army broke up into rival factions of political careerists and radicals, who took the place of dedicated Cromwellian members in Parliament. In 1657, the year before he died, Cromwell was offered the title 'King', which he thought about carefully before rejecting.

Oliver Cromwell was nearly 6 feet tall, with grey eyes and a large nose. He was not at all handsome, although he was once described as being 'of majestic deportment and comely presence'.

TIME LINE OF OLIVER CROMWELL 1599–1658

1644
Cromwell secured the victory of Marston Moor for parliament.

1645
The Battle of Naseby took place. The defeat of the Royalist army was decisive in giving victory to the Parliament in the Civil War.

1646
Charles I surrenders to the Scots at Newark, bringing the military phase of the Civil War to an end.

1647
Charles I is seized at Holmby House by the army. On the same day Cromwell flees Parliament to rejoin his army at Triptow Heath.

1648
Battle of Preston. A Scottish army under the Duke of Hamilton invades England in support of Charles I, but is beaten back by Cromwell. Charles onces again is seized by the army.

1649
Trial of Charles I. Charles is executed on scaffold outside the Banqueting House of Whitehall Palace.

1650
Battle of Dunbar where Cromwell's army defeats a Scottish army twice its size.

1653
Cromwell sets up a Protectorate with a Council of State and himself as Lord Protector.

1658
Cromwell dies of pneumonia in Whitehall (3 September).

THE COMMONWEALTH

1649–1660

The name 'Royal Oak' refers to the famous episode in English history when King Charles II attempted unsuccessfully to defeat Oliver Cromwell, win back the throne of England and avenge the execution of his father Charles I. He invaded England with an army of supporters but was beaten by Cromwell at the Battle of Worcester in 1651. It was after this battle that Charles reputedly escaped Cromwell's men by hiding in an oak tree.

AFTER THE EXECUTION of Charles I, a Council of State was formed with Cromwell at its head and England was declared a republic. Initially Cromwell did not intend to replace the King, but to oblige him to work with Parliament in a democratic manner. Initially, like Charles, who was convinced that he was carrying out God's will, there was a clash of interests and motives of diverse groups of members of Parliament. Among these were Puritans, Catholics and the new Levellers, who voted for a more tolerant application of laws. Deciding that a Parliament voicing too many different opinions was not workable, Cromwell and his minister, Pride, began to reduce the numbers of Parliamentarians. They created a Rump parliament, in 1649, of 53 members which renamed the government of England as the Commonwealth, at the same time abolishing the House of Lords and the monarchy. This was followed by further reducing the numbers of Parliamentarians to fifteen, and Cromwell naming himself Protector of England.

When Scotland and Ireland, which had been pacified by the army, were joined to the Common-wealth, Cromwell's problems increased. There was a body of Scots who supported the claims of Charles as the rightful heir to the throne. At this time Charles marched an army into England, but was defeated at Worcester. He also was faced with a war involving the Dutch. This resulted from the Navigation Act of 1652, passed by Parliament but opposed by Cromwell, who saw the Dutch as European Protestant allies. These, and other personal cares like the death of his daughter, undermined his health, and when he died on 3 September 1658, the Commonwealth died with him. His son, Richard, who was named his heir, was incapable of holding together the disparate groups that ruled England.

TIME LINE OF THE COMMONWEALTH

1649
Following the execution of Charles I, a Council of State is appointed with Oliver Cromwell as Chairman.
England is declared a republic.
Irish royalists defeated by Cromwell at Wexford and at the Siege of Drogheda.

1650
Scots royalists led by Charles II defeated at Worcester. Charles flees into exile.

1651
Navigation Act secures trade monopoly for English ships.

1652–4
First Dutch War.

1653
Cromwell expels the Rump Parliament. Cromwell becomes Lord Protector of England.

1654–5
First Protectorate Parliament sits.

1655
Cromwell dismisses Parliament and divides the country into 11 districts, each ruled by a Major-General.

1656
Second Protectorate Parliament abolishes rule of Major-Generals.

1657
Cromwell refuses an offer of the throne.

1658
Cromwell dies.

1660
A new Parliament is summoned and negotiates the restoration of the monarchy.

ART AND ARCHITECTURE

A portrait of Henrietta-Maria, wife of Charles I, by Anthony Van Dyck. Charles was so taken by the Flemish painter that he awarded him a pension and a knighthood as an inducement to stay in England.

WHATEVER THEIR DEFECTS as rulers, the Stuarts contributed positively to a new style in art and architecture in England. Much of this was due to a wave of interest in the Italian Renaissance and Classical style. Familiarity with continental developments, came with the growing popularity of travel for the educated classes. A habit which evolved into the Grand Tour.

James I, whose Scottish ancestry had long made him familiar with French culture, was well-versed in the art and architecture of the Renaissance. He encouraged the London-born architect Inigo Jones, who had studied architecture under the Italian, Antonio Palladio, in Venice. In 1616 Jones was commissioned to build the Queen's House in Greenwich, and to rebuild the burnt-out Whitehall Palace. The banqueting hall at Whitehall was decorated by the painter Peter Paul Rubens, and this still stands today.

He was also commissioned to design the layout of the Covent Garden quarter of London, and of Lincoln's Inn Fields. He thus set the scene for the classical masterpieces of Christopher Wren, James Gibbs, Nicholas Hawksmoor, Sir John Vanbrugh and Thomas Archer.

James also invited Dutch painters to England, notably Anthony Van Dyck who painted the King's full-length portrait at Windsor. Van Dyck was later invited by Charles II to reside in England, during which time he painted many magnificent pictures of Charles with his wife, Henrietta Maria, and their children. Van Dyck's success set the scene for the English school of portraiture of the seventeenth century. Peter Lely, whose real name was Pieter Van der Faes, painted portraits of Charles I, Cromwell, Charles II and thirteen admirals during the Dutch wars that are now treasures of the national collection.

Built in the classical style, the Banqueting House in Whitehall was designed by Inigo Jones. Peter Paul Rubens was commissioned by Charles I in 1635 to paint canvases for the ceiling in the Banqueting House.

Inigo Jones was an architect as well as a scenery and costume designer. Jones was one of the many versatile artists in the courts of James I and Charles I

CHARLES II

— 1660–1685 —

ROYAL BIOGRAPHY

BORN: 29 May 1630, St James's Palace. PARENTS: Charles I and Henrietta Maria.
ASCENDED THE THRONE: 30 January 1649 (by right); restored 29 May 1660.
CROWNED: As King of Scots, Scone, 1 January 1651; as King of England, Westminster Abbey,
23 April 1661. AUTHORITY: King of Great Britain and Ireland.
MARRIED: Catherine of Braganza, daughter of the King of Portugal. CHILDREN: Three children
still-born; about 17 illegitimate children, including the Duke of Monmouth.
DIED: 6 February 1685 Whitehall. BURIED: Westminster Abbey

WHEN CHARLES I was executed, his elder son, Charles, in exile in France, declared himself King. He began negotiations with the Covenanters in Scotland to lead an army against Cromwell's successor in England. Charles, having agreed to terms laid down by the Scottish Commissioners, was crowned King at Scone on 1 January 1651. The Covenanters supplied him with an ill-prepared and ill-led army, which was heavily defeated at Worcester in 1651. For the next nine years, Charles lived the life of an impoverished exile in France.

The failure of Oliver Cromwell's son, Richard, to control Parliament, aroused such fears in England of a repeat of Cromwellian military despotism, that it was not too difficult for General George Monck to engineer Charles's recall to England. His triumphant return in May 1660 began the Restoration period, when England, ruled by its self-indulgent, pleasure-loving 'Merrie Monarch', rejected Puritanism. Unlike his father, Charles was a shrewd politician and knew how to negotiate the minefield of public opinion and keep the country on an even keel.

Religious differences were still a major field of contention in England, and Charles, who privately had Catholic sympathies, supported the Act of

Uniformity of 1662. This Act obliged Puritans to accept the doctrines of the Church of England and ordered nonconformist clergy to remain five miles away from their parish. The Puritans were at one extreme of the religious spectrum, and at the other, was a Catholic element. The Puritans were accused of hatching the 'Popish Plot' to kill the King, though there was a strong suspicion that the plot was a fabrication to discredit Catholics.

Charles' means of dealing with enemies and financial problems were devious, but effective. By the secret Treaty of Dover with Louis XIV of France, Charles gained great support. This support was mainly financial. In his continuing battle with the Dutch over the valuable shipping trade, he managed to guide England back to Roman Catholicism without using the money, as Louis expected. The British navy was greatly strengthened and the Dutch quarrel was eventually settled by the marriage of Charles' niece, Mary, to the Prince of Orange.

Charles' peaceful and entertaining capital with its theatres and masques received a damaging blow in 1666 when a severe fire broke out following a plague. Both these disasters turned out to have a silver lining when the city was rebuilt with some of the superb buildings and churches that have survived to this day.

Although a married man Charles kept a succession of mistresses. His favourite was Nell Gwynne who was one of the leading actresses of the day and adored by the general public.

TIME LINE OF THE REIGN 1660–1685

1660
Charles returns to England from Holland and is restored to the throne. Pepys begins his diary. Edward Hyde becomes Charles's chief minister.

1661
Edward Hyde is created Earl of Clarendon. First Parliament of the reign meets at Westminster.

1662
Act of Uniformity compels Puritans to accept the doctrines of the Church of England. Royal Society given its royal charter by Charles.

1665–7
Second Dutch War, caused by commercial rivalry between England and Holland.

1665
Plague strikes London.

1666
Great Fire of London.

1670
Secret Treaty of Dover.

1672–4
Third Dutch War.

1678
Popish Plot fabricated by Titus Oates.

1679
Whig and Tory first used as names for political parties.

1683
Rye House Plot to murder Charles is discovered.

1685
Charles reveals his Catholicism on his deathbed.

THE GREAT FIRE

1666

LIKE NERO'S FIRE in Rome the Great Fire of London brought some benefits, for it destroyed large areas of crowded streets and unhealthy dwellings, which were later replaced by a modern city. The year before the Fire, London had been stricken by a plague that killed 100,000 inhabitants and brought daily life to a standstill. The fire claimed less victims, for many were able to escape the flames. It spread from Pudding Lane to the west, setting fire to the closely packed wooden houses and reaching the medieval cathedral of St Paul's on Ludgate Hill via the Guildhall and Royal Exchange.

There was little useful equipment to fight the blaze. Various statutes had forced the parishes to provide buckets, axes, ladders, squirts and fire hooks, but many were rotted through neglect, and water supplies, apart from the river, were minimal. So the means for fighting the raging flames, fanned by an east wind were minimal, consisting of buckets of water and hastily constructed fire breaks. In order to contain the fire, Londoners blew up or pulled down buildings in the path of the flames to create firebreaks.

The devastation caused by the fire can be clearly seen in this contemporary map.

The great fire raged for four days and three nights, destroying many famous buildings.

It is likely that London has had some form of firefighting from as early as the time of the Romans. However, after the Roman armies left Britain in 415 AD, any organised attempts to fight fires were abandoned. Following the Norman Conquest in 1066, William the Conqueror insisted that all fires should be put out at night to reduce the risk of fire in houses with straw 'carpets' and thatched roofs. William's law of *couvre-feu* (literally – cover fire) became the modern term *curfew*.

Despite these precautions, a huge fire destroyed a large part of the city in 1212 and was said to have killed some 3,000 people. This fire was known as the Great Fire of London – until 2 September 1666.

The fire began in the house and shop of Thomas Farynor, the King's baker, in Pudding Lane. His assistant awoke to find the house full of smoke. His master roused, the household tried to escape through a window and along a roof gutter to a neighbouring house. All were successful except for a maid servant who was said to be too frightened to clamber over the roof. She stayed and became the first victim of the fire.

Charles II, who had been driven out of the city by the plague of the previous year, stayed and appointed his brother to be in charge. He had to prevent looting and other crimes and start to plan the rebuilding of the city. London had lost 461 acres of buildings which included 87 parish churches, 52 halls of guilds and trading companies, the great medieval St. Paul's Cathedral and over 15,000 dwellings.

Christopher Wren, Surveyor of the King's works, was called in and put forward extensive plans for a new city. Various factions, however, opposed a scheme which would take some time to complete satisfactorily, and London lost the opportunity to have one of the best planned cities of Europe. Fortunately London did benefit from the scores of churches built by Wren and the glorious masterpiece of the new St. Pauls.

A monument to commemorate the disaster was erected at Pudding Lane in 1677 bearing the inscription 'But Popish frenzy which wrought such horrors is not yet quenched' – evidence of the religious animosity that still existed at that date. It was erased in 1830.

JAMES II

1685–1688

ROYAL BIOGRAPHY

BORN: 14 October 1633, St James's Palace. PARENTS: Charles I and Henrietta Maria. ASCENDED THE THRONE: 6 February 1685. CROWNED: 23 April 1685, Westminster Abbey. AUTHORITY: King of Great Britain and Ireland. MARRIED: (1) Anne Hyde, daughter of Edward Hyde, Earl of Clarendon, (2) Mary, daughter of the Duke of Modena. CHILDREN: With (1) four sons and four daughters, with (2) two sons, five daughters and five still-born babies. DEPOSED: 23 December 1688 DIED: September 1701, Château de Saint Germain-en-Laye, near Paris. BURIED: Saint Germain-en-Laye; later, the church of the English Benedictines in Paris; possibly returned to Saint Germain.

CHARLES II'S BROTHER James was a committed Catholic who resigned his post as Lord High Admiral, during the wars against the Dutch because of his beliefs. Prejudice against a Catholic monarch continued once he became King. An attempt by the Duke of Monmouth, Charles II's illegitimate son, to take his crown, failed when James defeated Monmouth at Sedgemoor, Somersetshire.

The difficult start to James's reign did not deter him from his ambition to restore Catholicism in England. The revocation of the Edict of Nantes, allowing religious tolerance in France, inspired James to start a campaign to limit Protestant power in England and to reinstall Catholicism. As he did not receive strong support from Parliament he gathered an army of 13,000 troops, which he placed on the outskirts of London in order to intimidate his opponents. This only served to drive his Protestant opponents to plan for the removal of the King. His marriage to Mary of Modena, a Catholic, exacerbated the situation. Making

matters worse James now tried to persecute seven bishops who contested the Declaration of Indulgence by which James had intended to suppress all laws against Catholic freedom of worship.

Believing that James would continue his campaign to re-establish Catholicism in England, and concerned about a Protestant succession, a group of ministers in Parliament drew up a Declaration of Rights. This Declaration accused James of unconstitutional behaviour, and made an approach to William of Orange. William's mother was Mary, eldest daughter of Charles I, and she was married to James II's elder daughter, Mary, a Protestant and James' heir. William responded favourably to the approach and arrived with a mixed Dutch and English army at Torbay on 5 November, 1688, thus bringing about what came to be known as the Glorious Revolution.

THE JACOBITES

'Jacobus' is the Latin word for 'James', so when King James II was forced to leave England at the time of the 'Glorious Revolution' in 1688, those who still supported him, even in exile, came to be known as 'Jacobites'. Most these supporters belonged to the Catholic faith.

Jacobite sympathizers would drink a toast 'to the King over the water' and if they wished to conceal their allegiance, their secret sign was to hold their drinking-glasses over finger-bowls, thus toasting 'over water'. Needless to say, when this secret sign was discovered, finger-bowls were banished from English royal tables. It wasn't until this century that the monarch, Edward VII by this time, felt it safe enough to re-introduce finger-bowls for his guests.

In the eighteenth century, when it was a treasonable offence to owe allegiance to the Jacobite cause, sympathizers had many secret devices. One of the most extraordinary is to be found in the West Highland Museum, Fort William, Scotland. It is a tray painted in apparently aimless scrawls, but when a glass is placed in the centre, the reflection bears a remarkable similarity to Bonnie Prince Charlie himself.

TIME LINE OF THE REIGN 1685–1688

1685
James succeeds his brother Charles II.
Rebellion of the Earl of Argyll in Scotland. This was designed to place Charles II's illegitimate son, the Duke of Monmouth, on the throne, but it is crushed and Argyll is executed.
Duke of Monmouth rebels against James but is defeated at Sedgemoor. Monmouth is captured, tried and executed.
Edict of Nantes – which resulted in thousands of Huguenot craftworkers and traders settling in England.
1686
James takes first measures to restore Catholicism in England.
1687
Nell Gwynne dies in London at the age of 37.
1688
Declaration of Indulgence suspends all laws against Catholics and non-Conformists.
Mary of Modena gives birth to James Edward, a Catholic heir for James. Seven leading statesmen invite William of Orange, son-in-law of James, to England to restore English liberties.
William lands at Torbay (5 November) and advances on London. James abdicates and after one failed attempt to escape (11 December) flees into exile in France (22 December).

THE CATHOLIC REVIVAL

JAMES II'S REIGN began with a challenge from the illegitimate son of Charles II, the Duke of Monmouth, who landed with a force at Lyme Regis in 1685. For many, he was the Protestant heir but once defeated at Sedgemoor, and later executed, the Protestant threat began to diminish and James II was able to devote himself to the dream of a Catholic revival.

James was converted to Catholicism in 1660 and, though Parliament tried to obstruct his accession, he became King with a mission to restore what he believed to be the true faith. In this he was following in the footsteps of Louis XIV of France who revoked the Edict of Nantes which allowed religious toleration. Like his father Charles I, James attempted to impose his will by gathering an army outside London to prevent disturbances caused by his pro-Catholic campaigns. In carrying these out, James was relieved of the need to ask Parliament for money by the good revenues available to him from foreign trade.

With the confidence that this allowed him, James set about dispensing offices among Catholic clergy. He also suspended discriminatory statutes, and encouraged the placing of Catholic clergy in important positions in Ireland. Such high-handed decisions aroused public fears of a return to autocratic government.

Whig ministers began to plot an appeal to William of Orange, James son-in-law, the Protestant leader of the Netherlands, to ensure a Protestant succession.

No action took place, however, for it was believed that James was ill and would not survive long, and that then William and Mary would succeed. However, in May 1688 James issued the Declaration of Indulgence, which suspended the penal laws against Roman Catholics and Protestant dissenters, and ordered the clergy to read the Declaration in their churches. Seven bishops, including the Archbishop of Canterbury, petitioned the King to be excused. James responded by treating their petition as an act of seditious libel and had them arrested and taken to the Tower of London. They arrived in the Tower in mid-June, where they were kept in one room. Their trial at Westminster Hall found them all not guilty.

The Queen's pregnancy and the possibility of a Catholic heir, James' re-issue of the Declaration of Indulgence favouring Catholics finally forced his opponents' hand and William of Orange was invited to England to stamp out the Catholic Revival.

James may have had many sins, but the greatest, in many people's view, was that of being a Catholic. During his three-year reign, Protestants lived in fear of their lives. Many were persecuted and even hanged.

TITUS OATES
1649–1705

Titus Oates was an Anglican priest whose whole career was marked with intrigue and scandal. He joined forces with one Israel Tonge to invent the story of the Popish Plot of 1678. Oates, who had been briefly a convert to Roman Catholicism, claimed that there was a Jesuit-guided plan to assassinate Charles II and to hasten the succession of the Catholic James, Duke of York (later James II). The account was completely fabricated. Oates, examined by the privy council, would perhaps have been immediately exposed had not treasonous letters from Edward Coleman to the French Jesuit, François La Chaise, been discovered as a result of his accusations. The unexplained death of Sir Edmund Berry Godfrey, the judge to whom Tonge and Oates first told their story, was attributed without evidence to the Catholics. Three innocent men were hanged for it. A frenzy of anti-Catholic hatred swept through England, resulting in the judicial murder of around 35 Roman Catholic peers and commoners. Oates enjoyed temporary eminence and even accused Queen Catherine of plotting to poison the King. In 1685, Oates was convicted of perjury, severely flogged, and imprisoned. Under William III he was released and pensioned.

WILLIAM AND MARY

— 1689–1702 —

ROYAL BIOGRAPHY

WILLIAM

BORN: 4 November 1650, The Hague. PARENTS: Prince William II of Orange, Stadtholder of the Netherlands, and Mary Henrietta, daughter of Charles I.
ASCENDED THE THRONE: 13 February 1689. CROWNED: 11 April 1689, Westminster Abbey.
AUTHORITY: King of England, Scotland and Ireland. MARRIED: Mary, daughter of James II.
CHILDREN: None born alive. DIED: 8 March 1702, Kensington Palace.
BURIED: Westminster Abbey.

MARY

BORN: 30 April 1662, St James's Palace. PARENTS: James II and Anne Hyde.
ASCENDED THE THRONE: 13 February 1689. CROWNED: 11 April 1689, Westminster Abbey.
AUTHORITY: Queen of England, Scotland and Ireland. MARRIED: William of Orange.
CHILDREN: None born alive. DIED: 28 December 1694, Kensington Palace.
BURIED: Westminster Abbey.

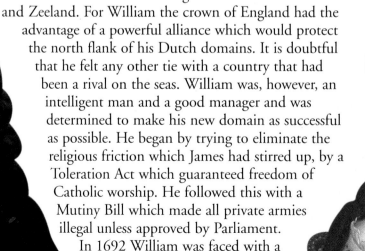

WHEN WILLIAM WAS approached by the English Parliament he was already a powerful figure in his own land as Prince of Orange and Stadtholder of Holland and Zeeland. For William the crown of England had the advantage of a powerful alliance which would protect the north flank of his Dutch domains. It is doubtful that he felt any other tie with a country that had been a rival on the seas. William was, however, an intelligent man and a good manager and was determined to make his new domain as successful as possible. He began by trying to eliminate the religious friction which James had stirred up, by a Toleration Act which guaranteed freedom of Catholic worship. He followed this with a Mutiny Bill which made all private armies illegal unless approved by Parliament. In 1692 William was faced with a

William and Mary purchased Kensington Palace from the Earl of Nottingham. They both died here, and it has been a royal residence ever since.

Jacobite rebellion led by James II and was obliged to repel the invaders at the Battle of the Boyne, north of Dublin, in which he personally took charge, forcing a Jacobite retreat. He wisely followed this by attending a mass at Dublin Cathedral and declaring himself in favour of religious freedom for Catholics by the Treaty of Limerick. This military truce lasted until 1697.

William's reign was not simply marked by religious compromise and wars, however, for his presence attracted Dutchmen to England. They continued the work instigated by James I in East Anglia, of turning wet fenland into an agriculturally wealthy area thanks to their long experience in draining the land by means of ditches and embankments.

William's influence also became evident in English architecture which erupted in neat brick houses with rounded gables. William's most notable contribution was the extension of Hampton Court Palace, on the banks of the Thames, where Christopher Wren added a Classical brick façade on the east and south sides of the Fountain Court. He also commissioned the Hospital for Seamen at Greenwich on the site of the former Tudor palace.

TIME LINE OF THE REIGN 1689–1702

1689
Parliament draws up the Declaration of Right detailing the unconstitutional acts of James II. Upon acceptance of this declaration, William and Mary become joint sovereigns. Toleration Act. First Mutiny Bill passed. Scottish rebellion against William put down. Catholic Forces loyal to James II land in Ireland from France and lay siege to Londonderry.

1690
William defeats James at the Battle of the Boyne (1 July).

1691
Treaty of Limerick. Outbreak of French war.

1692
Lloyds insurance office opens in London.

1693
National debt set up.

1694
Foundation of the Bank of England. Death of Mary, William now rules alone.

1697
Peace of Ryswick ends war with France.

1701
James II dies in exile in France.

1702
War of Spanish Succession breaks out in Europe, over the vacant Spanish throne.

1702
William dies after falling from his horse. He is succeeded by his sister-in-law Anne.

THE DUTCH INFLUENCE

THE WARS WITH the Dutch, which had strained relations with the Low countries for many years, came to an end when the Prince, who was to become Charles II, was in exile and conferred the Order of the Garter on William, Prince of Orange. This did not entirely banish the distrust that William felt about Charles but, when the future King promised support for a Protestant succession and he subsequently received an invitation from the English Parliament, William made up his mind to accept the British throne.

As a King in a land that had been an enemy, William moved cautiously and it is difficult to confirm his influence on various important events in his reign. For example, the founding of the Bank of England and the modern systems of banking, and the transfer of authority in the standing army to Parliament. The influence of Dutchmen who arrived in England with William is more discernible, however. Some of this had already made its appearance during the reign of James I when they commissioned the work of artists and architects. During William's reign and that of his sister-in-law Anne, there were some notable changes in architectural style. Houses were built in a classical style with rounded gables, and major works such as the façades of Hampton Court Palace and Kensington Palace, enlarged by Wren in a Dutch style, and the site of Greenwich Palace where William commissioned Wren to build a hospital for seamen.

Other evidence of Dutch influence is in the agricultural lands of East Anglia where Dutch, experts in the drainage of land, converted a swamp into a productive area where

Delft, in Holland, was important as a pottery centre from the mid-17th century to the end of the 18th century. This tulip vase is decorated with the intertwined initials of the two monarchs.

Dutch influence on English art and architecture was marked during William's reign. The picture above shows the ornate gate leading into The Hague.

THE INFLUENCE OF 'THE ARTS'

Art flourished in Flanders and the Low Countries in what is called the 'Baroque' period in the arts, whenever violent conflict did not disrupt the region. The Netherlands were divided: the northern Protestant Dutch provinces fought for independence, whilst the southern Catholic part remained under Spanish rule.

Faced with the threat of Protestantism, the Roman Catholic church spent lavishly on religious art to revive the faith of their congregations. Rich churches, abbeys and bishops commissioned leading artists such as Rubens. Many trained in Italy, and were influenced by Michelangelo, Raphael and the whole history of Italian art. In Antwerp, they had to paint religious subjects – aiming at spectacular, grand effects, whilst looking very realistic, and conveying a simple emotional message to the faithful.

Architects like artists were also commissioned by the rich. Kings, nobles and bishops wanted elaborately decorated buildings. New churches, palaces and public buildings were richly decorated. Both art and architecture were 'over the top'.

agriculture flourished and where today the bulbfields rival those of Holland.

Dutch styles also became fashionable in household ware, especially the blue and white Delft ware, and wooden furniture took on the simplicity of Dutch joinery.

ANNE

—— 1702–1714 ——

BORN: 6 February 1665, St James's Palace. PARENTS: James II and Anne Hyde.
ASCENDED THE THRONE: 8 March 1702. CROWNED: 23 April 1702, Westminster Abbey.
AUTHORITY: Queen of Great Britain and Ireland.
MARRIED: George, son of Frederick III of Denmark.
CHILDREN: 18, including those still-born and miscarried.
DIED: 1 August 1714, Kensington Palace. BURIED: Westminster Abbey.

ROYAL BIOGRAPHY

ANNE WAS A daughter of James II, yet an ardent Protestant. She carried on the pattern of life and political directions established by William and her sister, Mary. She had not expected to become Queen, but the death of her sister and William propelled her into a position of power and authority which at first she did not relish. Her source of strength and advice in the early years of her reign was Sarah Churchill, wife of John Churchill, the later Duke of Marlborough.

War with France began in 1702 and its political implications in Parliament drew Anne into the political arena. She was a partisan of Churchill's ideas and when he was derided for suggesting that the war should be waged at sea, she felt compelled to support him by making him a Duke. After the victory of Blenheim in 1704, Anne presented him with the Woodstock estate, now named after the battle.

The friendship with Sarah Churchill cooled when Anne began to feel that Sarah's self-interest was the main motive for their friendship, and she finally had the courage to dismiss her. She also broke away from Whig influence and began to take advice from the Tories, who had for some time protested at the cost and extension of the war. This led to a break with the Churchills, first the dismissal of Sarah from her position in court, and then the dismissal of Marlborough.

In 1713 Anne was able to report to Parliament that the war with France, known as the War of the Alliance, was over, and that Britain had gained from the terms of the Treaty of Utrecht, though this was in fact a compromise. At home, Anne was triumphant in having presided over the union of the parliaments of England and Scotland, creating the state of Great Britain.

Though never in good health, Anne presided over a splendid period of English history conscientiously and with good heart. The sad fact that none of the eighteen children she bore her husband, Prince George of Denmark, reached adulthood meant that the direct Stuart line died with her.

Anne will also be remembered for the distinctive taste in decorative arts that came to full flower in her reign. Furniture, in what is known as Queen Anne Style, was well-proportioned with elegant lines. It was usually veneered, notably with walnut, and inlaid rather than decorated with the elaborate wood-carving that was previously popular. New designs were also adopted from overseas: chairs and tables, for example, featured the curved cabriole leg, a design that had been brought into Europe from China.

TIME LINE OF THE REIGN 1702–1714

1702
Anne succeeds her brother-in-law, William III.
England declares war on France in the War of the Spanish Succession.
The first daily newspaper in London, *The Daily Courant*, is published.

1704
English, Bavarian and Austrian troops under Marlborough defeat the French at the Battle of Blenheim and save Austria from invasion.

1706
Marlborough defeats the French at the Battle of Ramillies and expels the French from the Netherlands.

1707
The Act of Union unites the kingdoms of England and Scotland.

1708
Prince George dies at Kensington Palace.

1709
Marlborough defeats the French at the Battle of Malplaquet.

1710
The Whig government falls and a Tory ministry is formed.

1711
Queen Anne establishes horse racing at Ascot.

1714
The Electress Sophia of Hanover dies, and her son George becomes heir to the throne.
Queen Anne dies at Kensington Palace, London, at the age of 49.

THE WARS OF SUCCESSION

1701–13

THE 17TH AND 18TH centuries were a period of warfare in which European nations attempted to influence the balance of power in Europe by supporting one or another dynasty that seemed to be in their own national interest. Austria, Spain under the Hapsburgs, France under Louis XIV, and England under the Stuarts, were all intent on playing a part in this game of political chess.

This commander's baton was used on the French side in the War of the Spanish Succession.

The Hapsburgs had the largest continental empire which had come together under Charles V and included Austria, the Netherlands and Spain, and the gold-rich empires of Central and South America. The French held the centre of the continent, and had a large navy which competed with the English for overseas trade routes. England at this time was emerging as a challenger to both.

The Spanish empire was the prize that stirred the greatest envy, especially that of Louis XIV who, according to the calculations of England, had his eye on the Spanish Netherlands and northern Italy. When the Spanish throne was bequeathed to the Prince of Aragon, grandson of Louis XIV, and Louis invaded the Netherlands, it obliged England, remembering the Spanish army encamped there at the time of the Armada, to take defensive action. The man of the hour for this campaign was John Churchill, who had fallen into disfavour on suspicion of being a Jacobite. But Anne, who was now Queen, did not hesitate to make him Supreme Commander of the armed forces. After a series of brilliant victories at Blenheim in 1704, Ramillies in 1706, Oudenarde in 1708 and Malplaquet in 1709, Marlborough was dismissed by a Parliament which had changed from Whig to Tory.

The Duke of Marlborough won a great victory against the French at Blenheim in 1704. Here he is seen signing the Despatch.

THE WARS OF SUCCESSION

1701
Outbreak of War of Spanish Succession. Prince Eugene of Savoy invades Italy.
1704
Battle of Blenheim, first of Marlborough's great victories over French armies.
1706
Battle of Ramillies, Marlborough's second victory.
1708
Battle of Oudenarde, Marlborough's third victory.
1709
Marlborough's fourth victory at the Battle of Malplaquet.
1711
Grand Alliance of powers against France dissolved; Marlborough dimissed by Queen Anne.
1712
French army under Marshall Villars gains a victory at Denain.
1713
Treaty of Utrecht. War ends with an equal redistribution of territory and power in Europe.
1713
Philip V, grandson of Louis XIV of France, confirmed as King of Spain. Louis agrees that France and Spain should never be united under the same ruler.

In 1740 another war of succession broke out, this time over Austria, a prize coveted by the rising power of the Prussians under the leadership of Frederick II. Austria was the heartland of the Austrian Empire and its influence spread over the Netherlands, Italy and Central Europe, the territory over which the war was fought for eight years. The English troops were largely under the command of the Duke of Cumberland, who destroyed Bonnie Prince Charlie's hopes at Culloden, and on one occasion at Dettingen, George II himself took part. Peace at this time was reached by the Treaty of Aix-la-Chapelle.

This was short-lived, however, for in 1756 the Seven Years War broke out. In this conflict, it was Frederick the Great's throne that was at stake. England helped to protect the throne against a coalition of states including France, Austria, Russia and Sweden. French involvement in the conflict provided an opportunity for the English to attack the French in Canada where General Wolfe took Quebec. The English also took advantage of the European entanglement for Robert Clive to defeat the pro-French Siruj-a-Dauda at Plassey and become masters of India.

THE DUKE OF MARLBOROUGH

1650–1722

JOHN CHURCHILL, later Duke of Marlborough, was the most successful general of his time and began his career as an emissary for James II. In helping to defeat the Monmouth rebellion, he gained the gratitude of the King. On the arrival of William III in England in 1688, Churchill deserted the catholic Stuarts and organised a group of officers to support the new King. As a reward he was made an Earl and rewarded the King by taking Cork and Kinsale in Ireland.

His career nearly ended here when, on learning that William was unwell, he became nervous about a return of the Catholic succession and once more became friendly with Jacobite supporters. The King's death and his wife Sarah's friendship with Queen Anne, saved him and he was made Commander of the English forces on the Continent, redeeming his name with a series of brilliant victories.

His final victory at Malplaquet was an expensive one in terms of men and materials. Parliament, where he had had his Whig supporters, had been lost to the Tories. The Tories were in favour of a peace compromise and agreed the Treaty of Utrecht, which undid the gains made by Marlborough. Despite his fame and reputation the great General was dismissed, and charges were made against him of having received money from the army's bread suppliers and for drawing an illegal commission from the pay of foreign auxiliaries.

During his years of success Marlborough had

Blenheim Palace was named after the Duke of Marlborough's famous victory in Bavaria. It was erected between 1705 and 1722, and was in fact not completed when Marlborough died in 1722.

A portrait of John Churchill, the 1st Duke of Marlborough,
painted by Robert Bing (or Byng).

HISTORY OF BLENHEIM PALACE

The name Blenheim derives from a decisive battle that took place on the 13 August 1704 on the north bank of the River Danube, near a small village called Blindheim or Blenheim. It was also here that John Churchill, the first Duke of Marlborough, won a great allied victory over the forces of Louis XIV, thus saving Europe from French domination.

In reward for his services in defending Holland and Austria from invasion by the French, a grateful Queen Anne granted to Marlborough the Royal Manor of Woodstock and signified that she would build him, at her own expense, a house to be called Blenheim.

Building, to a design by Vanbrugh and Hawksmoor, began in 1705, and there is an inscription on the East Gate that declares that:

'Under the auspices of a munificent sovereign this house was built for John Duke of Marlborough, and his Duchess Sarah, by Sir J Vanbrugh between the years 1705 and 1722. And this Royal manor of Woodstock, together with a grant of £240,000, towards the building of Blenheim was given by Her Majesty Queen Anne and confirmed by Act of Parliament . . .'

become famous and lived in a style which did not escape the eyes of satirists like Swift, who remarked that he was motivated by greed. If that was so, it raises a question about his being unable to complete the noble house that the Queen gave him at Woodstock, near Oxford, and named Blenheim in memory of his great victory.

Much of Marlborough's good fortune in the political web at home was his wife's close friendship with Queen Anne and, when this began to cool, he found himself deprived of his commanding role. He went into exile, though he was recalled to deal with the Jacobite rebellion of 1715.

THE HANOVERIANS

The succession of British Kings and Queens since William the Conqueror, passed through a series of monarchs of different nationalities. The French Plantagenets, the Scottish Stuarts, the Dutch William III, and finally to German Hanoverians. During the reigns of the Hanoverians Britain assumed a commanding role in world affairs and became the world's first industrial nation.

THE JACOBITE RISING

1745

THE JACOBITES, a name derived from the Latin for James 'Jacobus', were supporters of the Stuart dynasty. When James II was exiled they began a series of attempts to restore him and his descendants to the throne. In this they were aided by the French, who had their own motives for seeing England humbled. The Catholics wanted to see Protestantism defeated and also the Clans of central and western Scotland, many of whom were Catholics, and most of whom were much poorer that the Lowland Scots.

The first Jacobite rising took place in 1689 and was led by John Graham Dundee, 'Bonnie Dundee'. He withdrew from the Scottish Parliament with Lord Balcares and attacked the government and pro-William III forces. He died at the Battle of Killiecrankie in 1689 and the uprising came to an end the following year.

The Jacobite cause raised its standard again after the Act of Union of 1707, which aroused Scottish patriotic sentiment and received the support of Louis XIV. Louis saw an opportunity to install a Jacobite Scotland by supporting James Francis Edward Stuart, son of James II, and known as the Old Pretender. This attempt was aborted when the French expedition, then off the coast of Fife, came face to face with the British navy.

The next uprising was Scottish in origin and led by the Earl of Mar, but this was blocked by Argyll, chief of the Clan Campbell, and even the arrival of the Old

The Highland Scots defeated an English army at the Battle of Prestonpans on 21 September 1745. This painting by Frances Whittaker shows the scene after the battle was over.

Pretender was unable to save the day.

After war broke out between England and France in 1744 the French encouraged Charles Stuart, son of the Old Pretender, to lead an invasion of Scotland. However, they changed their minds, leaving Bonnie Prince Charlie alone to campaign with his loyal clansmen.

This was a success at first, with the Prince advancing into England as far as Derby. A superior English force under the Duke of Cumberland, son of George II, forced a retreat which ended with a total defeat at Culloden in 1746. Prince Charlie's flight and exile was followed by confiscation of clan lands, the emptying of the Highlands, the replacement of many clan chiefs, and the end of attempts to restore the Stuart dynasty.

THE BATTLE OF PRESTONPANS 1745

Bonnie Prince Charlie's landing on Scottish soil ignited a firestorm of incredible stories. Whilst these stories were drawing volunteers, they were also worrying the established powers.

Sir John Cope, commanding the Hanovarians, saw the need to crush the rebellion swiftly. He denied himself the use of the Corrieyairack Pass, however, convinced it was covered by 3,000 Jacobites.

This was not the case, and he made an unnecessary journey to Aberdeen to sail down to the Forth. He disembarked at Dunbar on 17 September while Prince Charles Edward was claiming Edinburgh.

Presuming the Jacobites would then challenge him from the west, Cope pitched his army at Prestonpans, near Musselburgh, where reinforcements from Berwick could reach him.

Reading Cope well, Lord George Murray brought his Jacobites right around to the south of the government force and attacked from the east. Reports time Murray's victory as taking either 10 or 15 minutes.

The rout of the Hanovarians meant that in the space of a month, Scotland was Jacobite except for the strong, important castles of Edinburgh, Stirling and Dumbarton.

BONNIE PRINCE CHARLIE

1720–1788

Bonnie Prince Charlie at the age of 12.

Bonnie Prince Charlie is one of the best-known historical Scottish heroes. He was not, however, Scottish, but was born into the Stuart Dynasty in Rome, Italy on December 31, 1720. His grandfather, James II of England had ruled that country from 1685–1689 at which time he was deposed by the Dutch protestant, William III of Orange. James II had aimed to bring England back into the Catholic fold and in the process had irritated and alarmed the powerful statesmen of the day. Since the exile of James II the so-called 'Jacobite Cause' had striven to return the Stuarts to the English and Scottish thrones. Bonnie Prince Charlie was to play a major part in this ultimate goal.

Charles Edward was also called the Young Pretender, the Young Chevalier, and later, Bonnie Prince Charlie.

The young Prince was trained in the military and from an early age was a pawn in the Jacobite Cause. His father managed to obtain the support of the French government in 1744, and Charles Edward travelled to France with the sole purpose of commanding a French army, which he would lead in an invasion of England. The invasion never materialized, principally due to the fact that the French were afraid of the strong British army and because of poor weather that prohibited sailing. Undeterred, Charles Edward was determined to carry on in his quest for reinstatement of the Stuarts regardless.

So, in 1745 he travelled to Scotland with a few supporters and, arriving on the Isle of Eriskay, he set about rousing the Highland Clans to support his cause. The Prince raised his father's standard at Glenfinnan in Scotland on 19 August, 1745, and so initiated what was to be referred to as the '45', effectively the last Jacobite Uprising. Among his supporters were 300 from clan Macdonald and 700 from clan Cameron. The rebels quickly took control of Edinburgh and by September 1745 had defeated the King's army at Prestonpans. Several victories followed and Bonnie Prince Charlie's army grew in number, at one point reaching over 6,000.

The Battle of Culloden, near Inverness, took place on April 16, 1746 and the Jacobite army suffered a crushing defeat at the hands of the 'Butcher of Cumberland', William Augustus the Duke of Cumberland. Thousands were killed and the Battle of Culloden Moor went down as one of the bloodiest in Scottish history. The defeat effectively put an end to the last Jacobite Uprising and the Prince was now a fugitive. On the run he spent the next five months in hiding in the Highlands and Islands of Scotland assisted by his supporters. A ransom of 30,000 pounds was placed on his head but, despite this, no one betrayed him to the authorities.

In conclusion, Bonnie Prince Charlie was a sad and tragic figure. Haunted throughout his life by the passion for Stuart kingship he ultimately ended his life as a pathetic drunk. He is remembered, however, as a Scottish hero, a reminder of bygone times when the Clans roamed the Highlands and his life is portrayed in many stories and folk songs which are recounted and sung across Scotland.

FLORA MACDONALD

The greatest manhunt in history culminated when Bonnie Prince Charlie arrived on the Island of Benbecula, where he met Flora Macdonald. Flora was not an ardent Jacobite supporter but felt that she could not betray the Prince. They met in the summer of 1746; the islanders aware of the Prince's presence on the island were frightened of British Government reprisals.

Flora helped to spirit him away to the Island of Skye, dressed in disguise as her maid 'Betty Burke'. Legend has it that Flora and Bonnie Prince Charlie fell in love that summer. He was assisted by supporters to escape to France where he lived a life of transient wandering throughout Europe before finally settling in Rome under the alias of the 'Duke of Albany'.

Flora was captured for her part in the Prince's escape and spent some time in the Tower of London before being released. She became famous for her role in the Jacobite matter, subsequently marrying her childhood sweetheart Alan Macdonald. They emigrated to North Carolina where her husband served on the British side during the American Revolution. When he was captured she returned to Scotland and Alan followed her back there when he was released. She died in 1790 and is buried on Skye. Legend has it that she was wrapped in the Prince's bed sheet.

GEORGE I

——— 1714–1727 ———

ROYAL BIOGRAPHY

BORN: 28 May 1660, Osnabrück, Hanover. PARENTS: Ernest Augustus, Elector of Hanover, and Sophia, daughter of Elizabeth of Bohemia. ASCENDED THE THRONE: 1 August 1714. CROWNED: 20 October 1714, Westminster Abbey. AUTHORITY: King of Great Britain and Ireland, Elector of Hanover. MARRIED: Sophia Dorothea of Celle. CHILDREN: One son, the future George II, and one daughter; three illegitimate children. DIED: 11 June 1727, Osnabrück. BURIED: Leineschlosskirche, Hanover; reinterred Herrenhausen, Hanover, 1957.

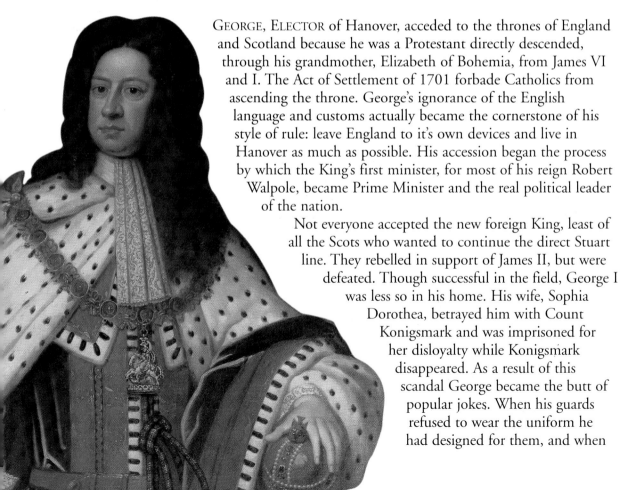

GEORGE, ELECTOR of Hanover, acceded to the thrones of England and Scotland because he was a Protestant directly descended, through his grandmother, Elizabeth of Bohemia, from James VI and I. The Act of Settlement of 1701 forbade Catholics from ascending the throne. George's ignorance of the English language and customs actually became the cornerstone of his style of rule: leave England to it's own devices and live in Hanover as much as possible. His accession began the process by which the King's first minister, for most of his reign Robert Walpole, became Prime Minister and the real political leader of the nation.

Not everyone accepted the new foreign King, least of all the Scots who wanted to continue the direct Stuart line. They rebelled in support of James II, but were defeated. Though successful in the field, George I was less so in his home. His wife, Sophia Dorothea, betrayed him with Count Konigsmark and was imprisoned for her disloyalty while Konigsmark disappeared. As a result of this scandal George became the butt of popular jokes. When his guards refused to wear the uniform he had designed for them, and when

Thackeray, in *The Four Georges*, allows both a glimpse of George I's character, and the circumstances under which he ruled England:

'Though a despot in Hanover, he was a moderate ruler in England. His aim was to leave it to itself as much as possible, and to live out of it as much as he could. His heart was in Hanover. He was more than fifty-four years of age when he came amongst us: we took him because we wanted him, because he served our turn; we laughed at his uncouth German ways, and sneered at him. He took our loyalty for what it was worth; laid hands on what money he could; kept us assuredly from Popery and wooden shoes. I, for one, would have been on his side in those days. Cynical, and selfish, as he was, he was better than a king out of St. Germains [the Old Pretender] with a French King's orders in his pocket, and a swarm of Jesuits in his train.'

TIME LINE OF THE REIGN 1714–1727

1714
George I succeeds his distant cousin Anne.
A new Parliament is elected with a strong Whig majority, led by Charles Townsend and Robert Walpole.
1715
Jacobite Rising in Scotland is easily defeated.
1716
The Septennial Act allows for General Elections to be held every seven years.
1717
Townsend is dismissed from the government by George, causing Walpole to resign.
1719
Daniel Defoe publishes *Robinson Crusoe*.
1720
South Sea Bubble bursts, leaving many investors ruined.
1721
Sir Robert Walpole returns to government as First Lord of the Treasury.
1722
Death of the Duke of Marlborough.
1726
Jonathan Swift publishes *Gulliver's Travels*.
Death of Sophia Dorothea, wife of George I.
1727
Death of the scientist, Isaac Newton.
Death of George I in Hanover.

it was discovered that he intended to plant turnips in St. James's Park, the jokes turned to ridicule. A further scandal was what came to be known as the South Sea Bubble, an investment scheme which ruined hundreds of George's subjects.

It was at this point that Walpole, who had resigned, was recalled and became first Lord of the Treasury and virtually took over running the country. Britain now became involved in a war over Spanish possessions in America and the Spaniards attempted to take Gibraltar. Both were fruitless exercises in which George showed very little interest. For him, his kingdom was Hanover and he spent a great deal of time there, dying at Osnabruck whilst travelling.

In the opinion of Lady Wortley Montague, a writer and traveller of the time, George was an honest blockhead.

GEORGE II

1727–1760

ROYAL BIOGRAPHY

BORN: 30 October 1683, Herrenhausen, Hanover. PARENTS: George I and Sophia Dorothea of Celle. ASCENDED THE THRONE: 11 June 1727. CROWNED: 11 October 1727, Westminster Abbey. AUTHORITY: King of Great Britain and Ireland. MARRIED: Caroline, daughter of the Margrave of Brandenburg-Ansbach. CHILDREN: Four sons and five daughters; probably one or more illegitimate children.
DIED: 25 October 1760, Kensington Palace. BURIED: Westminster Abbey.

Queen Caroline II.

WITH THE SUPPORT of his able first minister, Robert Walpole, George II ruled over a flourishing Britain. Although at war with European powers, it grew into an empire of worldwide trade thanks to the power of its navy.

The first skirmish on the high seas was the War of Jenkins' Ear. The war took its name from Robert Jenkins, captain of the ship *Rebecca*, who claimed Spanish coastguards had cut off his ear in 1731. He exhibited the ear in the House of Commons and so aroused public opinion, that the government of the British Prime Minister Robert Walpole reluctantly declared war on October 23, 1739. Basically, the war was one of commercial rivalry between England and Spain. This was followed by the War of the Austrian succession, in which Britain supported the claims of Maria Theresa against Prussian ambitions to take over the heart of the Hapsburg Empire. During this war George took part personally at the Battle of Dettingen, the last British King to go into battle. Before the war was over George was faced with the last Jacobite challenge. This was when Bonnie Prince Charlie led his clansmen army as far as Derby, but was finally defeated at Culloden thus concluding the Stuart challenge to the throne.

There now followed another European war that lasted seven years until 1763, but Britain's interest was now growing overseas, and victories in Canada and India brought these countries into Britain's possession. This laid the foundations for a new era with Britain as a world power.

Though not notable for his patronage of the arts, George was an enthusiastic supporter of George Frederick Handel, standing up at the 'Hallelujah Chorus' of the Messiah as a tribute to the composer – a ritual followed by audiences even today. George also commissioned Handel to compose special music for a firework display which celebrated the Treaty of Aix la Chapelle at the end of the War of the Austrian Succession in 1749. It is believed that Handel wrote the *Water Music* for George II to compensate for his long absences in England from the court at Hanover, by whom he was employed.

TIME LINE OF THE REIGN 1727–1760

1727
George succeeds his father George I.

1732
A royal charter is granted for the founding of Georgia.

1736
Witchcraft is finally abolished as a crime.

1737
Death of Queen Caroline.

1738
John and Charles Wesley start the Methodist movement.

1739
Britain goes to war with Spain.

1740–48
War of Austrian Succession breaks out in Europe.

1742
Walpole resigns as Prime Minister and is created Earl of Orford.

1743
George leads troops into battle at Dettingen in Bavaria.

1745
Jacobite Rising in Scotland.

1746
Scots crushed at the Battle of Culloden.

1756–63
Seven Years' War.

1757
Robert Clive wins Battle of Plassey and secures the Indian province of Bengal for Britain.
William Pitt becomes Prime Minister.

1760
George II dies at the age of 76.

ROBERT WALPOLE

1676–1745

WALPOLE WAS BORN on August 26, 1676, in Norfolk, England, and educated at the University of Cambridge. Though many historians would argue that Walpole was not the first Prime Minister, for others had held the important posts of Head of the Treasury and Chancellor of the Exchequer before him, none of them served a King who was unable to communicate with Parliament because he could not speak English. Walpole therefore occupied a unique position of power.

Early in his career, Walpole, who had served in the administration during the War of the Spanish Succession, had become an enemy of the Tory party and was expelled from office, impeached for corruption, and sent to the Tower of London. The triumph of the Whigs restored him and he regained his former offices. He was instrumental in saving the government and the crown after the debacle of the South Sea Bubble. This was a scheme by which the South Sea company offered to take over three-fifths of the national debt in exchange for trading privileges. After an initial boom there came a period of panic selling, corrected by Walpole by transferring stock to the Bank of England and the East India Company.

Apart from such coups as this, Walpole managed to change the systems of government by extending the power of a cabinet through the use of patronage, and making the Commons the centre of parliamentary power.

In order to strengthen Whig supremacy, Walpole used the fear of Jacobitism,

Robert Walpole remained an English country squire at heart.

for which he blamed the Tories, while ascribing to the Whigs the patriotism which supported the existing Protestant Hanoverians. By the use of patronage and the ruthless exclusion of certain peers who voted against the government, Walpole managed to exert a strict control over his administration. This was until 1742 when mismanagement of a war with Spain, decreased his hold on the House of Commons, though not the support of the monarch, who continued to value his advice. On retirement he accepted the title of Earl of Orford, an honour which he had refused earlier in his career.

THE ATTERBURY PLOT

Walpole's position as Prime or First Minister was solidified by his response to a Jacobite conspiracy uncovered in April, 1722, known as the *Atterbury Plot* after Francis Atterbury, the Tory bishop of Rochester. The conspiracy was to have taken control of the government, but was aborted.

Francis Atterbury was born in 1663. His upbringing was at the quiet Buckinghamshire rectory of Milton Keynes, by a father who had been suspect of disloyalty. A Westminster boy and student of Christ Church, he became prominent among the scholars of his day, and his contribution to the Phalaris controversy made him famous.

He took holy orders in 1687, and, before long, reached high preferment. Soon after the beginning of the century, he was Archdeacon of Totnes and Chaplain in Ordinary to Queen Anne. He became dean of Carlisle (1704), of Christ Church (1712) and of Westminster and bishop of Rochester (1713).

Seven years later, he was imprisoned in the Tower, without much evidence against him, for having been concerned in a plot to restore the Stuarts. Banishment followed, and he definitely threw in his lot with the exiled royal family. He lived till 1732.

GEORGE III

—— 1760–1820 ——

ROYAL BIOGRAPHY

BORN: 4 June 1738, Norfolk House, St James's Square, London.
PARENTS: Frederick, Prince of Wales, and Augusta, daughter of the Duke of Saxe-Coburg-Gotha.
ASCENDED THE THRONE: 25 October 1760. CROWNED: 22 September 1761, Westminster Abbey.
AUTHORITY: King of the United Kingdom of Great Britain and Ireland, Elector (later King) of Hanover. MARRIED: Charlotte, daughter of the Duke of Mecklenburg-Strelitz.
CHILDREN: Ten sons, including the future George IV and William IV, and six daughters.
DIED: 29 January 1820, Windsor. BURIED: St George's Chapel, Windsor.

WHEN GEORGE III succeeded his grandfather on the throne, Europe was about to enter a period of upheaval which would change the world. The Seven Years War had hardly finished when the American colonies rebelled and won their independence in 1783. This was followed by the French Revolution and a new doctrine of Equality, Fraternity and Liberty which was to become the battle cry of the politics of the future. The main threat for Britain was not ideological, but came in the person of Napoleon Bonaparte, a Corsican soldier who became Emperor of the French and master of Continental Europe.

Like his predecessors, George III hankered after personal rule, but the growing power of the Prime Minister and Parliament prevented his interference in politics becoming too overpowering, though he was able to exert influence on non-political matters such as farming. His own efforts at Windsor and Richmond showed how a crop could be multiplied, and his skill and knowledge spread through the

The royal coat of arms was changed in 1801 to remove the royal arms of France. In 1816 the arms were changed again when the Electorate of Hanover became a kingdom, the crown replacing the electoral bonnet.

countryside. He was nicknamed Farmer George. He was fortunate in having, on the whole, a good relationship with his ministers. One of the more prominent ones being Lord North who, though North America was lost during his long term of office, was able to follow George's wishes and to maintain a good relationship between the King and Parliament. Another was William Pitt the Younger, who dealt firmly with radicals who supported French Revolutionary ideas and steered the country through the worst of the Napoleonic Wars. He was also lucky to have two of the ablest sailors and soldiers in Europe in Nelson and Wellington.

In 1809 the King became blind. As early as 1765 he had suffered an apparent dementia, and in 1788 his derangement recurred to such a degree that a Regency Bill was passed, but the King recovered the following year. It is now thought likely that he had inherited porphyria, a defect of the metabolism that may in time lead to delirium. In 1811 he succumbed hopelessly, and his son, later George IV, acted as Regent for the rest of his reign. George III died at Windsor Palace on January 29, 1820.

TIME LINE OF THE REIGN 1760–1820

1760
George becomes king on the death of his grandfather George II.
1762
Earl of Bute is appointed Prime Minister.
1763
Peace of Paris ends Seven Years' War.
1769–70
James Cook's first voyage round the world.
1771
Encyclopedia Britannica is first published.
1773
Boston Tea Party.
1775–83
American War of Independence.
1783–1801
William Pitt the Younger serves as Prime Minister.
1789
Outbreak of French Revolution.
1793–1802
War between Britain and France.
1803–15
Napoleonic Wars.
1810
Illness of George III leads to his son becoming Regent in 1811.
1812
Prime Minister, Spencer Perceval is assassinated in the House of Commons (11 May).
1815
Defeat of Napoleon at Waterloo.
1818
Queen Charlotte dies.
1820
Death of George III.

AMERICAN INDEPENDENCE

1775–1783

BY THE MID-eighteenth century, the population of the British colonies in America had been swelled by influxes of Germans, French and other European emigrants. They lacked the strong sentimental ties with the home country of the original English settlers. There were also many Scottish and Irish. America was becoming a nation of thirteen states and was beginning to resent being regarded as a profitable overseas possession. The expense of wars with France and Spain over the new territories, however, was raising doubts in England and increasing the national debt.

Britain's success in defeating the French in Canada gave the colonists confidence, as the threat of occupation by another foreign power receded and they began to resent the taxes levied by the government in England. This came to a head in Boston where, in 1770, British troops fired on and caused the death of six protesters. Again in 1773 when the unpopular tea duty was rejected by Americans, dressed as Indians, emptying chests of tea into the sea.

The war that now broke out began in Lexington in 1775. The first phase ended at Saratoga, where a misconceived advance down the Hudson by General Burgoyne was defeated.

'What Wants me' – cartoon showing Tom Paine and the Rights of Man by Isaac Cruikshank. Paine passionately argued for independence from Great Britain and the ability of the young country to prosper unfettered .

A delegation, led by Thomas Jefferson and Benjamin Franklin, presented the draft of the Declaration of Independence to the Continental Congress for debate in July 1776.

Britain's defeat brought support for the American colonists from France and Spain and threatened Britain's naval supremacy. But George Washington, in command of the American troops, was also having some difficulty in keeping his troops fed, paid and together. The southern states of America appeared to remain loyal to Britain, which encouraged Cornwallis to lead an expedition there. He was stopped at Yorktown where he surrendered in 1781, thus ending the War of Independence.

George Washington's role in gaining independence for the American colonies and later in unifying them under the new U.S. Federal Government cannot be overestimated. Labouring against great difficulties, he created the Continental Army, which fought and won the American Revolution (1775–1783), out of what was little more than an armed mob. After an eight-year struggle, his design for victory brought final defeat to the British at Yorktown, Virginia, and forced Great Britain to grant independence to its overseas possession.

Though to many of Britain's enemies this seemed to be a major blow to her overseas expansion, this was not the case. Free of her costly American adventure, Britain was able to undertake the conquest and expansion of other territories in Africa, Australia, New Zealand and the East.

THE FRENCH REVOLUTION

— 1789–1799 —

THE FRENCH REVOLUTION was an exciting, dramatic, and violent episode in western history. The rise of the middle class, the use of the guillotine, the fall of monarchy, the outbreak of European warfare, the growing role of women, and the harsh realities of mob violence all contributed to making this episode truly significant and memorable.

The Revolution, which led to the death of Louis XVI and his Queen Marie Antoinette, had its roots in the debts accumulated by Louis XIV and Louis XV in foreign wars to establish French supremacy in Europe. When Louis XVI came to the throne French finances were in a parlous state, and poverty and unemployment were rife. The rich and noble, however, ignored this and continued their traditional privileged way of life.

After a number of abortive attempts to bring in reforms, some agreed by Louis XVI, the King dissolved parliament. The people of the Third Estate then formed a National Assembly which challenged the King and established authority. The Revolution began on July 14, 1789, with the taking of the Bastille prison fortress by a huge crowd of Parisians.

Britain looked on with interest as these

Introduced to France by Dr. Guillotin, the guillotine became the symbol of the French Revolution. It stood in what is now the Place de la Concorde in central Paris.

Storming the Bastille: The Bastille prison was a symbol of royal and aristocratic tyranny. It held only seven prisoners when the mob attacked and captured it in 1789. This scene was sketched by one of the revolutionaries.

developments took place. Many Britons, including Wordsworth, at first applauded the principles of liberty and equality of the revolutionaries. However, as matters got out of hand and the King was sentenced to death for acts of treason against the republic, the mood changed and Pitt the Younger, who had been derided by Charles James Fox for his Tory policies, gained supporters for his stand on the Rights of Kings and the privileges of Parliament.

His hopes for a peaceful and profitable relationship with France collapsed and he was obliged to take on the role of the defender of the British way of life.

When Napoleon entered the European scene Pitt recognised the danger for Britain and built up a coalition against him. While in office Pitt counted on and received the support of King George III which enabled him to carry out his duties to the satisfaction of both monarch and country. After his death his policies were carried on by younger men whose talents he had encouraged and whose grasp of the broader issues of Britain's role in Europe helped to shape the post-revolutionary world.

THE NAPOLEONIC WARS

1803–1815

Battle of Trafalgar which took place on 21 October, 1805.

AFTER NAPOLEON had defeated the Austrians in Italy and had established himself as a political force in the Directory, which governed France after the Revolution, he was given command of the army of England. It was an attempt to get him away from the political centre of Paris but also a recognition that Britain was a dangerous enemy. Realizing that he could not hope to cross the Channel while the British navy guarded it, Napoleon set off for Egypt intending to cut Britain's route to the lucrative markets of India and the East. He was foiled in Egypt by the brilliance of Nelson who destroyed his fleet on the Nile.

Returning to Paris to find a *coup d'etat* being prepared against him, Napoleon overthrew the plotters and formed a consulate of which he was named First Consul. His offers of peace with Britain were refused, though later in 1802 after a victory against the Austrians in Italy, a truce was agreed. It was only a temporary interruption, however, and by 1805 war had broken out again and Napoleon was preparing an army to invade Britain. Once again, on the eve of invasion, he changed his mind and set off for Central Europe, leaving Admiral Villeneuve and his fleet to cope with the British.

Napoleon's next confrontation with the British came in Spain, where he had made his brother Joseph King, and in Portugal where a British army under Wellington had landed in 1808. Wellington's army and Spanish irregulars now fought a bitter war, which finally drove the French out of Spain in 1813. Convinced that England was now going to make an alliance with Russia, Napoleon made the fatal mistake of invading Russia. From here on the defeats

Napoleon Bonaparte was one of the greatest military commanders in history.

grew as he retreated from Moscow in dire mid-winter conditions, and was faced with a coalition of allies including Austria, Prussia and Saxony. In the west, meanwhile, Wellington was crossing into France behind the retreating French army. It was almost the end, but the resilient Napoleon won four more battles before retreating to Fontainebleau, where his marshals forced him to abdicate. He was exiled to Elba from which he escaped to survive another hundred days before the Battle of Waterloo on June 18, 1815.

Here he was comprehensively defeated by an allied army led by the Duke of Wellington. He returned to Paris to abdicate (22 June) and throw himself on the mercy of the British. He was exiled to St Helena, a lonely island in the Atlantic where he spent the rest of his days, dying there under mysterious circumstances on 5 May, 1821.

WELLINGTON'S DISPATCHES 1808–1815

THE PENINSULAR CAMPAIGN

June, 1808
Wellington receives news of the impending assignment.

July 7–21, 1808
Assignment to the Spanish expedition.

July 21–30, 1808
The preparation for departure to Spain.

July 1–6, 1809
Prelude to the battle of Talavera.

July 8–14, 1809
Prelude to the battle of Talavera, including the capture of Soult's orders and problems moving the army military chest.

July 15–19, 1809
Prelude to the battle of Talavera. Preparations to move against the French Army in Spain.

September 18–24, 1810
Prelude to the battle of Busaco.

September 27–30, 1810
The battle of Busaco and its aftermath.

May 8, 1811
The aftermath of the battle of Fuentes de Onoro.

July 14–21, 1812
Prelude to the battle of Salamanca.

July 23–25, 1812
The battle of Salamanca and its aftermath.

July 28, 1812
Conclusion of Battle of Talavera; victory over Soult.

THE WATERLOO CAMPAIGN

June 1–5th, 1815
Mobilization, organizing the Army.

June 6–7, 1815
Mobilization, organizing the Army.

June 8–14, 1815
The beginning of the Campaign.

June 15–18, 1815
Quatre Bras and Waterloo.

June 19, 1815
Post battle reports and letters to dead and wounded officer's families.

NELSON AND WELLINGTON

TWO OF THE ablest military men of Britain played vital parts in the long war against the French and Napoleon. Early in his already distinguished career, Nelson was retired in poor health for five years to Burnham Thorpe in Norfolk. In 1793 he was recalled to serve on the Agamemmnon with Hood in the Mediterranean and, it was while here that he fought in the battle of Cape St Vincent and lost an arm, shattered by enemy grapeshot. Once restored to health, Nelson was sent to the Mediterranean once more where, following Napoleon's fleet, he destroyed it at Aboukir Bay in Egypt.

On returning to Naples he met Lady Hamilton who became his mistress and the love of his life. A more serious misdemeanour was his refusal to leave Malta, which he was blockading. Censured by the Admiralty, he resigned his command. Only after the French Revolution did his efforts to gain a new sea command finally pay off, and he entered the phase of his life that would make him famous. However it also cost him dearly. While doing joint operations with the army ashore at Calvi he was wounded in the face, costing him the sight of his right eye. This was not the end, however, for he was next ordered to Toulon to observe the French fleet under Villeneuve. The French admiral escaped to the West Indies and it was not until his return that he and Nelson met at the decisive Battle of Trafalgar in 1805. This resulted in victory for the British, but cost Nelson his life.

Arthur Wellesley had a distinguished career in India, thanks to his brother buying him a commission in the regiment of the 33rd Foot. He returned to Britain at the age of thirty-six and

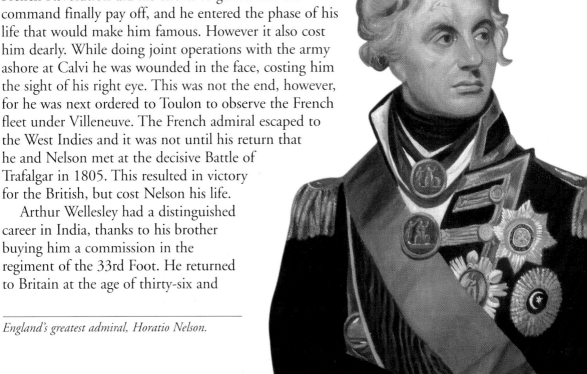

England's greatest admiral, Horatio Nelson.

210

married Kitty Pakenham. As a colonial soldier, he was not highly regarded by his fellow officers and was known as the 'Sepoy General'.

His experience of warfare was, nevertheless, exceptional and gained from personal experience as well as his studies. His appointment in 1808 was fortunate for, after fighting and defeating a French force under Junot in Portugal, he was returned to England where he once more took up his duties as MP for Rye and Irish Secretary, a post he had gained in 1806.

In 1809, after Sir John Moore's retreat and death, Wellesley was recalled to take command of the forces on the Iberian Peninsula. Unlike Nelson, who was an impulsive and aggressive fighter, Wellesley's strategy was to wait until his enemies' difficulties with supplies so far from their base began to weaken their forces. He entrenched himself behind the lines of Torres Vedras on the Lisbon peninsula until he was ready to move, and then advanced steadily until the French were driven out of Spain. It was while in Madrid that the Spanish painter Goya painted his portrait, a faithful interpretation of a doughty man who was to be the Nemesis of Napoleon at Waterloo.

The Duke of Wellington and his charger 'Copenhagen' by Sir David Wilkie.

BATTLE OF WATERLOO

The Duke of Wellington is best known for his victory over Napoleon in the Battle of Waterloo.

The Battle of Waterloo was the final and decisive action of the Napoleonic Wars. It effectively ended French domination of the European continent and brought about drastic changes in the political boundaries and the power balance of Europe.

Fought on 18 June, 1815, near Waterloo, in what is now Belgium, the battle ranks as a great turning point in modern history.

The Battle of Waterloo was one of the bloodiest in modern history. During the fighting of 18 June, French casualties totalled about 40,000, British and Dutch about 15,000 and Prussian about 7,000. At one point about 45,000 men lay dead or wounded within an area of 8 sq km. Additional thousands of casualties were suffered by both sides during the three-day campaign that preceded the final battle.

In his reminiscences about the Waterloo campaign, Napoleon severely criticized General Grouchy for his failure to intercept the Prussians after their retreat from Ligny. Finally, Napoleon himself erred in massing only 124,000 men before Charleroi when he might easily have marshalled more by drawing on reserve troops left in secondary positions.

GEORGE IV

1820–1830

BORN: 12 August 1762, St James's Palace. PARENTS: George III and Charlotte of Mecklenburg-Strelitz. ASCENDED THE THRONE: 28 January 1820.
CROWNED: 19 July 1821, Westminster Abbey. AUTHORITY: King of the United Kingdom of Great Britain and Ireland, King of Hanover. MARRIED: Caroline, daughter of the Duke of Brunswick.
CHILDREN: One daughter, Charlotte Augusta; two illegitimate children.
DIED: 26 June 1830, Windsor. BURIED: St George's Chapel, Windsor.

ROYAL BIOGRAPHY

LIKE MOST OF the Hanoverian kings, George IV, when Prince of Wales, did not get on with his father. As a young man, the Prince of Wales enjoyed the good life with his mistresses, good food and the arts. In 1785 he went through a form of marriage with Maria Fitzherbert, a Catholic, which would have prevented his succession if the marriage had been made public. Ten years later, he was forced into marriage with a Protestant princess, Caroline of Brunswick, in order to obtain money from Parliament to pay his debts. The marriage was a disaster almost from the outset and, after the birth of a daughter, the two lived apart. After having tried unsuccessfully to divorce her, George excluded her from his coronation ceremony.

Once he became King, George succeeded in bringing about a measure of Catholic emancipation, and Catholics were given the vote. His political influence was slight, however, for being always in debt, he had to depend on Parliament for financial help. His weak political status was worsened by quarrelling with Charles James Fox and the Whigs, who had voted for him to be Prince

Regent. When the Tories came to power with ministers like Wellington and Liverpool, George was forced to accept a repeal of religious discrimination against dissenters and Catholics, and his one political achievement, was nullified. (In 1829, Catholics were allowed to become members of Parliament.)

Culturally George did a good deal for the nation. He commissioned work from John Nash, the architect, for a park in London now known as Regent's Park, the colonnaded Regent's Street and, most remarkable of all, the Royal Pavilion at Brighton. During his reign the British Museum was extended in 1823, the National Gallery established in 1824, and the first rail passenger service in the world was established from Stockton to Darlington. He was the first Hanoverian to visit his Scottish realm, and in 1822 made a triumphant visit to Edinburgh clad in tartan and tights, his reception having been orchestrated by the great Scottish novelist Walter Scott.

George secretly married a 28-year-old widow, Maria Fitzherbert, in 1785.

TIME LINE OF THE REIGN 1820–1830

1820
George IV acedes to the throne after the death of his father George III.
Failure of the Cato Street Conspiracy, a radical plot to murder the Cabinet.
Trial of Queen Caroline in which George IV attempts to divorce her for adultery.

1821
Queen Caroline excluded from George IV's coronation.

1823
British Museum is extended and extensively rebuilt to house expanding collection.

1824
The National Gallery is established in London.

1825
The world's first railway service is opened – Stockton and Darlington Railway.
Trade unions are legalized.

1826
The Royal Zoological Society is founded in London by Sir Stamford Raffles.

1828
Wellington becomes British Prime Minister.

1829
Robert Peel sets up the Metropolitcan Police Force.
The Catholic Relief Act is passed, permitting Catholics to become Members of Parliament.

1830
George IV dies at Windsor.

WILLIAM IV

— 1830–1837 —

ROYAL BIOGRAPHY

BORN: 21 August 1765, Buckingham Palace. PARENTS: George III and Charlotte of Mecklenburg-Strelitz. ASCENDED THE THRONE: 26 June 1830.
CROWNED: 8 September 1831, Westminster Abbey.
AUTHORITY: King of the United Kingdom of Great Britain and Ireland, King of Hanover.
MARRIED: Adelaide, daughter of the Duke of Saxe-Meinigen.
CHILDREN: Four, none of whom survived infancy. DIED: 20 June 1837, Windsor.
BURIED: St George's Chapel, Windsor.

WILLIAM SUCCEEDED his brother, George IV, and was welcomed with open arms by the British public, who had grown weary of the excesses of the fourth George. William possessed an unassuming character, exemplary private life and disdain for pomp and ceremony.

The third son of George III, he moved up the line of succession when his elder brother, the Duke of York, died. While following a naval career that took him to the office of Lord High Admiral, he had lived out of the public eye with his mistress, Dorothea Jordan. She was an actress who bore him ten illegitimate children. In 1818, beset by debts and also aware that the death of the Prince Regent's daughter in childbirth left the Hanoverians without heirs, William married Adelaide of Saxe Meiningen. The two daughters born to them died in infancy.

Not politically minded, William depended on his ministers for advice and when, in 1831, the Whigs became the most powerful party in Parliament, a movement for parliamentary reform began that would change the political scene in Britain.

The first Reform Act in 1832, extended the franchise to some 300,000 middle-class citizens and redistributed parliamentary seats. It was the beginnings of the process that would lead to a truly democratic system. The following year colonial slavery was abolished, and a Factory Act prohibited the use of children under nine from working in factories. The Poor Laws were reformed and the Municipal Reform Act of 1835 greatly advanced constitutional change.

The radically changed life of working people had been brought about by the industrial revolution and the establishment of industries which were to make Britain the wealthiest country in the world. It is doubtful, however, that William IV was even aware of the conditions of life of his subjects. Society was divided between the rich, who were often landowners, and the poor, many of whom had been agricultural workers who were driven into the cities by the poverty of farming. The new society was to be the focal point of national life in the next reign.

William IV died at Windsor early in the morning of June 20, 1837.

William's death separated the joint rule of England and Hanover. His niece Victoria ascended the throne of England, but was barred by Salic law from ruling in Hanover, which passed into the hands of William's brother Ernest, Duke of Cumberland.

TIME LINE OF THE REIGN 1830–1837

1830
William IV succeeds his brother George IV.
Liverpool–Manchester railway line opened.

1831
The new London Bridge is opened over the River Thames.

1832
The First Reform Act is passed.

1833
Slavery abolished throughout the British Empire.
Factory Act passed, prohibiting children under the age of nine working in factories and reducing the working hours of women and older children.

1834
Poor Law Act passed, creating workhouses for the poor.
The Tolpuddle Martyrs sentenced to transporation to Australia for attempting to form a trade union.
The Houses of Parliament are destroyed by fire.
Lord Melbourne resigns as Prime Minister, he is succeeded by Sir Robert Peel.

1835
The Municipal Reform Act is passed.

1836
Births, deaths, and marriages must be registered by law.

1837
Charles Dickens publishes *The Pickwick Papers*.
William IV dies at Windsor Castle.

VICTORIA

——— 1837–1901 ———

ROYAL BIOGRAPHY

BORN: 24 May 1819, Kensington Palace, London.
PARENTS: Edward, Duke of Kent and Victoria of Saxe-Coburg.
ASCENDED THE THRONE: 20 June 1837.
CROWNED: 28 June 1838, Westminster Abbey.
AUTHORITY: Queen of the United Kingdom of Great Britain and
Ireland, Empress of India (from 1 May 1876).
MARRIED: Albert, son of Duke of Saxe-Coburg.
CHILDREN: Four sons. DIED: 22 January 1901, Osborne,
Isle of White. BURIED: Frogmore, Windsor.

*A painting of Queen Victor
by Sir Francis Gra*

QUEEN VICTORIA was the longest reigning of the British monarchs, coming to the throne at the age of eighteen. She was the daughter of the Duke of Kent, fourth son of George III and of Princess Victoria Leiningen of Saxe-Coburg. It seemed likely from her earliest years that she would one day inherit the throne, and so was carefully brought up, under the care of a Hanoverian governess, Fraulein Louise Lehzen.

The two major influences in her first years as Queen were her uncle, Prince Leopold, and Lord Melbourne, her first Prime Minister. Both were sophisticated men of the world and politically wise. Their example and her own strong will formed the character of the later Queen. Her first tussle with the established order occurred in May 1839 when Melbourne resigned, to be succeeded by the Tory Sir Robert Peel. The new Prime Minister insisted that the ladies of the Queen's Bedchamber should all be Tories, like the new government. The Queen refused to dismiss the Whig women in her household and the affair quickly became a crisis, leading to a vote in Parliament that Peel lost. Melbourne took up the prime ministership again.

By the autumn of 1839, a much more important influence on Victoria had been brought into her life by her mother and Uncle Leopold, both intent on marrying off the young Queen suitably.

Balmoral Castle in Scotland, (left) was rebuilt in the 1850s following Prince Albert's plans. It was Queen Victoria's favourite home and is still a favourite of today's Royal family.

Their candidate for the role of royal consort was a relative, Prince Albert of the small German principality of Saxe-Coburg-Gotha. Albert was handsome, intelligent and well educated, and Victoria was immediately attracted. They were married in the Chapel Royal, St James Palace in February 1840. Their first child, Victoria, was born in November, to be followed over the next 16 years by another eight children, all of whom grew up to be married into the royal families of Europe. Victoria and Albert's close-knit family life set the pattern for the Victorian Age.

Albert was decisive and ambitious, and had to overcome much early criticism in Britain because of his German origins and comparative poverty. Albert's ambitions were not for himself but for his adopted country; he wished to make Britain the greatest nation in the world. Victoria adored him and

TIME LINE OF THE REIGN 1837–1901

1837
Victoria succeeds William IV.
1840
Victoria marries Prince Albert.
1840
Penny post introduced.
1845-9
Potato famine in Ireland.
1852
Death of the Duke of Wellington.
1854-56
Crimean War fought by Britain and France against Russia.
1856
Victoria Cross instituted for military bravery.
1859
Charles Darwin writes
On the Origin of the Species.
1861
Death of Prince Albert.
1863
Edward, Prince of Wales, marries Alexandra of Denmark.
1863
Salvation Army founded.
1876
Victoria becomes Empress of India.
1887
Victoria celebrates her Golden Jubilee.
1897
Victoria celebrates her Diamond Jubilee.
1899-1902
Boer War in South Africa.
1901
Death of Queen Victoria.

Queen Victoria with her grandchildren, Prince Arthur (b. 1883) and Princess Margaret of Connaught (b. 1882).

together they made an indelible impression on British life.

The Great Exhibition of 1851, which was Albert's idea, increased his popularity, as did his desire for change and improvement for the working people of Britain. This was a subject which Victoria had at first given little thought to, for Melbourne had nurtured in her the idea that change was better left to itself and not encouraged. But Victoria had a more liberal and tolerant view of the world, more, it can be said, than many of her subjects. This became evident in her attitude, for instance, to the instigators of the Indian Mutiny in 1857, against whom, unlike the rest of her subjects, she did not demand revenge.

In 1861, Albert died of typhoid. Unable to face public life without him, Victoria retired for thirteen years and was seldom seen by her subjects. That was until her Prime Minister, the clever and astute Benjamin Disraeli, restored her sense of her duty to the imperial destiny of her country by making her Empress of India in 1877. This move ensured the protection of the short sea route to Britain's possessions in India, south-east Asia and the Pacific.

The latter part of Victoria's reign was a triumphal march of an empire on which, it was thought, the sun would never set. Britain's world influence grew with her colonies and mandates and the home country prospered as never before. In 1887 her Golden Jubilee became an occasion for national rejoicing, only surpassed by her Diamond Jubilee ten years later.

PRINCE ALBERT

1819–1861

VICTORIA'S CHOICE Albert of Saxe-Coburg-Gotha as a husband was not universally approved and she had to wrestle with Parliament to obtain an allowance for him. Nor could she obtain agreement to her idea of making him King Consort or, indeed, of getting him a simple British peerage. It was not until 1853 that Victoria was able to have her husband made Prince Consort.

Albert was an ambitious young man and devoted all his energies to establishing Britain's greatness. His most ambitious idea was to hold a great international fair of science and invention in London's Hyde Park. This was housed in a vast glass palace with 100,000 square feet of floor space. This fabulous project was entrusted to Joseph Paxton, a landscape gardener famous for the lily house and other glasshouses at Chatsworth in Derbyshire.

This new Crystal Palace was filled with all the technical innovations of the age and with a vast array of treasures from all over the world, particularly the countries of the British Empire. The Great Exhibition was opened by Albert's immensely proud wife in 1851 and was an enormous success. Visitors came from all levels of society, many of whom were brought to London by that great Victorian innovator, Thomas Cook, a friend of Paxton's from Leicester. The Great Exhibition brought Albert much praise and popularity and left a permanent mark on the cultural life of the nation. South Kensington in London became an important museum area, where the Victoria and Albert, Natural History, Science and other world-famous museums were built out of the profits of the Exhibition.

Albert made other, less tangible, but no less important contributions to life in Britain. He was concerned with social conditions, with attitudes to imperial domains and exerted an enlightening influence on his wife, encouraging her interest in Scotland, where they established a holiday home at Balmoral.

THE INDUSTRIAL REVOLUTION

DEFORESTATION, SHORTAGE of charcoal for smelting and a growing demand for iron stimulated major changes in the iron and steel making process; coal was used instead (Abraham Darby, 1709). Coal mines became deeper and needed more effective pumps. This prompted the invention of the steam engine (Thomas Newcomen, 1712). The new machines made mass production in many industries possible, and brought together huge numbers of factory workers in ever-growing towns.

John Kay, an English weaver met the high demand for cotton products by introducing his flying shuttle, an invention that could cut cotton twice as fast (1733). The scene was now set for many other inventors to revolutionize the cotton industry. Another problem arose – yarn was not being fed fast enough to the weaver, but in 1769, two new inventions solved the problem, the spinning jenny and the water-powered frame, both of which provided yarn faster. Edmund Cartwright, who invented the power loom, combined the machine's characteristics and purposes into one machine in 1800.

In 1829 George Stephenson built a steam engine that he named 'The Rocket'. Stephenson adapted the locomotive to pull carriages with passengers and by 1855 thousands of kilometres of railway covered Britain.

Abraham Darby and his son discovered how to make iron using coal. It was Darby's grandson that constructed the first iron bridge, over the River Severn in Western Britain.

The fundamental conditions for industrial growth in Britain were established with the discovery of how coal and coke could be used for energy. Coke provided a cheap way of smelting iron and its by-product, gas, provided a means for lighting streets and warming homes. Cheap power expanded the textile industries, encouraged the invention of new machinery and created the railway networks which facilitated transport of people and goods. Britain led the world in the use of industrial power and its naval pre-eminence ensured the spread of the benefits of industry world wide.

With industrial success came social change as workers, moving from poorly paid agricultural work (or no work at all) into factory towns, began to demand better conditions of work and a say in how those conditions were established by law.

Soon, there were violent encounters between groups of workers and groups, like the Chartists, demanding parliamentary reform and the guardians of law and order, the police. This body of men, first created as the Metropolitan police of London by Prime Minister Robert Peel in 1829, established a means of keeping order in the new crowded cities, and replaced the system of deterrence by harsh punishments, like death sentences for stealing.

These new conditions created by industry and the growth of towns brought more humane and tolerant means of dealing with the problems of society. It also achieved the standards of civilized living which, broadly speaking, prevail today and which have led to such concepts as human rights and the protection of the individual.

A PENNY POST

A penny post on all letters was initiated in Britain in 1840 after it was discovered that handling, not the distance sent, was the critical cost in delivering mail. All letters weighing a half-ounce or less could be carried for an English penny.

By 1875 the Universal Postal Union had been established to facilitate the transmission of mail between foreign countries.

In 1871 telegraph cables reached from London to Australia; messages could be flashed halfway around the globe in a matter of minutes, speeding commercial transactions.

In 1876 Alexander Graham Bell transmitted the human voice over a wire, although it was several decades before the telephone became popular.

THE EMPIRE

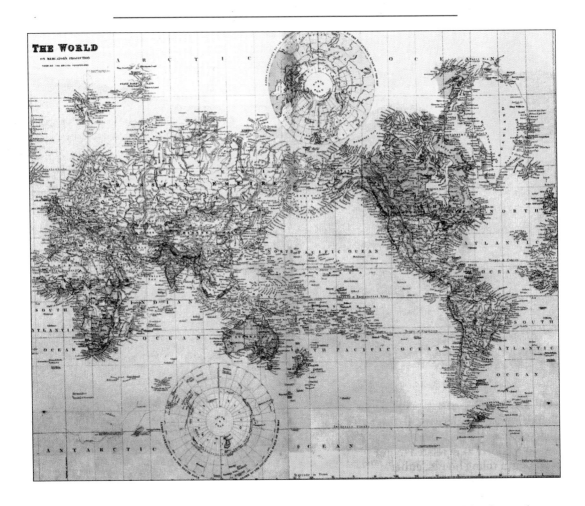

AT ITS PEAK, the British Empire was the largest formal empire that the world had ever known. As such, its power and influence stretched all over the globe; shaping it in all manner of ways – the triumphs, the humiliations, the good that it brought and the bad that it inflicted. For better or worse the British Empire had a massive impact on the history of the world.

The Plantagenets had a small empire in France which they lost and it was not until Tudor times that another wider empire was created by the sea adventurers of the reign of Elizabeth I. England was then trailing behind the Spanish and Portuguese who had claimed territories and trade routes in the Far East and the Americas.

By 1886 the British Empire (shown in pink on the map below) was reaching the height of its power. Its greatest extent came in 1920 when the former German colonies in Africa and the Far East came under British control.

The Boer War (1899–1902) was one of the most vicious imperial wars fought in South Africa. In 1902 the Boers surrendered and their republics were reduced to colonial status.

Despite the loss of the English colonies in North America in the eighteenth century, Great Britain still retained large holdings in the world from India to Australia and, after the defeat of Napoleon and with its navy unchallenged on the world's oceans, saw its empire expand even more as the nineteenth century progressed.

In 1824 Britain acquired Singapore and captured Rangoon, then came Malacca. The colonization of western Australia began in 1829. An opium war with China in 1842 left Britain in possession of Hong Kong. All Canada was united under Britain in 1841, a year after New Zealand became a separate British colony. Meanwhile in India, where Clive had succeeded in enlarging British influence, the Punjab was taken over. In 1850 Britain acquired Danish West African settlements and in South Africa Britain set up responsible government in Cape Colony. In 1858 the Indian Mutiny decided Britain to take charge of all India. In the new world, Vancouver and British Columbia joined the Dominion of Canada and in Africa the dream of Cecil Rhodes of a map coloured in red from Egypt to the Cape was becoming a reality.

By the time that Disraeli proclaimed Victoria Empress of India the British Empire was at its peak. It had grown piece by piece and even where it did not have colonies, Britain's influence was unchallenged.

To most people in Britain, the Empire was somewhere far away, where a few other Britons worked on colonial service. Colonials were a different breed from those who stayed at home, though those who remained benefited enormously from the bankers, merchants, traders, tea planters, rubber planters, timber merchants, cotton growers, cattle and sheep farmers and others who kept the raw materials of the world pouring into Britain and shipped back the products of Britain's industrial cities. The period of the British Empire coincided with a remarkable flourishing of European art and culture. Britain would make its own contributions to European cultural life but it would also spread its art and culture to the far flung corners of the world.

EDWARD VII

1901–1910

ROYAL BIOGRAPHY

BORN: 9 November 1841, Buckingham Palace. PARENTS: Victoria and Albert.
ASCENDED THE THRONE: 22 January 1901. CROWNED: 9 August 1902, Westminster Abbey.
AUTHORITY: King of Great Britain and Ireland and of British Dominions overseas, Emperor of India. MARRIED: Alexandra, daughter of Christian IX of Denmark.
CHILDREN: Three sons, including the future George V, and three daughters.
DIED: 6 May 1910, Buckingham Palace. BURIED: St George's Chapel, Windsor.

THOUGH EDWARD VII was renowned for his hedonistic lifestyle rather than for the political achievements of his reign he nevertheless created the cultural ambience of the twentieth century. The Edwardian Age, which he exemplified, was a period when self-assurance and complacency of the Victorian Age was giving way to doubts and self-examination about Britain's world role. This was accompanied by a new frivolity in the pursuit of leisure.

Edward had waited fifty-nine years to become king and as Prince of Wales had never gained his mother's approval, either as an international ambassador or as a king in waiting. Though he travelled extensively, he spent most of his visits abroad indulging his pleasures, which were a love of women and horses, the arts, theatre and motor cars. In 1863 he married the beautiful Alexandra of Denmark and she bore him six children, though this did not slow down his lifestyle.

In his public presence, however, Edward personified the Britain that ruled the world. In his state robes, painted by Sir Luke Fildes, he looks as much a *roi soleil* as Louis XIV. Edward's contribution to the social life had far-reaching effects in the Entente Cordiale between Britain and France, which replaced the Anglo-German inclinations of his mother.

Though he seemed little interested in science, industry or social reform his reign was marked by considerable advances in these quarters, and his misdemeanours were easily forgiven by his adoring subjects.

Victoria, true to the Hanoverian name, saw the worst in Edward. She and Albert imposed a strict regime upon Edward, who proved resistant and resentful throughout his youth. His marriage at age twenty-two to Alexandra afforded him some relief from his mother's domination, but even after Albert's death in 1863, Victoria consistently denied her son any official governmental role. Edward rebelled by completely indulging himself in women, food, drink, gambling, sport and travel. Alexandra turned a blind eye to his extramarital activities, which continued well into his sixties and found him implicated in several divorce cases.

Edward became the first reigning British monarch to visit Russia, and his presence there in 1908 strengthened the Anglo-Russian agreement of 1907.

TIME LINE OF THE REIGN 1901–1910

1901

Edward VII becomes King on the death of his mother, Queen Victoria.

Australia granted dominion status.

1902

Edward institutes the Order of Merit.

1903

Wilbur and Orville Wright make the first flight.

Emmeline Pankhurst founded the Women's Social and Political Union, demanding votes for women.

1904

Britain and France sign the *Entente Cordiale*, settling outstanding territorial claims.

1907

New Zealand granted dominion status.

1908

The Fourth Olympic Games are held in London.

Herbert Henry Asquith becomes Liberal Prime Minister.

The Triple Entente is signed between Russia, France and Britain.

1909

Lloyd George, the Chancellor of the Exchequer, introduces the People's Budget.

1910

Parliament Bill introduced to curb the power of the House of Lords.

Edward dies at Buckingham Palace, aged 68.

ENTENTE CORDIALE

THE ENTENTE CORDIALE, established by treaty in 1903 and strengthened in 1904, is sometimes thought to be solely the result of Edward VII's fondness for France and especially Paris, but the phrase was used as early as 1843 by a French *chargé d'affaires*, the Comte de Jarnac. At the time he was referring to the friendly welcome Britain had accorded Louis Philippe when he became King of France in 1830, after the deposition of Charles X. British friendship with France, after the enmity of centuries and in particular the Napoleonic Wars, was a matter of international diplomacy. It was essential to maintain the balance of power threatened by the revival of Austria and the rise of Prussia and Russia.

Although Queen Victoria was attached to Germany by many family threads, not least the marriage of her daughter Victoria to Frederick, Crown Prince of Prussia, the British government did not let this influence their international diplomacy. Robert Peel, her Prime Minister, and the Foreign Secretary Lord Aberdeen were particularly in favour of a closer relationship with France. They persuaded the Queen to visit both Louis Philippe and his successor, Napoleon III, and to offer Napoleon a haven after France's defeat in the Franco-Prussian War of 1870 and his subsequent exile.

Britain's strength and world supremacy meant that the government did not much fear, at least in mid-century, a German political and commercial challenge but, when in 1904 Germany tried to persuade Russia and France to form a league to undermine the Entente Cordiale, Britain became uneasy. The suspicions about German intentions grew as the German navy increased in size, so that from 1909 the British navy was concentrated in home waters to counter the German threat.

The Entente Cordiale was often represented by cartoonists as a French woman flirting with an English soldier.

In 1903 Edward VII visited Paris, which paved the way for an Entente Cordiale *between Britain and France. He is seen here shaking hands with George Clemenceau, the future Prime Minister.*

Edward VII had approved the Entente Cordiale alliance, made by the Liberal government of Herbert Asquith, against the alliance of Germany, Austria and Italy. He had also supported the naval reforms by Admiral Fisher and the reform of the army, which had been humiliated during the Boer War. It could be said, therefore, that despite his constitutional position, weakened by the Reform Acts and other legislation, he had some influence in the events which were to come to a head so dramatically after his death.

THE FRANCO-BRITISH DECLARATION, 1904

(Article One)

His Britannic Majesty's Government declare that they have no intention of altering the political status of Egypt.

The Government of the French Republic, for their part, declare that they will not obstruct the action of Great Britain in that country . . .

It is agreed that the post of Director-General of Antiquities in Egypt shall continue, as in the past, to be entrusted to a French savant.

The French schools in Egypt shall continue to enjoy the same liberty as in the past.

(Article Two)

The Government of the French Republic declare that they have no intention of altering the political status of Morocco.

His Britannic Majesty's Government, for their part, recognise that it appertains to France, more particularly as a Power whose dominions are conterminous for a great distance with those of Morocco, to preserve order in that country, and to provide assistance for the purpose of all administrative, economic, financial, and military reforms which it may require.

They declare that they will not obstruct the action taken by France for this purpose, provided that such action shall leave intact the rights which Great Britain, in virtue of treaties, conventions, and usage, enjoys in Morocco, including the right of coasting trade between the ports of Morocco, enjoyed by British vessels since 1901.

THE HOUSE OF WINDSOR

*The family name of Windsor, adopted by George V in
1917, is appropriate for it recalls that the town on the
Thames has long connections with royalty from the
time that William the Conqueror hunted there.
Henry VI founded Eton College in the fields by the
river and Charles II provided a home for his beautiful
mistress, Nell Gwynne, in the old village by the castle.
During their reign the Windsors have seen
contemporary British history being made.*

GEORGE V

— 1910–1936 —

BORN: 3 June 1865, Marlborough House, London. PARENTS: Edward VII and Alexandra.
ASCENDED THE THRONE: 6 May 1910. CROWNED: 22 June 1911, Westminster Abbey.
AUTHORITY: King of Great Britain and Ireland and British Dominions overseas, Emperor of India.
MARRIED: Mary, daughter of the Duke of Teck. CHILDREN: Four sons, including the future
Edward VIII and George VI, and one daughter. DIED: 20 January 1936, Sandringham, Norfolk.
BURIED: St George's Chapel, Windsor.

THE SECOND SON of Edward VII was quite unlike his father. He brought up his children with a severity that was intended to prevent a resurgence of Edward VII's libertine ways, and to restore dignity and decorum to the royal household and the life of the nation. He was also concerned about the role of King and Parliament and refused to create new members of the House of Lords for political purposes, as requested by his Prime Minister. In 1914 the outbreak of war with Germany saw him standing firmly against his cousin the Emperor of Germany whom he later called 'the greatest criminal'.

Like his grandmother, Queen Victoria, George V was only dimly aware of the undercurrent of discontent among his less privileged subjects. The General Strike of 1926 was almost as much of a shock to him as the Russian Revolution of 1917. The Wall Street crash and its after effects in Britain was another sobering fact of George V's reign, and perhaps prompted his first royal broadcast to the nation in 1931.

The inter-war period during which George V reigned may have appeared broadly unruffled on the surface to most middle-class Britons, but there were

George married Mary of Teck (affectionately called May) in 1893 and she reigned with him as Queen Mary from 1910. She bore him four sons and one daughter. She set a social example even more formidable than that of her husband, and she moulded her own family, including her grandchildren, in a most definite fashion.

1910
George V bcomes King and Emperor of India on the death of his father Edward VII.
1911
Parliament Act ensures the sovereignty of the House of Commons. National Insurance Act provides sickness and unemployment benefits.
1912
SS Titanic sinks on her maiden voyage; more than 1,500 lives are lost.
1914–18
First World War.
1914
Battles of Mons, the Marne and Ypres.
1916
Battle of the Somme.
David Lloyd George becomes Prime Minister.
1924
First Labour government formed by Ramsay MacDonald.
1926
General Strike in support of the coalminers.
1928
All women over 21 get the vote.
1931
Great Depression leads to the formation of a national government of all three political parties.
1935
George celebrates his Silver Jubilee: 25 years on the throne.
1936
George V dies at Sandringham.

strong currents of change at work under the surface of working class life and the young educated classes. While writers like Noel Coward and P. G. Wodehouse were poking fun at middle-class morals, others like D. H. Lawrence and J. B. Priestly were undermining accepted ideas about sex and society, while the cartoonist Low was lampooning politics and politicians. But for George V and Queen Mary it was a regrettable development, one they hoped was a passing phase.

THE GREAT WAR
1914–1918

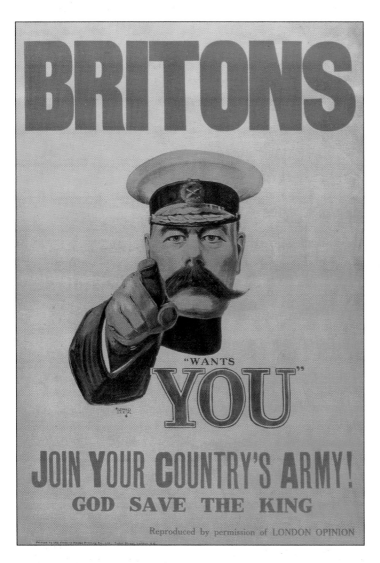

'Your Country Needs You': First World War Recruitment Poster, with a portrait of Secretary for War, Lord Kitchener.

THE IMMEDIATE cause of the First World War was the assassination of the Archduke Franz Ferdinand in Sarajevo in 1914. Britain's entry was due to its treaty commitment to defend Belgium against attack. But the War's underlying reasons were the rivalry amongst the great powers of Europe, and Germany's ambitions to weigh more heavily in the scales of power. This ambition led to a network of treaties and alliances fatally linking the great powers.

It was a baptism by fire for the new King, George V, but like his Prime Minister Herbert Henry Asquith, he believed that Britain and the Allies would triumph before long, especially as the Royal Navy could blockade all German ports. This calculation had not taken into account the growth of Germany's U-boat fleet, which now began to threaten Britain's lifelines. Nor did he allow for the diminishing resolution of the French and Russian armies that were receiving inadequate support on land from Britain.

A new government with Lloyd George at its head came to the conclusion that there would not be a speedy end to the conflict. It seemed that victory would depend on industrial power, the weight of armaments, and the will for victory of the people.

Longer hours at work and a more disciplined labour force increased the production of armaments and of new weapons of war such as the tank and the aeroplane. George V and his wife, Mary, devoted themselves to the upholding of the nation's morale. It was an example to be repeated in the Second World War when aerial bombardment made all Britain a battlefield.

The collapse of the Russian government in the revolution in 1917 was a bitter blow, but an alliance with the USA restored the spirits of the British and French. It was a year, though, before enough troops could cross the Atlantic. Meanwhile, the war continued with the invaluable contribution of Australia, Canadia, New Zealand and other imperial forces. Finally, Germany gave way, defeated and exhausted, but not persuaded to give up the ambition of dominating the world.

he Battle of the Somme was the scene of the 'Big Push' from July to November 016 when over a million soldiers died.

BATTLES OF WORLD WAR ONE 1914–1918

1914
Battle of Liege, Battle of the Frontiers, Battle of Mulhouse, Invasion of Lorraine, Battle of Stalluponen, Battle of Gumbinnen, Battle of the Ardennes, Battle of Charleroi, Siege of Namur, Battle of Mons, Battle of Le Cateau, Battle of Tannenberg, Battle of Heligoland Bight, 1st Battle of the Marne, 1st Battle of the Masurian Lakes, 1st Battle of the Aisne, 1st Battle of Albert, Siege of Antwerp, Battle of Arras, 1st Battle of Ypres, Battle of Yser, Battle of Coronel, Battle of Tanga, Battle of the Falkland Islands, 1st Battle of Champagne, Battle of Dogger Bank, 2nd Battle of the Masurian Lakes

1915
Battle of Neuve Chapelle, 2nd Battle of Ypres, Battle of Festubert, Battle of Loos, Battle of Verdun

1916
Battle of Jutland, Battle of the Somme, Battle of Bazentin Ridge, Battle of Delville Wood, Battle of Pozieres Ridge, Battle of Guillemont, Battle of Flers-Courcelette, 2nd Battle of the Aisne

1917
Battle of Messines, 3rd Battle of Ypres, 3rd Battle of the Aisne

1918
Battle of Cantigny, Battle of Chateau-Thierry, Battle of Belleau Wood, 2nd Battle of the Marne, Battle of Havrincourt, Battle of Epehy

EDWARD VIII
— JAN–DEC 1936 —

ROYAL BIOGRAPHY

BORN: 23 June 1894, White Lodge, Richmond, Surrey. PARENTS: George V and Mary of Teck.
ASCENDED THE THRONE: 20 January 1936. CROWNED: Never crowned.
AUTHORITY: King of Great Britain and Ireland and British Dominions overseas,
Emperor of India. MARRIED: Mrs Wallis Simpson. CHILDREN: None.
DIED: 28 May 1972, May. BURIED: Frogmore, Windsor.

THE PRINCE of Wales, who had a non-combatant role in the British Expeditionary force in France during World War I, had a natural talent for communication with men in all walks of life. He also had a love of women which became a subject of popular gossip.

After the War, at the suggestion of the Prime Minister, Lloyd George, he travelled worldwide and charmed everyone he met. At home, he showed concern for victims of the world recession which reached its lowest point in Britain in 1931. The conditions of the people in mining villages and factory towns prompted him to comment that something should be done to improve matters. This was construed by the Conservative government in office as a political criticism. This made him enemies, whose numbers increased when it became known that the future King was emotionally entangled with a twice-divorced American woman, Wallis Simpson.

Once Edward became King – and head of the Church of England, which did not permit divorce – the question of his possible marriage to Mrs Simpson became a hugely serious matter for the government. Although few ordinary citizens knew anything about the matter because the newspapers of the day said nothing, there was a great division of opinion among those who did know. While the government, led by Stanley Baldwin, and the Church opposed him, Winston Churchill and other liberal-minded peers supported him. When the matter became public knowledge, Edward found, to his dismay, that he had the support of the British Union of Fascists. Ordinary citizens were also divided, but the heads of other Commonwealth states were not – they opposed the marriage. In the end, after less than a year as King, Edward resolved the crisis by abdicating. He signed the abdication agreement, witnessed by his brothers, on 10 December 1936. Given the courtesy title of Duke of Windsor, he left Britain and, apart from a few brief visits, never returned.

When war broke out in 1939 Edward offered his services but a visit his wife had made to Hitler in 1937 and the suspicion that he had fascist sympathizers brought his loyalty into question and prejudiced his appointment to an important war job in Britain. Instead he was offered the Governorship of the Bahamas, a post he filled conscientiously and well, though his unauthorized meetings with Roosevelt were criticized. After the war the Windsors made their home in Paris. They were unwelcome visitors to Britain and ignored by most of the Royal Family, who felt that his behaviour had discredited them. On his death his wife, the Duchess of Windsor was invited to stay at Buckingham Palace before attending his funeral and burial at the Royal Mausoleum at Frogmore in Windsor.

EVENTS OF THE REIGN 1936

Edward VIII succeeds his father, George V, as King in January.

Outbreak of Spanish Civil War.

Germany, under Hitler, reoccupies the demilitarized left bank of the Rhine.

Britain begins to re-arm as political tension increases in Europe and the prospect of military conflict arises.

The Crystal Palace is destroyed by fire.

Maiden voyage of luxury ocean liner, the *Queen Mary*.

Gatwick Airport opens.

BBC inaugurates the world's first television service in London.

Pinewood Film Studios open.

The Jarrow Hunger March begins.

Edward abdicates in December after a reign of only 325 days. His younger brother, the Duke of York, becomes George VI.

GEORGE VI

1936–1952

ROYAL BIOGRAPHY

BORN: 14 December 1895, Sandringham, Norfolk. PARENTS: George V and Mary of Teck. ASCENDED THE THRONE: 11 December 1936. CROWNED: 12 May 1937, Westminster Abbey. AUTHORITY: King of the United Kingdom of Great Britain and Northern Ireland and British Dominions overseas, Emperor of India (until 1947). MARRIED: Elizabeth Bowes-Lyon, daughter of the Earl of Strathmore and Kinghorne. CHILDREN: Two daughters, the future Elizabeth II and Margaret. DIED: 6 February 1952, Sandringham. BURIED: St George's Chapel, Windsor.

WHEN HIS BROTHER abdicated, Albert Arthur George Windsor, Duke of York, known as Bertie to his family, was thrust into a situation that he did not relish. He would have preferred to remain as just another member of the royal family, living as a country squire. His duty lay in accepting the role of King, however, and taking the name of George VI to stress the continuity of the crown, he assumed the throne. He was greatly helped by his wife, the former Lady Elizabeth Bowes-Lyon. She gave him the strong moral support and confidence to speak in public, despite his stammer, and to overcome his awareness that he lacked the natural charisma of his brother. Despite his doubts, George made a great success of his reign.

As a young man he had served in the Royal Navy at the Battle of Jutland and later in the Royal Naval air service. On leaving the services he became interested in factory conditions and the social structure of postwar Britain. He set up the Duke of York camps where boys

*George VI created two
new decorations for acts of
civilian gallantry: the
George Cross and the
George Medal.*

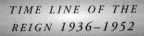

TIME LINE OF THE
REIGN 1936–1952

1936
George VI accedes to the throne
upon the abdication of his
brother, Edward VIII.

1938
Prime Minister Neville
Chamberlain signs agreement with
Hitler at Munich in an attempt to
stop outbreak of war in Europe.

1939
Outbreak of Second World War.

1940
Retreating British troops
evacuated from beaches of
Dunkirk as Germans advance.
Winston Churchill becomes Prime
Minister.
Battle of Britain.
Heavy aerial bombing raids on
British cities.

1941
USA enters War after Japanese
surprise air raid on Pearl Harbor.

1942
Decisive British victory over
Germans at El Alamein.

1944
D-Day landings in Normandy.

1945
Defeat of Germany marks end of
the War in Europe (8 May).
Japan surrenders, after US drops
atomic bombs (14 August).
United Nations formed.
Labour Government in Britain.

1951
Festival of Britain.

1952
George VI dies.

of private and state schools
could meet in a holiday
atmosphere. He also began a
series of royal visits abroad
which made Britain, and its
monarchy, more familiar
throughout the Empire.

When war broke out in
1939, it was suggested
that he – or at least his
two young daughters,
Elizabeth and Margaret – should go to Canada.
But he and the Queen refused to leave
England, despite the air raids, and
concerned themselves with the victims of
the bombardments of London. This
added to his, and the Queen's
popularity, especially when
Buckingham Palace was
bombed nine times. In order
to recognize the valour of
his subjects he created
two new decorations,
the George Cross and
the George Medal, both
awarded to men and women
for civilian acts of gallantry.

WORLD WAR II

1939–1945

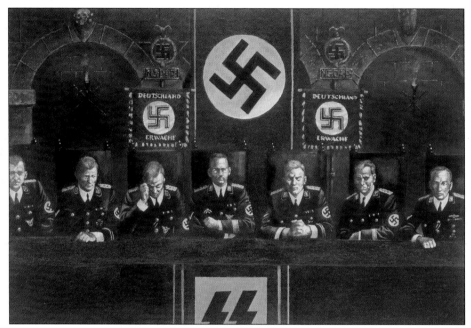

Heinrich Himmler and his SS Council by Gianetto Coppola.

IN 1940 GERMANY was triumphant: France had fallen, Scandinavia had been invaded, Italy had become a German ally and Japan had joined the Berlin/Rome Axis. At this dark moment in history the British, normally cool towards authority, rallied round their leader Winston Churchill. He had become the Prime Minister of a coalition government and managed to turn the dramatic snatching of a large, defeated British expeditionary force from the beaches of Dunkirk, in France, into a great moral victory.

Churchill and George VII were instantly in agreement on the need for a national morale-strengthening campaign and both set about creating an image of cool, courageous resolution. Though the King offered to visit the troops abroad, Churchill dissuaded him because of the possibility of death or capture. When the bombings began, the King and Queen set an example by refusing to move out of London and enjoyed a certain grim satisfaction when Buckingham Palace was bombed. This happened nine times, the first being in September 1940. They felt that this identified the Royal Family with the stress being suffered by Londoners, especially those who lived in the East End near the docks.

Aware that the front line of the war was as much at home as abroad, the King created two awards for acts of bravery and gallantry by civilians. One of these was the George Cross. One of the earliest recipients of the George Cross was the population of the island of Malta for their courage under the bombardment of the German Luftwaffe. The other was the George Medal which, like the George Cross, was regarded as a civilian equivalent of the Victoria Cross which was awarded to the armed services.

The royal children, Elizabeth and Margaret, spent the war at Windsor. On her eighteenth birthday Elizabeth joined the Auxiliary Transport Service and learned to drive ambulances and trucks.

By 1943 the tide of war had begun to turn. The allies were driving the Axis powers out of North Africa and beginning to land on the Italian mainland, and George VI made his first visit to the troops in Africa. The welcome he received was a tribute to the royal contribution to the war, as were the massive crowds which gathered outside Buckingham Palace on V-E Day in 1945.

On 7 December 1941, the Japanese attacked Pearl Harbor, the main US naval base in Hawaii. Five US battleships and 15 other ships were sunk or crippled.

WINSTON CHURCHILL

Churchill came from a military dynasty. His ancestor John Churchill had been created first Duke of Marlborough in 1702 for his victories against Louis XIV early in the War of the Spanish Succession. Churchill was born in 1874 in Blenheim Palace, the house built by the nation for Marlborough. As a young man of undistinguished academic accomplishment – he was admitted to Sandhurst after two failed attempts – he entered the army as a cavalry officer. He took enthusiastically to soldiering (and perhaps even more enthusiastically to regimental polo playing) and between 1895 and 1898 managed to see three campaigns: Spain's struggle in Cuba in 1895, the North-West Frontier campaign in India 1897 and the Sudan campaign of 1898, where he took part in what is often described as the British Army's last cavalry charge, at Omdurman. Even at 24, Churchill was steely: 'I never felt the slightest nervousness,' he wrote to his mother. '[I] felt as cool as I do now.' In Cuba he was present as a war correspondent, and in India and the Sudan he was present both as a war correspondent and as a serving officer. Thus he revealed two other aspects of his character: a literary bent and an interest in public affairs.

ELIZABETH II

1952–

ROYAL BIOGRAPHY

BORN: 21 April 1926, 17 Bruton Street, London. PARENTS: George VI and
Elizabeth Bowes-Lyon. ASCENDED THE THRONE: 6 February 1952.
CROWNED: 2 June 1953, Westminster Abbey. AUTHORITY: Queen of the
United Kingdom of Great Britain and Northern Ireland, Head of the
Commonwealth. MARRIED: Philip, son of Prince Andrew of Greece.
CHILDREN: Three sons, Charles, Andrew and Edward, and
one daughter, Anne.

*It has been said ab
the young Elizabet.
that she was grave,
reserved and wise
beyond her years. I
many years as reig
monarch have mac
her utterly professi
and mindful of the
seriousness of her r*

THE REIGN OF Elizabeth II has been no less eventful or hazardous for Britain than that of her Tudor predecessor. It has included war, political and social upheaval, and one threat that the first Elizabeth did not have to defend herself against – the attacks of an intrusive and often malicious mass media.

When her father died in 1952 Elizabeth was in Kenya with her husband, Prince Philip. It was the start of a trip that should have taken her to the furthest points of the Empire and Commonwealth, a demanding job which, in subsequent years, would make her the most travelled monarch in British history.

The new Queen had also soon to deal with a break-up of the social structure at home, as a tide of change in social attitudes, which became more of a tidal wave in the 'Swinging Sixties', swept away established social forms. Brought up in a traditional manner by her parents in an aristocratic Court, not known for its modernity, the Queen and her family had to find a way to meet the demands of a more democratic, media-driven society. That she did not immediately succeed was made clear in 1957 by the furore that greeted an article in a national magazine. It was written up by a former Lord turned commoner, Lord Altrincham, and criticized her staff as being out-of-touch and narrow-minded. It also said that her own style was 'priggish' and 'schoolgirlish'. Wisely, the Queen did not respond, adopting a low profile while the torrents of criticism, satire and even abuse swirled about the monarchy.

With the support of her husband, Prince Philip, she made her family more accessible, encouraging them in their public duties and providing opportunities for media coverage. During her reign she has worked with ten Prime Ministers representing Conservative and Labour governments, and has lived through the labour crises of the three-day week, miners and newspaper strikes, and the problem of Northern Ireland and the Falklands War.

In 1997, faced with the breakdown of marriages in the royal family she swept away former accusations that the monarchy had little in common with ordinary people, by referring to a year of unhappiness in her own family as the *Annus Horribilis*. Now, as she approaches the Golden Jubilee of her reign, there are few who would not agree that the young woman who became a Queen at the age of twenty-five has made a success of a very difficult job.

TIME LINE OF THE REIGN 1952–1979

1952
Elizabeth accedes to the throne on the death of her father George VI.

1953
Edmund Hillary and Tenzing Norgay climb Everest just before Coronation Day.

1955
Winston Churchill resigns as Prime Minister and is succeeded by Anthony Eden.

1957
Harold Macmillan succeeds Eden as Prime Minister.

1959
Oil is discovered in the North Sea.

1963
Alec Douglas-Hume replaces Harold Macmillan as Prime Minister.
The Beatles release their first LP.

1964
Labour government of Harold Wilson takes office.

1969
Charles invested as Prince of Wales.

1970
Edward Heath becomes Conservative Prime Minister.

1971
Decimal currency is introduced.

1973
Britain joins the European Community.

1974
Harold Wilson returns as Prime Minister.

1979
Margaret Thatcher becomes Britain's first woman Prime Minister.

ROYAL RESIDENCES

Windsor Castle the largest occupied castle in the world.

WINDSOR CASTLE is the largest castle in Britain. Set in its own Great Park, it was once used as a hunting ground for kings. The castle is dominated by a powerful Round Tower and the splendid St George's Chapel, the burial place for many Kings and Queen. From its commanding position above the Thames, the castle has splendid views of the Thames Valley and Eton College and its chapel.

The castle was first a simple structure used by William I as a hunting lodge. It was not until the reign of Charles II that it became a well-appointed royal residence. Since then, it has been a favourite home for the royal family, made all the more so by a disastrous fire in 1992. Restoration, funded partly by opening Buckingham Palace to the public, was carried out to the highest standard and the Castle is once again a favourite place with royalty and tourists alike.

Buckingham Palace is the London home of the sovereign. Set at the top of The Mall, close to the Tudor St James Palace and Clarence House, and surrounded by Green Park and St James Park, it is the centre of royal London. The original house was built in 1677 and was bought by George III in 1762. It was later enlarged by George IV, who engaged the architect John Nash, who was creator of Regent's Park and Regent Street, to carry out the work. Queen Victoria was the first sovereign to live in Buckingham Palace, moving there from Kensington Palace shortly after her accession. Since 1993, the State Rooms of Buckingham Palace have been open to the public in the summer. The Queen's Gallery, built by the Queen on the site of the palace's bombed chapel has been considerably enlarged in time for her Golden Jubilee. It will provide an opportunity to see some of the art masterpieces of the Royal Collection.

The Royal Family's favourite private residence in Scotland is Balmoral Castle, set on the River Dee in Aberdeenshire. The original building, acquired by Queen Victoria and Prince Albert, who had a particular fondness for Scotland, was rebuilt to the royal couple's own design. It greatly pleased Victoria, who, in her book *Leaves from My Journal of Our Life in the Highlands*, called it her 'dear paradise'.

Another favourite private residence is Sandringham in Norfolk, which was bought by Bertie, the Prince of Wales, in 1860. It was redesigned in an Elizabethan style in red brick, according to the ideas of the Prince and his beautiful bride, Alexandra of Denmark. It was their country home and has continued to offer the Royal Family a rare degree of privacy.

No longer a royal residence, but an imposing building with a regal appearance, is Osborne House on the Isle of Wight. This was built for Victoria and Albert as a private family home by the seaside, by the architect Thomas Cubbitt, who also built the East front of Buckingham Palace. He gave Osborne House an Italian style with a large square tower and terraces with views over the Solent. It was here that Edward VII, George V and George VI later indulged their love of yachting – though not from Osborne House, because Edward VII had already sold it. The Solent, which borders the house grounds, was where Queen Victoria tried the prevailing fashion for sea bathing for the first time.

Buckingham Palace has served as the official London residence of Britain's sovereigns since 1837.

THE FAMILY

ALTHOUGH THE Queen is the head of state, at home her husband Philip, who became Duke of Edinburgh on their marriage in 1947, is head of the family and a strict but loving father. In the demanding job of untitled Prince Consort he has been supportive of his wife and among his duties has been the management of the royal estates. He is the patron of many charities, in particular the World Wild Fund for Nature and he founded the Duke of Edinburgh Award Scheme for young people. During World War II Philip served in the navy and was mentioned in despatches at the Battle of Cape Matapan, Italy. He is a keen sportsman and until recently played polo, sailed yachts and competed in carriage driving competitions.

Anne, the Princess Royal, who was born in 1950, inherited her father's outspokenness and for a while was unpopular with the media for her firm refusal to be taken advantage of. Her work as patron of over five hundred charities, and especially Save the Children, have made her much admired, especially as she carries out her work without a fanfare of publicity. She is also admired as a woman of spirit who has distinguished herself as a three-day event rider,

The royal family on the balcony at Buckingham Palace to celebrate the Queen Mother's 100th birthday.

representing the UK at the Montreal Olympics. Her divorce from Captain Mark Philips was handled with quiet discretion as was her subsequent marriage to Commander Timothy Lawrence. Her children, Peter and Zara, have grown up largely out of the public eye.

Andrew, the second son of Elizabeth and Philip, born in 1960, made a career in the Royal Navy, perhaps following his father's example, though Andrew chose to be a pilot rather than follow a more deck-bound role. During the Falklands War he served as a naval helicopter pilot, and was often in the thick of the action. Since his retirement from the Royal Navy, Prince Andrew, who has been Duke of York since his marriage to Sarah Ferguson in 1986, has taken on many more public duties. A role he has inherited from his second cousin, the Duke of Kent, is president of the Football Association. Prince Andrew's many duties abroad and the high life of his spirited wife eventually led to another divorce in the Royal Family, but this time a much more friendly one.

TIME LINE OF THE REIGN 1981–2002

1981
Prince Charles marries Lady Diana Spencer.
1982
Unemployment tops three million. Britain goes to war with Argentina over control of the Falkland Islands.
1989–90
Poll tax introduced amid widespread protest.
1990
Margaret Thatcher resigns as Prime Minister and is succeeded by John Major.
1996
Both the Prince and Princess of Wales, and the Duke and Duchess of York divorce.
1997
Labour Party under Tony Blair ends 18 years of Conservative government.
Hong Kong reverts to China after 155 years of British rule.
1998
Structure of Millennium Dome completed.
1999
National Maritime Museum reopens after being refurbished.
2000
Queen Mother celebrates her 100th birthday.
2001
Prince William starts at St Andrews University.
2002
Queen Elizabeth marks 50 years of rule. Princess Margaret dies.

The Duke and Duchess of York are often together with their children, the Princesses Beatrice and Eugenie, on holidays at home and abroad.

Edward, the youngest of the Queen's four children, was born in 1964. After taking a degree at Cambridge, he joined the Royal Marines but decided that he was not suited to the sort of military life of action expected of sons of the monarch. Instead, he followed another interest, perhaps inherited from his royal ancestors, for art and theatre. He now has his own television production company, making documentaries, largely on royal subjects – and not always with success. On his marriage to Miss Sophie Rhys Jones, he was given the title of Earl of Wessex. For a time after their marriage, the new Countess continued with her job of public relations consultant.

Princess Margaret, the Queen's sister, always liked more glamorous aspects of life than her serious-minded sister. She had always carried out many public engagements at home and abroad for the numerous charities with which she was connected, but these activities were somewhat curbed due

Princess Margaret always took a keen interest in the arts, particularly dance and modern art.

to ill health in her latter years. After a sense of public duty made her renounce her plan to marry a divorced man, Group Captain Peter Townsend, she married the photographer Anthony Armstrong-Jones, who was given the title Earl of Snowdon on their marriage in 1960. The couple had two children, David, Viscount Linley who has pursued a successful career as a furniture designer, and Sarah, who, as an artist, has exhibited at the Royal Academy and elsewhere. After her divorce from Lord Snowdon, Princess Margaret chose to live without a partner. Princess Margaret died in the early hours of Saturday morning on February 9, 2002, at the age of 71, following a third stroke.

THE QUEEN MOTHER
— 1900–2002 —

ELIZABETH BOWES-LYON was, essentially, a family woman. Behind all the pomp and majesty which surrounded her public duties was a contented family life made sadder by the events of

The Queen Mother's coffin lying-in-state at Westminster Hall.

later years. There can be little doubt that the Queen Mother re-invented the idea of an active Royal Family. Her powerful personality brought about many changes including the now-ubiquitous 'walkabout'. From the day of her accession as George VI's Queen, she dedicated her life and that of her family to serving the nation and to supporting the shy and retiring King in his onerous duties as sovereign. Testing times were ahead – World War II brought the terrors of the Blitz to Britain. The King and Queen brought comfort to those left homeless by the Luftwaffe's bombs. With the death of her husband in 1952 and the coronation of her daughter a year later many would have expected the Queen Mother to take a back seat. But she continued to work at her royal duties, continually supporting her daughter just as she had supported her husband. As a grandmother, the Queen Mother played an active role, looking after her grandchildren when the Queen was away on official business. She was particularly close to the Prince of Wales and the two were often seen at royal engagements in her later years.

The Queen Mother died peacefully in her sleep at the age of 101, at Royal Lodge, Windsor, on Saturday 30 March, 2002, with her daughter at her bedside. This news came only six weeks after her last public appearance, at the funeral of her daughter Princess Margaret. Princess Margaret's ashes were interred with the Queen Mother's coffin, in the George VI Memorial Chapel at Windsor.

The Queen Mother lived longer than any other King or Queen in British history. The Prince of Wales said of his beloved grandmother, 'the Queen Mother served the UK with panache, style and unswerving dignity for nearly 80 years, enriching the life of the nation and beyond'.

THE PRINCE OF WALES

1948–

PRINCE CHARLES has been heir to the throne for most of his life. Born in November 1948, he was just three years old when his mother became Queen. The Prince of Wales is the 21st holder of the title in 700 years – but the role of The Prince has not been defined over the centuries. It has always been for each Prince of Wales to interpret his position as he wishes.

Charles has been sometimes admired, but more often criticised, for his personal opinions as well as for his handling of the pitfalls of life for a person not aptly prepared for modern society. However, as an intelligent and cultured man he has learned to adapt to his changing role without losing his individuality. During all this time he has, mostly, managed to preserve a cool and reasonable demeanour, interpreted by those who wish to do so, as lack of feeling. It is a criticism that has been largely vanquished by the care he has shown for his children, William and Harry, after the tragic death of their mother.

Charles' marriage in 1981 to the personable Lady Diana Spencer, daughter of Earl Spencer, seemed at the time an idyllic partnership and the very public breakdown of the marriage had world-wide repercussions for the Royal Family. Princess Diana's death, a year after her divorce, in a car crash in Paris which also claimed the life of her lover, Dodi El Fayed, produced a tidal wave of sentiment and criticism that threatened to engulf the whole Royal Family. Though he is well aware of his non-political role, Charles feels free to give his opinions on such matters as architecture, the environment and organic farming – which he practises at his home, Highgrove, in Gloucestershire – and is sometimes criticised for expressing an opinion at all.

Being a patron of over 500 charities and having a round of royal duties to fulfil as well as giving time to his various environmental projects, Charles has little time for leisure. However, when he does he plays polo, flies aircraft, shoots game birds, fishes for salmon and goes hunting, which some people find reprehensible.

In 1976 Charles founded the Prince's Trust out of a conviction that a way should be found to tackle the alienation of many young people in society, by encouraging challenge, adventure and self-help. Today, a decade later, fund-raising rock concerts and royal film premieres helped the Trust to hand out more than £300,000 a year in grants to disadvantaged young people between the ages of 14 and 25.

Even older is the Welsh organization set up by the Prince in 1971, two years after his Investiture, and now known as The Prince's Trust 'Bro' – from the Welsh for 'community'. It has supported more than 4,000 projects, helping Welsh communities cope with the effects of change, backed by nearly £4 million in grants.

Prince Charles, Prince of Wales, in Hong Kong on 29 June 1997

PRINCE WILLIAM

Following the death of the Princess of Wales in 1997, not only did her family grieve at the terrible loss, but the whole nation was in shock as well. The Queen said it was 'a chance to show to the whole world the British nation united in grief and respect'.

PRINCE WILLIAM Arthur Philip Louis was born on June 21, 1982 at St Mary's Hospital in London. From the start his parents, the Prince and Princess of Wales, tried to give him as normal a life as possible. Prince William has one sibling, his brother Harry, who was born in 1984 and it is said that they get along well together. At first Prince William was a boisterous little boy – known to have flushed his father's shoes down the toilet, and fighting with a flower girl at his uncle Andrew's wedding. As he grew older he became more quiet and thoughtful. At age eight Prince William was sent to Ludgrove, a boarding school, where he shared a room with four other boys. He spent five years there and proved to be an excellent athlete. He was on the school soccer, basketball, and swimming teams, and became captain of hockey and rugby teams. He also participated in clay pigeon shooting and cross country running. Another of his interests was acting and he appeared in several school plays and said in 1993 that he would like to become a professional actor.

In 1995 Prince William left Ludgrove and entered exclusive Eton College. In August of 1996 Prince Charles and Princess Diana were divorced. Prince William's housemaster at Eton, Dr. Andrew Gailey, is said to have helped William deal with the trauma, but unfortunately, a worse blow was to follow. On August 31, 1997 his mother, Princess Diana, was killed in a car crash in Paris. Prince William helped to make the arrangements for his mother's unusual funeral. It was his idea for Elton John to sing 'Candle in the Wind.' Prince William walked in the funeral procession with his father, brother and grandfather. In 2000, Prince William graduated from Eton and passed three A-level exams. He was accepted by the University of St Andrews in Scotland. Before attending the university he spent a year travelling and pursuing educational projects. His first stop was a jungle in Belize, where he took part in military exercises with the Welsh Guards. Later that year he visited Chile which was organized by a group called Raleigh International, which takes young people on a three-month expedition that included environmental and community projects. After graduating from St Andrews, Prince William will probably be expected to follow the family tradition and enter one of the armed forces.

GOLDEN JUBILEE YEAR

The Queen's Golden Jubilee was a once in a lifetime event which marked the 50th anniversary of Her Majesty The Queen's Accession to the Throne. It was an occasion both to look back at the role that The Queen has played in the affairs of the United Kingdom and the Commonwealth over the last fifty years and also to look forwards. This special milestone has previously been achieved by only four earlier British monarchs – King Henry III, King Edward III, King George III and Queen Victoria.

The celebrations took place between May and July 2002 when Her Majesty toured the regions of England and paid visits to Scotland, Wales and Northern Ireland. The Jubilee Weekend saw the focus of national celebrations, including major events in London. In the spring and autumn of 2002 The Queen visited the Commonwealth countries including Australia, New Zealand, Jamaica and Canada.

Although the Queen's Golden Jubilee was a momentous celebration it was tinged with sadness marred by the death of the sister she loved, Princess Margaret. It was also the fiftieth anniversary of the death of her father, King George VI; the anniversary still awakens painful memories.

INDEX

Page numbers in **bold** refer to major entries.

Picture Credits
Abbreviations: b = bottom; c = centre; l = left; r = right; t = top.

Bridgeman Art Library: 8 l & r, 9 r, 14/15 c, 18/19 c, 21 b, 22/23 c, 26 b,
28 bl, 30/31 c, 33 br, 38/39 c, 40 bl, 41 tr, 42/43 c, 44 bl, 45 tl, 48/49 c,
50/51 c, 52/53 c, 54/55 c, 59 c, 60/61 c, 65 t, 66 b, 68 bl, 73, 74/75 c,
76/77 c, 78/79 c, 83 t, 84/85 c, 88/89 c, 90/91 c, 92 r, 96.97 c, 100 bl,
103 tc, 104/105 c, 108/109 c, 112, 114/115 c, 118 l, c & r, 119 l, c & r,
120/121 c, 122/123 c, 126/127 c, 128/129 c, 130 t, 138 l, 139 t, 140/141 c,
143, 145, 150 l, 151 bl, 154 bl, 156/157, 158/159 c, 162/163 c, 164 tl,
166/167 c, 168, 172/173 c, 174 b, 176 br, 180 bl & br, 184/185 c, 187 tl,
189 t, 192/193 c, 194 l, 195 bl, 196 bl, 198/199 c, 200 bl, 201 tl, 202 b,
204 l, 205 t, 208 l, 210 br, 211 br, 212 br, 214/215 c, 216/217 c, 218 tl,
219 tl, 221 tl, 225, 230/231 c, 232 l, 233 bl, 234/235 c, 236/237 c, 238 t,
243 b. Getty Images: 36, 62/63 c, 70 b, 80, 102 bl, 112 bl & r, 113, 117 t,
171 tl, 183 t, 228/229, 242 tl. Mirror Syndication International: 37 br,
55 bl, 132 bl, 133 tl, 175 t, 244 t, 255 tl, 246 tr, 247 br, 248 bl, 250 l,
250/251 c. National Portrait Gallery: 110/111 c. Magic Dragon Multimedia:
146/147 c.